ROOJAK

William D. Northcott

TEMPLE

TEMPLE PUBLISHING COMPANY
London, England

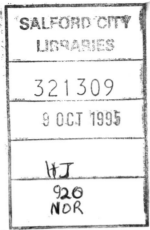
First published in Great Britain 1995
by Temple Publishing Company
London, England

Copyright © William D. Northcott 1995

**British Library Cataloguing-in-Publication Data.
A catalogue record for this book is available
from the British Library**

ISBN 1 85977010 X

Cover design by Harold King

Printed & bound in England by
Antony Rowe Ltd, Chippenham, Wiltshire

WHEN A MARRIAGE GIVES OUT, THERE
USUALLY HASN'T BEEN ENOUGH PUT IN

To my loving daughter Anne and my dear sons
David, Peter William and Christopher . . . at least
Dad tried

WHITE MAN'S BURDEN

But Why Bwana why?

I stared out at the tiny thatched house on stilts, in
which he lived. There was nothing for me to say,
but at that moment the dignity of man walked out
of books and became as real to me as the bread I
eat.
YES . . . FOR ME NOW ONE IS DEFINITELY
STRONGER ALONE

PREFACE

Every thinking man at some time or other in his lifetime is aware of, and feels his own originality.

We are all individuals – each made in a different mould from his neighbour.

Some of us, perhaps the more ductile, travel serenely through life, on established societies and accepted roads.

Others, less conventional, are often erroneously labelled non-conformist, nihilistic, or even worse.

Pushed by events, or becoming a casualty of their own weakness, they sometimes stray from the highway, and fall painfully out of step.

I claim no immunity, however, and ask for no licence.

I am what my own God has made me.

INTRODUCTION

At nearly seventy-two years of age – this being my first experience of writing such a manuscript – I must ask myself, why am I attempting such a formidable task?

I have always been keenly aware of a gut feeling, about most big decisions I have had to make, and no matter how much I weigh up the pros and cons of an issue – think long and logically – in the final analysis, when action is called for this intuition makes the final decision and takes over.

So, I have a tale to tell, and I feel I must endeavour to get into print the motivation and driving force, which has alternately inspired, betrayed and eventually rewarded me.

Memory, as one gets older, is somewhat fragile, and although dates and times seem less important now, the various episodes enumerated are factual. Where it has been felt necessary to recall individual conversations, the content and meaning, if not the actual words, are completely truthful. The characters I have met and described are still very real to me, but for obvious reasons, those individuals encountered as clients or adversaries during my period as a private investigator in Australia will bear a suitable pseudonym.

My life, like so many others, does seem to have been a rather perplexing struggle – not without humour fortunately – against stupidity, prejudice and perhaps, not least of all, the undesirable consequences of my own weakness.

Perhaps I have been too dogmatic in questioning the validity and significance of some of the events I have been associated with, but only because their future implications have to me been most important. To be able to say that I am a really happy man, at my comfortable 'Tribal Elders' age, must, however, mean something. I feel much pleasure when I reflect nostalgically on some of my marvellous memories – even the difficult and more embarrassing moments have now faded gratefully below the horizon.

I should mention that some of my more erudite friends have counselled me as to how I should layout my story. I prefer, however, to tell this in my own way, in a straightforward fashion. After all, I am writing it as much for my own nostalgic pleasure as for anyone else!

I nevertheless thank my well-wishers for their interest in both myself and the things I stand for. The many thought-provoking sessions we have shared have been of immense help, and from them I have been able to formulate a better perspective of the real me. Any conclusions I have reached or views I express, remain completely my own, except for what I feel are relevant quotes, and these are marked accordingly.

I am a fortunate man – blessed with good health, a love of mankind, and enjoy a lively sense of humour. Despite the unpleasant traumas I have experienced in my long journey through life, I have at last found a very real and complete peace.

There is a crucial turning point in most mens' lives, and mine came, as it did no doubt for many others, when I made a very human mistake during the Second World War.

It has taken me all of fifty years to find my way out of the wilderness, and this I am sure, was only through a return to my early Christian faith.

This last paragraph will, I know, raise a wry smile from my few agnostic friends. But I really believe that prayer has had a lot to do with my recent good fortune. So to my story . . . and where to begin?

1. Wheel of Fortune

Whose hand guided me from the desolate wastes of Australia to the lush green valleys and spirituality of Thailand?

I was sixty-eight years of age, had been retired from business for five years, and lived on a small hobby farm in the southwest corner of Western Australia.

Here I had intended to lick my spiritual wounds, let the farcical pantomime of the world go by and live on a small British and Australian Veteran Affairs pension.

It had originally been a rewarding experience – taking a 'bare paddock' as the Australian says, building a house, guest chalet and swimming pool . . . way out in the 'bush'. I planted hundreds of trees and shrubs, bushy yates and melaleuca for shade and wind breaks, impressive poplars up the long driveway to the house. We had river gums around the dam, together with a variety of citrus and other fruit trees.

All very English, I had thought nostalgically and landscaped accordingly. I had even planted an English oak in a commanding position on the circular driveway.

Most city men dream of having such a property . . . I did . . . until I became crippled with osteoarthritis. Then, as if aware of my predicament, the wind blew almost continuously and the leaves and branches came down. Algae from the dam water supply filtered into the swimming pool, mostly at times when guests were expected. Cattle broke through the fences, and, despite all my efforts, the ferns and bracken continued their relentless invasion, providing cover for the multitude of rabbits, which quickly reached plague proportions.

My meagre efforts, even supported by mechanical tools, were ineffective. It was a painful struggle even to climb aboard the small Bolen tractor and soon my peaceful rural haven became an endless round of pain, work and worry.

At this time I was also experiencing an unpleasant interlude with a live-in girlfriend, one whom I had nurtured for well over a year. This relationship, slowly deterioratimg, had finally culminated in an unholy row. Then after her threatening, theatrical but most welcome departure, I settled down to enjoy, if possible, a little peace. A bachelor state, even for a semi-invalid, proved to have so many advantages.

I should have learned my lesson with the fairer sex long ago. I nearly said 'weaker', but that would have been a misnomer, wouldn't it? Two broken marriages behind me and numerous affaire-de-coeur . . . some men never learn!

A fortuitous spell in hospital for my first hip replacement gave me ample opportunity to evaluate my position carefully. Where had I previously gone wrong? A very foolish marriage de convenience conforming to the social norms during the war of 1939-1945 had not helped to strike a good foundation. But what was I still searching for? What was life all about? What rules does one apply and whose?

How many of you have asked yourselves the same questions?

I had put my little farm on the market some time before, as I had long ago realised I would soon be incapable of running it. I sold the little remaining stock, and had arranged with a neighbour to graze a few sheep on the property to keep the grass under control.

I now badly needed a change of scenery and felt that I had

to get away from Australia.

A travel agent contact, a brief discussion, and I had booked a fourteen-day visit to Thailand, a few days in Bangkok and the remainder in Phuket. I arranged with an Australian mate to check the farm occasionally and service the swimming pool. Locking the house up, taking a last look around, I placed my valise in the car, drove to Perth and boarded the Singapore Airlines flight to Bangkok in the Kingdom of Thailand.

2. Thailand

Now I began to feel alive again!

Gracious, soft spoken, smiling servants . . . the artificial world of luxury hotels . . . beautiful, elegant and intriguing Thai ladies everywhere.

I had the time, money and opportunity to indulge myself . . . I did. I had a ball . . . my isolated little Australian farm, with all its petty problems, was forgotten. So many new friends . . . such exotic foods and surroundings. I immediately felt at one with the tempo of Thailand, and wished I could have stayed forever, but all too soon the party was over and the smiling Thai faces were soon replaced by the dour unsmiling custom officers at Perth Airport.

I was back home . . . back to reality.

On my return to the farm the gods smiled on me favourably with great news. A note informed me that a prospective buyer was interested in the property. A month or so later the sale of my property was finalised and the settlement date just six weeks away. Was this to be my salvation? Now I faced a mild dilemma. My children were all doing well, had lives and interests of their own, and as in so many fragmented Western-style families, I rarely saw them. Realising, that time was slowly running out for me, and after mentally exploring the options open, I tidied up my affairs in Western Australia, dissipated my personal treasures and paintings amongst the children, and booked a one-way ticket back to Thailand.

I learned from one of my sons that my dear daughter thought I was terminally ill when I made this move. She was very upset, but as I explained to her later, it was now 'dad's time'.

I had made a reservation for one night at the Airport Hotel, Bangkok, and from there an overnight sleeper on the train, up to Chiang Mai in the Northern Province, a city of which I had heard such good reports. During the thirty years I was domiciled in Australia, I had built up three different type of enterprises. The first driven by financial necessity – a firm of private investigators. The second, a wholesale fashion agency, and my last company an engineering personnel consultancy business. The investigation business I had eventually been forced to sell . . . but more of this later.

All three had been started with very little capital, but considering all the aspects, I was quite pleased with my achievements, although, if outside pressures had been eased, I would no doubt have done a lot better financially.

I will try, as I said in my introduction, to spell out my story as simply as possible, but with so many anomalies I ask my reader to look between the lines, and, like myself, ask why things happened the way they did.

Freedom is a God-given right, and as my story unfolds, one can well imagine the carefree state of mind I enjoyed as I stood on the Bangkok railway station awaiting the train departure for Chiang Mai. The last overnight journey I had made by train had been some thirty years earlier, from Nairobi to Mombasa in East Africa en route to my second honeymoon on the island of Zanzibar. I did not expect to see the same fascinating wild game as in Africa, but I was not disappointed with what I did encounter.

The kaleidoscope of people intrigued me: colourful hill tribe people with strangely packed luggage; distinguished-looking Sikhs and two uniformed policemen; chests emblazoned with medal ribbons, one sporting a parachute insignia, their arms around each others' waists, striking a humorous note to western eyes as they strolled along the platform, apparently oblivious to the world around them.

I had sensed a feeling of freedom in Thailand even on my previous short visit – something that I had never really experienced in Australia. Could the fact that I was no longer responsible for crippling maintenance payments have had something to do with this? But one must be fair.

This feeling of freedom was to become increasingly noticeable the longer I stayed in the country. The Thais are an independent, proud people, who adopt a low-key, cheerful approach to life. I can readily understand why they have never been colonised.

At last, exhilaration. I arrived in Chiang Mai, the second largest city in Thailand. I have no immediate plans of leaving.

5

During the first week, staying at the Rincombe Hotel, I met Ao, A twenty-eight-year-old Thai, tall, beautiful and intelligent. One night, sitting quietly in a romantic setting, reminiscing over our past back-grounds and diversities, Ao explained to me details of her early childhood, her secret feelings, wishes and fears. Despite our different cultures, ages, backgrounds and experiences, I felt I understood her, and in return she took away all my hurt and gave me back a new life. I shall be forever grateful.

Ao

We moved into a furnished house at Santitam, directly opposite the YMCA where Ao (pronounced 'or') soon convinced me of her culinary skills, both Thai and European, and her organisational abilities when entertaining and house-keeping. Her narratives on the history of her country were fascinating, and together we explored Chiang Mai, discussing our future – whether to stay in Thailand, or move to a western country?

6

Another setback, albeit only temporarily, was that I had to have another hip operation, which gave us little choice. We returned to Western Australia, where Ao met my family, the five children two ex-wives, and savoured a little of the Western life style.

After staying for a while with my son William we rented a very nice furnished townhouse in South Perth equipped with a swimming pool, which I knew would be useful when I was convalescing from my impending operation. This was finally undertaken at the Mount Hospital – my second hip joint replacement the first was undertaken in 1984.

As I had sold my property, thereby increasing my paper assets, I had completely lost my Veteran Affairs pension and the health cover that it provided. The medicare payments I had made since were insufficient in number to qualify as any tangible relief. The operation cost me about $7,000 Australian. Had I realised and known more about the medical services in Thailand, I could have had the same operation performed in Chiang Mai for about $2,500, and, as I understand it, quite safely. Medical services in Thailand are excellent and most inexpensive by Western standards. When I think of the many hours I have wasted in doctors' reception rooms in Perth just to get a prescription signed, for a fee of twenty-seven dollars, and having then to go to the chemist to get and pay for the prescribed medicine . . .

Shortly afterwards I had an acute shoulder pain – my osteoarthritis. I visited a small village clinic and waited about ten minutes to see the doctor. There followed a quick diagnosis, an injection and the issue of pills from the pharmacy attached to the surgery. Total cost was 50 baht – approximately two dollars fifty – and almost instant relief. Needless to say, I do not worry about health insurance. The convalescent period for my second operation was like a dream. Ao was just magnificent. Whereas previously I had driven two hundred miles from the hospital to a lonely farm house, doing my shopping en route, now I lay back in a comfortable South Perth townhouse, having every want and whim cheerfully attended to.

The swimming pool attached to the unit helped accelerate my period of recovery and soon I was able to drive again and show Ao a little of Western Australia.

We visited Augusta, and as we turned off the main road onto the winding bush track that led to my late property Ao, with a tear in her eye, said, 'you came all that way from this little red road to find me in Chiang Mai'! I realised then how my prayers had really been answered.

A good Australian friend, Stuart Ridley, flew us around the district in his tiny Cessna, over the Blackwood River and my old home – yet another pleasant experience for Ao. We travelled to Wongan Hills, and stayed with another friendly couple, Joan and Dennis Lord, on their large sheep station. The vastness of the property was such a contrast to my small holding in Augusta.

During our travels in Western Australia we discussed the possibility of purchasing a house in WA and looked at several properties. I felt, though, that our happiness together could only lie in Thailand. I had already sacrificed too much of my life, and my feelings toward Australia were becoming more and more negative.

So, just six months after our arrival, we stood once again at Perth International Airport, surrounded by family, friends and one ex-wife, waiting to board our flight, destination Bangkok.

LEFT TO RIGHT: *Chris, Peter, Anne, Dad, David & William*

8

I had happily achieved a reconciliation with my eldest son David after a period of several years. A rupture in our relationship, emanating, indirectly I am sure, from the consequence of my divorce from his mother. Photographs were taken at the airport – my four sons, daughter and myself – the very first time we had all been together.

I had been instrumental in bringing the three elder children from England to Australia, where they had taken advantage of the opportunities offered and were all doing well. Whilst Australia had not been a very uplifting experience for me, as the reader will shortly see, I shall always be grateful to the country for giving my children such a chance.

Perhaps on my arrival at thirty-nine years of age, I had too many preconceived ideas, or my critical faculties had not been sufficiently blunted.

Coming, as I had from the rather refined, if not always efficient colonial service, was it that I could not quite accept the rather plebian and disparaging 'Pommy bastard' bigotry?

Or was I just being too sensitive?

Handicapped also by the twenty-pounds-a-week maintenance payments to England, I had of necessity to earn good money. I have been informed by some of my good 'Aussie' friends, that the average Australian does not take too kindly to 'pushy' immigrants . . . Was I too considered a pushy immigrant, or was there something else? I have speculated over this question for so long that it doesn't hurt now or matter to me. Time cures every problem.

Back to my story . . . We set off eventually on our return trip to Thailand. As we were processed through the metal detector checkpoint at Perth Airport, the X-ray picked up a metal object in my hand luggage. A large and surly looking immigration officer checked the bag. Helpfully, I informed him that the object in question would be a pewter goblet, a gift from my daughter that I had packed at the last minute. He glowered angrily at me. 'I'll decide what it bloody well is,f he replied, in quite a hostile manner.

What a difference this was to the smiling reception we were to have in Bangkok! I greeted the immigration officer who was, checking my passport in Thai, yin dee tee die roujak khun krap! which means 'very nice to meet you' He broke into a broad grin, as did his companion. Yes, I remember feeling; this must be the country for me. I felt surprisingly more at home and in an Asian country! When we arrived in Chiang Mai, we were fortunate in being able to re-lease the house at Santitam. The Chinese owner was obviously glad to see us return. So we settled down once again, and after two or so weeks invested in a small Suzuki four-wheel-drive vehicle which made life considerably easier.

A New Zealand school teacher, Vicki Stint, was the first of our many European guests, we had met originally when she was caretaking the old property at Augusta, in Australia. Vicki stayed with us for nearly three months, introduced Ao to aerobics, and was a keen swimmer and card player. She was a cheerful and interesting visitor, and we missed her when she left.

It was whilst we were at Santitam that we disturbed a bandit, endeavouring to break into the house. A heavy rainstorm was in progress, apparently ideal conditions favoured by Thai criminals, as the noise factor from entering is deadened. We first heard the thud of a fallen body, and, grabbing two souvenir African spears, flew into action. As the bandit heard us shout, he took off, leaping the six-foot-high front gate like a frightened gazelle. Searching the back of the property in the pouring rain, I found his work bag, full of skeleton keys, tools, metal saws etc, together with an umbrella and sandals. Ao and I were both soaked through to the skin, but we had saved the day, or night.

When the police very promptly arrived on the scene, Ao and I were still armed with the spears, causing the Thai police much amusement. I reflected that under similar circumstances in Australia we would no doubt have been charged with 'being in possession of offensive weapons'. After all the preliminaries and excitement had died down, we started to reflect on a possible move away from the city, and began to look around for a more permanent home.

3. Mae Sa – Idyllic Haven

After viewing several properties, we extended our field of search, and finally in the beautiful Mae Sa Valley, found a delightful townhouse. It was situated only some twenty kilometres north-east of Chiang Mai, two miles from an elephant training camp, and near an orchid and butterfly farm.

The house was set at the foot of a range of hills surrounded by paddy fields and bush vegetation, and overlooked by a Buddhist temple. Water buffalos worked, or wallowed, in the paddy fields, and the scenery was quite magnificent.

We decided to purchase the house, but first arranged for several modifications to satisfy my western background. Windows and doors were knocked out; hot water pipes installed; toilet and shower facilities changed. In fact, the inside of the house was almost completely renovated. During the important phase of our new life together, Ao's linguistic abilities speeded things up considerably, and her short experience in Australia proved of immense help. Building standards are unique in Thailand, but by persevering in visiting the site two or three times daily, supervising the progress and oiling the social cogs with innumerable bottles of Mekon whisky for the labour, we were eventually satisfied. This was a busy period for Ao and I, as we were also carefully shopping around for furniture, electrical appliances, curtains and the myriad of small items that go to make up a comfortable home.

To a Thai, it is important to remember that thought is more important than action, meditation is valued over the incessant search for material goods. The building foreman and labourers working on the house must have concluded that we were really unbalanced, as we fussed over very detail, and to them, set an incredibly high and unnecessary standard. Wealth and power are important goals in life, but spiritual realisation and self-contemplation to the Thai rank higher in the scale of cosmic values. However, in the end we were well satisfied. After my experiences of the hedonistic life style of Australia, I slowly began to feel whole again.

Older civilisations have so much more in the spiritual sense to offer. Their people prize the gift of time, which has given them so many centuries to think, to experience, change, reject and finally forge together a life style which is acceptable and can withstand the restlessness of man. I feel that Thailand, in fact, has much in commom with my birthplace England; it is an old monarchy; its people know and value freedom; it is an island surrounded by socialist-controlled countries; it has a well defined identity and a heritage to be proud of. I felt completely at one with both the country and the people – the English too at one time were PIRATES.

Now, with abundant time to indulge in the luxury of quiet reflection, I am able to piece together the story of my life's experiences. I have no doubt been variously described, but I prefer to think of myself as an ordinary man, who has been driven by some indefinable force to struggle constantly against the outmoded values of a failing society.

As Adlai Stevenson, the American democrat, wrote in Harpers magazine:

'Criticism . . . is an ugly word. It suggests non-comformity, and non-comformity suggests disloyalty, and disloyalty suggests treason, and before we know where we are, the process has all but identified the critic with the saboteur and turned criticism into an un-American activity, instead of democracy's greatest safeguard. The concern of a democracy is that no honest man shall feel uncomfortable, I don't care who he is . . . or how nutty he is!'

Please remember these words as you read my story. It could explain the iniquitous pressures that have been applied, for which at the time there appeared to be no logical explanation.

4. Roots

I was born on 10th October 1919 in Plymouth, the second child of my parents and had a sister Betty, just eighteen months older. My father was a chief engine-room artificer in the Royal Navy, eventually serving some forty-three years in that service, and seeing action in both World Wars. My mother came from a religious Devon family the Sleeps, who ran a humble greengrocer's shop in Plymouth. Her three brothers were Methodist ministers for many years, the eldest brother Bert, obtaining a Doctorate of Divinity, from a Canadian University. It is obviously from this side of the family that I got my strong sense of justice and my own critical, moralising mixture of honesty and hypocrisy. After all, none of us are really perfect.

My mother had a caring, compassionate nature and possessed the true gift of a clairvoyant. When I was hit by a car near my home in an accident, at the age of about eleven, my mother was actually at the scene whilst I was still lying unconscious. She had told the neighbours, "quickly, look after the children. Billy has had an accident"!

On her brother Bert's return to England from the university in Canada, he obtained a post as secretary to the Methodist Overseas Mission. The wild behaviour of his younger brothers had at this time become an embarrassment to him, but he was able to provide them with an assisted passage as missionaries to Australia. They could do no damage to his career there!

One of the brothers, Harold, whom I was to meet in Adelaide shortly before his death, never forgave Bert for sending the two young boys to Australia. As he recounted, they were poorly equipped and trained; couldn't even say Grace at the table, and, were in his opinion, a pair of con men in clerical collars.

I asked him why he had been influenced into leaving the church.

'Bill, I had a wedding ceremony to perform in the morning,

followed afterwards by the usual type of wedding breakfast. You know the Sleeps are partial to a drink. I was, and the day was hot. In the afternoon I officiated at a funeral, and during the service. . . 'earth to earth, ashes to ashes, dust to dust' I sprinkled the earth with solemn dignity over the coffin, but to my discomfort, confetti from the morning's wedding service also fell out of my cassock sleeve. I decided then that I was unable to continue my ministry.'

Like myself, Harold appeared to have had a pretty turbulent life in Australia. He had been a police sergeant in Adelaide; a captain in the Australian army, had various businesses; worked as a labourer on the railway line then being built across the Nullabor Plain, and eventually found solace in the bottle, becoming a confirmed alcoholic. To his great credit, however, he did eventually rehabilitate himself, securing a cleaner's job at the Royal Adelaide Hospital where he progressed slowly, finally retiring as the domestic supervisor. And once again, he became a devout practising Christian.

The Sleeps were a strange and amusing mixture. Harold told me that he once preached a service in Perth with a loaded pistol in his hip pocket. I must have inherited some of their peculiarities.

The third brother Alfred, after seventeen years in the church, came under fire from the hierarchy during a period of economic depression in Australia, and was told to modify his sermons. As this, he felt was against his conscience, 'the fateful Sleep conscience', and he was morally unable to follow orders, he resigned from the church.

I am digressing slightly, but it is quite amusing to recount the events that followed Alfred's resignation. His last church was at Merredin in Western Australia, from where he left by train to travel to Perth. This would have been in 1928. He decided on arrival in Perth to open a small office in William Street, with the intention of running some sort of welfare agency. Remember, at that time, there was much poverty and hardship in Australia, and soup kitchens were then providing meals for hungry people.

Shortly after opening the office, a farmer visited the premises and asked Alfred to help locate his wife who had left the farm several days earlier after a heated argument. He placed a banknote on the desk to defray any expenses incurred.

It was an exceedingly hot day, and his client having departed, Alfred closed the office and walked across to the Royal Hotel. To his request for a drink, the barman questioned, 'A pot'?

Alfred, who had never up to this point touched alcohol, replied in the affirmative and placed the farmer's banknote on the bar. On being served with a pot of beer and receiving change, Alfred said, 'you've given me too much here'!

'Don't you know a ten-pound note when you see one?'

Alfred sipped his beer, didn't like the taste, put the glass down, collected his change and left the hotel. Returning to the office, he placed the nine-pound notes and silver, on the desk, and reflected on the small pittance of a salary he had been getting as a Methodist minister.

A further visit from his farmer client, a few days later, followed by another payment of ten pounds in exchange for Alfred's explanation of the difficulties involved in such a case, and a new career was launched as one of Australia's most successful private investigators.

Such is fate. Alfred had christened children, married and buried people, and now he was being handsomely paid to assist in securing divorce evidence. As he stated years later, though, when I first met him, he too, like his brother, had become a confirmed alcoholic, albeit a very wealthy one, and he deeply regretted ever leaving the church.

So much for my mother's family.

We were brought up as children to believe in the religiosity of the Sleep family. Photographs of the three brothers in their clerical vestments were always proudly displayed on the mantelpiece in my parents' bedroom. The hard, seafaring background of the Northcott family was constantly compared to the spirituality of the Sleeps. Actually, a complete reversal of roles came about, as I was to learn years later.

With my father constantly at sea - three-year commissions were normal in those days - we children, three of us, Betty, myself and younger brother Jack, looked mainly to my mother for support and comfort.

During my parents' marriage, my father was at sea for a total of seventeen years. I am sure few modern couples could survive such a prolonged separation. Promotion in the regular Royal Navy was extremely slow, but by the time I was at primary school, my father had reached warrant officer's rank, and was soon to be commissioned. Most 'upper deck' officers in the

RN had a separate income to augment their naval salary. Once my father was commissioned and living in a ward room, he had the added expense of mess bills to pay each month, as well as the allotment, to provide for wife and children.

Whilst we were never short of food, as a family we always seemed to be short of money. It seems illogical in these days of generous welfare provisions, readily available in most of the Western world to recall that when the Royal Navy was at the peak of its power, its officers were treated so shabbily. Each month we used to walk several miles to 'Joliffes', the naval tailor in Devonport, to pay off the instalments due on my father's uniforms. We were unable to afford a bus or tram ticket, and Jack, my younger brother, about three or four years old at the time, gamely stepped out with the rest of the family. Such was the hidden price that English naval families paid, so that our mighty fleet could show the flag.

The only school suit I possessed was one that my mother had knitted - a navy blue, carefully darned in the trousers, where I had snagged a thread, climbing a tree, or during some such boyhood activity. How I hated that suit which I was forced to wear until just before I took the eleven plus examination. Years later, I was to show my twelve-year-old Australian son, on a visit to England, the very tree, in the playground of Hyde Park School, where I had stood being jeered at by boys ridiculing that horrible suit. It was on this occassion in fact, when I first learned that violence, as a last resort, does at least command a certain respect. I picked the most vocal boy in the crowd and laid into him. My mother, God bless her, endeavoured to give us a happy childhood. We made regular weekend excursions to Cawsand, Bovisand, across the river Tamar, and out to the edges of Dartmoor. We walked miles into the Devon countryside, taking a picnic lunch, and swimming in the sea and rivers, beautiful spots I recall, for which Devon is famous.

How different though when Father came home from sea. An iron discipline descended on the household, and our regular weekend excursions were suspended for another two or three years. Both my parents had strong personalities, and the atmosphere when they were together was hardly conducive to a peaceful family situation. As the years passed, my mother began to loathe the Navy and all it stood for - a feeling she persisted with, until her death at eighty-nine years of age.

I had an undistinguished period at school, which I never

really enjoyed, secondary and grammar schools, and was educated to the Cambridge School Certificate standard. I was no more than an average student, always somewhat mystified by the impracticality of Latin grammar, and the complexities of trigonometry and algebraic equations at the secondary school. Nor was I assisted by my transfer from Tamar secondary school in Plymouth, where they specialised in training boys educationally for future careers in the dockyard or navy as engineering or shipwright apprentices. I then went to a grammar school at Weymouth, where I lost ground and time spent in Latin exercises and the school officer cadet corps.

On my return to Tamar secondary, I discovered I was well behind in the mathematical subjects and could not even then read a logarithm table - the move was for me an educational disaster. I failed too, an entry examination for an engineering apprentice course in the Royal Navy, much to my father's disgust and certainly not good for my ego!

On a lighter note, my dear brother, an old Tamaritan like myself, wrote to me recently, seventy-two years of age remember, telling me that Tamar secondary school had been renamed Tamar High school, and had recently been closed down. He kindly sent me an old boys association tie, and in his letter emphasised that we could now honestly say we in a resume, that went to a high school which should help us to further our careers. Better late than never, but then, the school motto was: 'The best is yet to be.'

Whilst speaking of education, I have been surprised at the number of Englishmen I have met, then in responsible positions, who told me they had failed the Eleven Plus exam. It shows the educational system at this time was by no means foolproof.

5. Pre-war years

England in 1935 was just coming out of the depression and when I wished to leave school, start work and contribute to the feeble, family finances, I began to realise that I was faced with a difficult task.

I was fortunate eventually in securing a position as a junior salesman with Prices Tailoring Ltd, a multiple tailoring organisation, at one of their Plymouth branches. They traded under the name of 'The fifty-shilling tailors'. I started by learning how to pack parcels, sweep floors, brush stock, and make myself generally useful. They were long hours, I recall, working from 8.30 am to 7.00 pm on weekdays, and until 8.00 pm Fridays, and 9.00 pm on Saturdays. One half-day off a week, for the magnificent sum of fifteen shillings a week.

When the family transferred to Manchester I was faced with an hour's travelling time, on top of the normal working day, that is, one hour each way. But now I was getting twenty-seven shillings a week. I considered myself lucky at the time, if nothing else, the position gave me a dress sense, and with my gregarious nature, the useful basic knowledge of how to handle people. My pleasure when I first secured this position was somewhat dampened by my father's anger. 'I'm not having my son working in a tailor's shop' and down he stormed to see the manager, but was soon completely mollified upon learning the remuneration that could be earned as a branch manager – with no overseas posting either.

The fact that Sir Henry Price, the founder of the business, had himself started out sweeping stock room floors also helped. The naval engineer lieutenant ashore was obviously no match for an astute business manager.

These were difficult times for employment. I once remember seeing a grown man cry when he was threatened with dismissal. He had been out of work for many years, and with the responsibility of a family, fully realised the consequences. An ex-school mate, Bill Wadge, also worked with me at the Plymouth branch. Like myself, he was a tall gangling youth, I can see him now, dressed self-consciously as I was, in a black jacket and striped trousers.

During the war, Bill became a paratrooper, decorated for bravery, and I was told by a police lieutenant in Kenya years later, he had won a General Police medal in Malaysia when he served with the Malaysia Police during the emergency – which goes to prove that clothes don't really make the man.

I worked with this tailoring company until I finally joined the Royal Air Force in 1939. Most of the younger men in the company joined the Colours at the outbreak of war. I remember with sadness the number who never returned.

Whilst in Manchester, I worked with an older man called Jim Cain, who had a vivid scar on the back of his neck. As war became a regular subject of discussion, Jim explained how he had served in the 1914-1918 War with a Lancashire division who had suffered appalling casualties in just one day's fighting. Whilst fighting for possession of Hill 66, most of it in fearful bayonet, hand-to-hand skirmishes, he had received a bayonet slash across the neck. The toll was terrible on both sides.

During a further discussion in the small staff room, Jim told us that he had no intention of allowing his son to go through such an experience, and was arranging to get him a job exempt from military service on a farm in Wales. Coming from a naval family and brought up on tales of Jutland and other naval engagements, this presented a different side for me to the glories of empire and war. This is perhaps when I first really began to earnestly question, some of the things I had previously taken for granted. Why is war necessary? What inspires men to such madness? What are they really dying for? And for whom? Where does all the money suddenly come from? Perhaps it will be interesting to quote from the book by Leon Wolfe, In Flanders Field.

'In March 1922, the British War Office published its statistics of the military effort of the British Empire during the Great War. Released as soon as possible after the event, it flatly lists British casualties between July and December 1917 (the Flanders campaign and Cambrai) at 448,614. This does not include French losses on the North flank, which may conservatively be reckoned at 50,000 for the same period. Thus the total allied loss comes to half a million. The Flanders campaign was normal for the Western Front, in which the proportion of dead to other casualties, almost always ran at thirty per cent. Therefore, 150,000 approximately were killed in five months, some 30,000 a month. In the same report, German casualties were listed as 270,710.'

On a more personal level, I had become friendly with a young chap at work, called Kinsella. One Sunday I invited him to lunch at home. Imagine my surprise and horror, when just as my father was preparing to carve the Sunday joint, Kinsella proudly started telling us that he was a full-time member of the British Union of Fascists, then commanded in England by Sir Oswald Moseley. My father went white, then threw down the carving knife, and, his face drained of blood, stormed out of the room. Although I was genuinely unaware of Kinsella's political beliefs, ignorance was considered no excuse, and I was firmly ordered to see that my friend never set foot in the house again.

Kinsella got married shortly afterwards, with a total capital of twenty pounds, his honeymoon, a tram ride around Manchester.

Father, needing Naval epaulettes when he was awarded the MBE as he had to visit Buckingham Palace, had difficulty affording a second-hand set from Joliffes the tailor. Such were the times.

I was beginning to find my father's opinion of things, other than English, a little dogmatic and prejudiced, and had several heated arguments with him regarding events in the colonies, especially, I remember, about Africa.

Books too had always intrigued me. I had read a lot, on a wide spectrum of subjects: history, world events and foreign peoples had since an early age been of great interest. Years later in Africa, I realised that my early impressions of that continent had not been far wrong, despite my father's earlier assertation that I didn't know what I was talking about.

Incidentally, these arguments often ended in violence, much to my mother's chagrin. Dad had a violent temper; was quick with his fists, and is in fact the only man who has ever knocked me unconscious. I was fifteen years old at the time. I remember now seeing bright crescents, moons and stars, on a vivid black velvet background. Looking at his life and early naval training, I can now better understand him. He was a scrupulously honest man, and apart from his violent temperament, I am sure he was a good husband.

I remember drinking in a pub with my brother during the war when he got into a heated altercation with a soldier who shouted, 'I've got a good mind to knock your head off!' Jack looked at me and grinned, replying, 'we've been knocked around for years mate, and I'm quite used to it!'

Ironicaly, Jack, who as a child experienced the greatest violence, was the one who finally provided a comfortable home for the 'old seadog', who finally died in Plymouth, his birthplace, at the ripe old age of ninety-six.

I have met several men, though, who served under my father. They obviously had the greatest respect and affection for him. It must have been difficult for him on his return from a commission, to be faced with three young children, not always obedient, or accepting a comparative stranger, with authority, into the family. My sister-in-law Joan, Jack's wife, was magnficent for years, cheerfully tolerating the old man's garrulous and impatient ways when he lived with them before his death.

6. Bless 'em all

When war finally broke out in September 1939, my friends were enthusiastically talking of joining up.

Despite the proliferation of posters, 'Your Country needs you' I kept thinking of Jim Cains's abortive experiences in the earlier conflict. However, I finally joined the RAF volunteer reserve, on the 11th October 1939, where I served in the police section until I was released on the 18th April 1946. My six years' service was spent mainly on security work at radar installations, on mobile police squads, and later with an air disarmament wing in Germany.

Whilst on my initial police course number 138 at Uxbridge, I trained with the Bedser Twins, Alex and Eric of cricket fame. I remember Eric, or was it Alex, telling me that when he was seconded as a bodyguard to an Air Vice Marshall, how he lay on his back on a sand dune at Dunkirk, firing at Stuka dive bombers with a .303 Lee Enfield rifle. I fared better, when I was shooting at a Dornier once when it was endeavouring to bomb the Firth of Forth bridge in Scotland. At least I was armed with a Lewis gun, having just completed a ground gunner's course whilst awaiting further police training.

Like many servicemen in England I saw as much action when I was on leave, or travelling between stations. I spent many terrible nights in Plymouth during their heaviest blitz, and was once travelling in a train en-route from Edinburgh to London that was heavily machine-gunned at night by a German raider.

My military service taught me a lot, but, as it did for so many others, it changed the whole course of my life. At least I am still alive, unlike my closest school friend, Geoffrey Tinkler – 'Tink' who was shot down over the Rhine in Germany on the 21st April 1944. 'Tink' was a qualified shipwright working in Devonport dockyard, doing a useful war job. At the time he was engaged in sea-trials on old Polish destroyers being structurally modified to take heavier guns. His fiançe wanted him to join the RAF and 'Tink', although not enamoured with the idea, eventually succumbed to her entreaties. He did his ITW Initial Training Wing, a few operations and then he was shot down. Another wasted life. Mary, his fiançe, suffered a mental breakdown and entered a mental hospital.

F O. G.C. TINCLER
R A F

K
A
21.4.44

'Tink' and Bill   'Tink' – The Folly War

Bettina my sister and our parents

23

With my father at sea, my mother remained in Plymouth throughout the Blitz period. The windows of the house were blown out on several occasions, but miraculously without major damage. My mother was magnificent at this time, and several neighbours spoke to me after the war and confirmed how much sympathy and support she had been able to offer.

My grandmother had a flat nearby, and once when on leave during the opening stages of a German air raid, I assisted her across the road, into an air raid shelter. As we stood unprotected in the middle of the road amidst the scream of falling bombs, thunder of ack-ack fire, punctuated by the splatter of falling shrapnel, dear old Grandma remembered that she had forgotten her handbag; so back we went to the flat.

It's all a matter of individual priorities – your money or your life!

Eventually we decided to make her comfortable in a cubby hole under the stairs to which she retreated during an air raid alarm, praying that she would soon join her deceased husband, dear Albert. Of course she survived for many years.

My father eventually returned to England from the Persian Gulf. For six months he had not received a letter from home, just radio descriptions of the heavy raids on Plymouth. The first and only time I have seen a tear in the old boy's eye was as he greeted my mother on alighting from the taxi.

He was next posted as the chief engineer to a fleet of motor torpedo boats at Falmouth in Cornwall.

My parents rented a house Rydall Cottage opposite the Greenbank Hotel in Falmouth, and on one occasion, when I was on leave, there was a daylight raid by a small force of six German bombers. The alert had been sounded, and my mother was busy making Cornish pasties for lunch. My father had just arrived home from the base, resplendent in his naval officers's uniform, wearing campaign medal ribbons, a holstered pistol and tin hat.

'Come along, Edith. The alarm has been sounded!'

My mother was experienced enough to realise that the planes were still some way off, and that it was only a light force. 'Shan't be a minute, dear. Must get these pasties in the oven'.

'Alright then. I can see it's every man for himself!' And down to the shelter went the mighty head of the household. The family never forgave him, and his excuse that he felt happier when attacked at sea was never totally accepted.

24

Police School Uxbridge

Everyone in England at that time was in the front line – so different to previous wars fought overseas.

As a family, we were exceptionally lucky. Dad was at one time the chief engineer of the infamous HMS Lucia out in the Persian Gulf. My brother Jack was serving with the 'Devons', and my sister was nursing with the VADs (Voluntary Nursing Auxilary) in London, first in the tube stations and later at Stoke Mandeville hospital in the skin grafting wards. We all had some narrow escapes, but came through, at least physically, unscathed.

Recapturing the stupidities of war, I can visualise quite easily the police school at Uxbridge. Early morning reveille: cold, dark, often foggy, or raining heavily. Hundreds of trainees poured out of the grey, grim, four-storeyed billets, to form up for early morning parade and inspection. Webbing belts blancoed, buttons and boots highly polished, caps on at the correct angle. The stamp of steel heeled boots and rifle butts slamming to the ground as 'flights' sized off and formed up, prior to marching off towards the parade ground. NCOs barking orders, the shouts of men counting off and shuffling feet, as they dressed off into position.

No wonder I needed two hip replacements in later years. I

was too enthusiastic. I remember standing to attention for what seemed hours, in rain, snow or sunshine, as an assistant provost marshall, meticulously inspected each individual of the five flights.

Suddenly one heard the sound of a falling rifle, as some luckless man slumped to the ground, unable to hold his rigid position any longer. The show must go on though.

Co-ordination drill on the huge parade ground where one man gave drill commands to another, who as directed, performed various movements. A deep grey fog, visability less than one yard was not allowed to interfere with the syllabus. Orders shouted to invisible men who moved smoothly through the fog . . . 'saluting to the front . . . turn about – about turn! Slope arms' etc. Finally it developed into a complete farce, as men realised the sheer futility of the exercise.

Causing more and more merriment as the densely fog-covered square echoed and re-echoed to an endless series of barked orders, and men suddenly appeared ghostlike and grinning, apparently from nowhere. Accompanied by caustic, ribald comments, some NCOs foolishly stumbled through the fog, as they unsuccessfully endeavoured to restore some semblance of order.

There was more farce as one of my police colleagues, Acting Corporal Shearer, was given a trade test. Locked in a cell, as was the custom at that unit, he duly headed his test paper with his number, rank and name, lit a cigarette and reflected. He made no attempt to answer any of the questions. The flight sergeant in-charge of the examination, was a peace-time house painter and decorator. At the end of the time limit, he collected the papers and remonstrated with Shearer, as to his failure in not even attempting an answer to one question. Shearer defended himself by explaining that he was by profession a solicitor, and his law practice continued to make up his peace-time salary, and he was quite indifferent as to whether he held the rank of temporary corporal, sergeant or even flight sergeant. One of the lucky ones.

7. The Turning Point

I had always been able to converse quite freely with my parents about personal problems and the mysteries of sex were for that period quite openly aired. But I was still, at twenty-one years of age, somewhat unsophisticated and innocent when it came to any real intimacy with the opposite sex. An admission which now sounds quite ridiculous, doesn't it, that is, until I met Barbara – a nineteen-year-old radar operator. She was woman-wise beyond her years, and within a few days of our first meeting I was an innocent no longer. Yes, I know it takes two to tango, but at that time I was certainly no dancer. This brief period of ecstasy was soon to be transformed into years of self-incrimination, doubt, heartache and financial hardship. This is difficult for me even now, but I must tell it as it happened.

A few weeks after our relationship had commenced, I was posted to a police unit in Norfolk, being billeted with three other men in a post offfice at Somerton. The post office was run by a lovely lady and her husband Charlie. Some seven months elapsed, and one evening, after the usual cooked meal when we were nicely relaxed, Mrs Pritchard said, 'Bill, I have a telegram for you.' It read, 'received an important letter from Brigadier Armstring. Play the game, son. Love, Dad.'

Barbara

I realised immediately I was in trouble, as the only Armstring I knew was Barbara, but could this really mean what my instinct told me?

Much later, I realised, to my cost, I was about to play everybody else's game but mine. How foolish the young are. How differently I should have tackled that situation. A few days later, after several phone calls and telegrams, I was on my way to Scarborough in Yorkshire. Temporary Corporal Northcott was about to meet his nemesis.

Barbara, it appeared, was seven months' pregnant, and it needs little imagination to realise my state of mind as I saluted Brigadier General John Cardew Armstring CBE MC for the first time at the Scarborough railway station. After Barbara and her mother had gone shopping, the Brigadier and I walked along the promenade and my interrogation began. When finally he asked if I loved his daughter, I replied truthfully with a firm 'No.'

It took me only a few hours to realise that the situation was as embarrassing for the Armstrings as it was for me. The severity of their attitude towards Barbara indicated that there was no sympathy, or love, in that family relationship.

After a civil registrar's wedding, I made my second mistake. Compassion took over and a quick call to the Pritchards requesting their permission to bring Barbara back with me to Somerton met with their agreement.

The Armstrings were obviously delighted to clear the matter up so easily. The outcome was that Barbara eventually travelled down to Cornwall to my parents, and gave birth to my first child, Anne, at a hospital in Falmouth. Anne is clearly recognisable as my daughter. We have always enjoyed a very special relationship.

So, catapulted suddenly into marriage and fatherhood, I endeavoured to make the best of a bad start. Posted to a unit on the Yorkshire Moors, I managed to secure a furnished cottage, and sent a message to Falmouth requesting Barbara and Anne to join me. Shortly after their arrival I received another disastrous shock.

I was wearing civilian clothes when I boarded a service liberty truck, also containing a number of service personnel. Directly opposite me sat a WAAF wearing the radar insignia flash. She was accompanied for some reason by her mother. I asked her what group and wing she belonged to, and receiving appropriate answers, enquired if she knew Barbara Armstring. 'Oh yes, Barbara; she was in love with a Canadian, but her parents made her marry a policeman, called Bill something or other.'

Naturally, this came as a shock to me, and I must have looked somewhat stunned, because she spoke again. 'Are you – are you a policeman?

'Yes.'

'Are you called Bill . . . ?'

'Yes.'

Her mother wisely intervened, saying, 'shut up. You always talk too much.'

But the damage was done. I got out of the truck in a daze.

A few days later I was back in the cottage with my new family. I questioned Barbara as to her relationship with a Canadian airman whilst she was carrying my baby and I, the father, wasn't even aware that she was pregnant. I received an emphatic denial.

A few days later, however, she admitted that there had been a Canadian lover with whom she had spent several weekends at a hotel. Her admission, whilst not altogether unexpected, still came as a big shock to me. From an early age I had been taught to respect the opposite sex. In fact, in my naivety, I had placed them on a pedestal.

Now I felt so outraged, I left the room and loaded my revolver . . . until sanity returned and I left the cottage, and, coatless, walked up the snow-covered hill towards the moor, revolver still in my right hand.

A middle-aged home guard major with whom I was acquainted came walking down the hill towards me. We sat in the snow-covered hedge whilst I explained my dilemma to him. I shall always be grateful to this fortuitous mentor for the advice and compassion he gave me on that occasion. This was the first of many lies Barbara had told me, and I never ever believed in her again. The agony of my marriage had now started. The cards were well and truly weighted against us, sex being the only common denominator. Not enough for any successful relationship. Some thirteen months later, a second child, David, was born.

Before I get too far ahead, I must recount a few impressions I had formed of my worthy father-in-law, who died ultimately at the age of 66 years. Barbara's twin brother was slightly wounded in the Italian campaign. I was present when the Brigadier rang up the war office in London, requesting that Richard be moved back from the front line.

'When your brother-in-law is C in C of all the medical forces in Italy, you should be able to do something for your own son.'

I mentally agreed, but thought of the less privileged wounded without such connections. On another occasion when Richard was on leave in England, and staying at the house in Shooters Hill Road, Blackheath, one night he was late returning home.

'Out with some slut of a shop girl, I suppose!' the Brigadier said. 'What makes you think, sir, that all shop girls are sluts?'

He was relating some of his experiences in India. Once, as a young Subaltern he was acting adjutant and had to hear a charge brought against a Hindu soldier.

'What is, 'what have you got to say for yourself' in Hindustani?' he enquired from his English-speaking Sgt major.

'And what is fourteen days field punishment?'

He made appropriate notes.

The offender was briskly marched in and asked by Armstring in Hindustani what he had to say for himself. Listening to the lengthy explanation for a while, the Brigadier cut the man short, and glancing at his notes, gave sentence.

'Fourteen days field punishment.'

This was my first really intimate contact with this privileged, yet uncompassionate class of people. I was not impressed.

He took great delight in reminding me that a Lieutenant commander was a comparatively junior rank. It had taken my father thirty odd years to attain that exalted position. I can now laugh at the farcial comedy we call life, but at the time these conversations left a deep impression.

An amusing and associated incident was told to me once by a friend in Africa, Harry Mathews. Harry was an ex-airborne captain in the war, then commanding an isolated, snake-infested station, called Malango-ya-simba – gateway to the lions.

One day, the district commander, an ex-navy type and a reservist, visited the post.

'Good morning, Mathews!'

'Good morning, Stacey!'

'Commander Stacey Marks' barked the old man.

'Captain Harry Mathews' bellowed back Harry.

Two Englishmen stacking on side in the African bush, and no audience to appreciate the performance. In retrospect I see how much easier now I could have handled the Brigadier but everyone needs time to mature and grow.

When my second child David was born he was a healthy baby, of average weight, but whilst serving on a mobile police unit at Blackpool, I received a telegram informing me that he was dangerously ill in the Greenwich hospital. Quickly obtaining a few days' compassionate leave, I visited the hospital. My previously healthy son was lying, a small, frail, emaciated skeleton, in an oxygen tent, in which he had been christened. I learned that Barbara had been unable to breast-feed the child, and neither she nor her mother had recognised that, in fact, the baby had been starving. Such incompetence is hard to believe, and certainly difficult to forgive.

The Armstrings owned a house in Devon near Barnstaple, but the Brigadier, who was on sick leave, wished to be near the war office in London. As Barbara, with two babies and Joan, her sister, with another two young children were also staying with her parents, I once questioned the desirability of them living in Blackheath, subjected at the time to the V1 and V2 bombardment of London, when they had an empty house in peaceful Devon.

'Do you think, Bill, I'm going to let a few German bombers frighten me from my home?'

With the thought of a bomb falling on so many defenceless young lives, and being yet another responsibility for the already overworked national fire service, I could not quite see the logic of this argument.

Not long after, David came out of hospital. He had showed so much courage in just surviving, I was posted to an air disarmament wing in Germany. After the usual preliminaries in preparing such a unit we set sail from Tilbury docks, aboard a large tank-landing craft, our destination – Ostend.

Upon landing, we formed up in convoy and while sitting in a police jeep, parked on the dock, I watched the remainder of the personnel disembark. Sitting on the wharf, waiting to be sent as prisoners of war to England, were a corps of battle-hardened, war-weary German Panzer troops, some with blood-soaked, bandaged limbs. As the bespectacled RAF clerks, fat

31

cooks and unmilitary-looking storemen shuffled down the ramp, I could well imagine the fleeting thoughts of our watching enemies.

Eventually formed up, we headed east through Belgium, across the Rhine, over a Bailey bridge and into Cologne. The devastation was appalling. Death was in the air, evidence of war and destruction everywhere.

Once on the autobahn, we made good speed, but huge amphibious vehicles, called ducks, still roared past our convoy, driven by grinning, coloured American soldiers.

I remember being most impressed with the American supply units: huge stacks of petrol cans as high as a house. No red tape. Pull up, fill up and get moving.

The Germans had retreated, but fought tenaciously. Every bridge, every strong-point had been vigorously defended.

I served in Germany for some eleven months, for most of the time stationed in the beautiful town of Detmold, temporarily then part of the American sector.

At night, remnants of the German forces hiding in the woods above Detmold would creep into the town for supplies and food. There were always minor skirmishes and shoot-outs.

On one occasion I called at an isolated farmhouse for some fresh eggs, and was given some by a middle-aged woman who looked at me with hate-filled eyes. I did not offer to pay her. The next day, after ascertaining the price of eggs, I returned to the farmhouse, where the same woman was working in the yard. I paid her for the eggs, saluted and left. It had been a small gesture which made me feel good, but which caused some wry amusement amongst my colleagues.

After all, we were British, you know! And I must say, I felt proud to be British when the sector was finally handed over to the English administration. A small contingent of our red-cap military police marched into the square at Detmold, immaculately dressed and sized off, preceded by a lone Scottish piper playing his haunting melody.

The Germans, one could see and feel, were impressed with the sight of this small unit and its significance. I had previously watched a civilian standing on the balcony of the Gauliters house, by his bearing obviously a Wermacht officer, observing a party of GIs in uniform seated on a pavement kerbstone, playing crap. The contempt on his face was easy to read.

Another small incident that happened whilst we were still

at war with Germany. In company with another RAF man, we visited a barbers shop for a haircut. The barber, a huge, closely-cropped German worked on me in silence. When he started stropping a cut-throat razor to clean up my neck, I realised the temptation and the possibility. He had lost his family of loved ones in one of our bombing raids. I philosophically submitted to this ordeal, however, loosening my revolver under the barber's sheet, as a futile precaution. These are the foolish little memories that leave an impression.

We would drink some evenings in one of the undamaged, but open beer taverns in Detmold. Officially though, they were closed, as the Non-fraternisation ban was then in force, and peace had not yet been declared. The Germans in civilian clothes, but quite obviously by their bearing, military personnel, would keep to their end of the bar, and the allied personnel to theirs. There was little bother. The average man in such a situation of no matter what nationality does not want or go looking for trouble. Back to Blighty by plane – an old Dakota, no formalities. It was so different to modern travel with security checks, luggage inspection, loading passes and visas, passports etc. A short period on a maintenance unit at Stafford, and then the magic moment of demobilisation.

8. Civvy Street

Under the re-instatement act employers were obliged to offer positions to returning ex-servicemen, so back I went to the tailoring company.

At the brief refresher course at Bristol, I was standing with a fellow trainee an ex-Eighth army man from North Africa. Bowler-hatted, rolled umbrella – all the trimmings of our civilian status. He turned to me and said: 'Bill, this life is not for me anymore, I'll never make it.' The roles we play in life can be sometimes a little confusing.

After the brief training at Bristol, I was transferred to Taunton, where I was obliged to find lodgings. No houses were available for rent, and I certainly had no savings with which to purchase a property. Barbara and the children were staying at the time with her parents in Blackheath.

I had been in touch with my local MP on several occasions, complaining of the lack of accomodation. One day he contacted me at work, requesting an immediate interview. Ex-servicemen in a similar plight to myself, it appeared, were starting to occupy unused army establishments throughout the country. He asked if I was prepared to lead a handful of such homeless men into a local army camp. I agreed to do so, and accompanied one evening by a friend, Les Hodder from Cornwall, led a few men and their wives into Nunsfield army camp, in Taunton.

After we had selected a suitable hut, making our beds down and settling in, an Orderly Officer and Sergeant appeared. We were told this was army property, and ordered to leave. Naturally, we refused, so the Officer and NCO quietly left.

I telephoned Barbara to come down, and a few days later we started furnishing the hut and making a home for ourselves and the children.

The authorities were not to be taken lightly though, and soon the power and the water facilities to the camp were cut off. It was winter, snowing and bitterly cold. I remember walking up the road with two buckets of water needed for breakfast one day, when I passed a priest.

'You should be ashamed to wear that that clerical collar,' I exclaimed.

'Why, son?'

'There are young babies and women in that camp; cold and without water, or electricity . . . what are you doing about it?'

After several days , making petitions and what publicity we could get from the local press, the water and the power was resumed, and we were soon comparatively comfortable.

The intense bombing of England, the destruction of thousands of houses, plus wartime material shortages, together with the huge number of newly wed ex-service people, created an almost insoluble problem. The situation was somewhat different to our Australian opposite numbers, who were granted a cheap housing loan almost automatically on demobilisation. But so be it . . .. we survived.

It still amazes me, though. Emergency powers can be quickly voted by government to cover just about any eventuality, but at that time in England returned ex-servicemen, their wives and children were subjected to conditions that should never have been allowed.

Sensibilities can become blunted after six years of war, and I realise there were strong political forces in England endeavouring to hold back the new spirit that was sweeping through the country. The clock of progress must under no circumstances be allowed to turn too quickly.

This has always been my main criticism of governments. They seem unable to feel the pulse, the mood of the moment. They are pushed often by events, instead of leading, and this despite the prohibitive cost to the taxpayer, supporting a multiplicity of bureaucratic departments, set up ostensibly for the public welfare. As Louis Napoleon wrote: It compromises society instead of protecting it.

Seeking better money, my brother Jack and I had changed jobs, and were at the time area representatives for a well known American electrical company, Hoover Ltd. We both had old pre-war cars – all we could afford, – travelled extensively and worked long hours, to secure an adequate income. When I consider now the working conditions of my children and their salaries, together with their high standard of living, I realise how disadvantaged we really were. Progress . . . No doubt every generation feels the same.

After one particularly exhausting sales campaign, when the company called incessantly for higher figures, Jack and I decided to 'call it a day' and both resigned. At the time we gave notice we were averaging about twenty-two pounds a week – good money in 1947, but running costs for the cars, insurance, taxes and other expenses, together with the extremely long hours, made it an uneconomical proposition. Various local employment offices were unable to offer work paying anything like the amount we had been earning. Jack was offered a secretary's position, to an author, at four pounds ten a week. He naturally declined.

A government office in Taunton informed us that an ex-army full colonel was working as a postman in the town, for a salary of five pounds a week. As we were quick to explain, we had neither held this exalted rank nor wished to be postmen. I had at that time progressed domestically from Nunsfield army camp to a pre-fabricated house, one of thousands springing up on estates throughout the country. My brother Jack finally secured a position as a secretary to a district manager, with the oil firm Esso, eventually becoming an area representative, circuit manager and later, taking his own service station. He did quite well out of the petrol business, staying in it until he finally retired.

I, on the other hand, was destined yet to fill many further roles in life.

A telephone call to my sister in Slough informed me that work was plentiful in that area. I travelled on the train to Reading, where Betty kindly met me.

9. Tinker Tailor

Four days later I commenced work as an assistant manager with a well known Slough store. The position was a remunerative one, and I lived temporarily with my sister and her husband, Bunty, a medical practitioner. I will always be grateful for their sympathy and hospitality at that time.

My life was busy and happy until I returned to Taunton and realised the perplexing situation I had to contend with.

Since meeting her parents, I had in many ways sympathised with Barbara, as they obviously had no real love for her and she had been parked away at a boarding school as soon as possible. There had always been servants in her family too, but for years I could never really forgive her for the negligent way she looked after the children. Time, however, heals all wounds.

One very obvious solution which we never even thought of was for Barbara to have a full-time job, enabling us to afford a surrogate mother for the children. This could have been the answer, but most mothers of young children in that period traditionally stayed at home.

Authoritarian families remember Victorian rules!

Back to the store . . . This was in the days of clothing coupons, and I had so much to learn. A sales girl once asked, 'what are these coupons worth, Mr Northcott?' 'Three and a half' was the quick reply. A check with my office . . . green coupons were worth only two units each. I went back to the counter, and said in a confidential tone: 'what colour were those coupons you showed me, miss? 'Green, you say . . . oh, those are only worth two units each. Don't tell anyone please, but I've been colour blind since birth!' I sound like the Brigadier now, don't I, but nobody was hurt.

So it went on. A salesman on the drapery counter once asked me in front of a customer, what the correct name of a particular material was.

'Now what do you think it is?' as I inspected the roll of cloth.

'Moygashel!'

I had never heard of such a material, and even now cannot spell it.

'Of course, it's Moygashel!'

An amusing character I had engaged as a casual storeman, an Irish ex-seaman – short, thickset, with heavily tattooed arms – requested that I give him a permanent job. As he was a good worker and had obviously kissed the Blarney Stone, I agreed.

Somehow, whenever the Jewish directors came to visit the store, accompanied by their very chic American wives, Paddy always seemed to be hanging around the fashion department, looking, of course, invariably like a pirate, about to take part in a boarding party. A muttered, 'Bugger off, Paddy, lose yourself' usually effected his rapid departure, but he was completely unaware of the incongruous note he was striking as he strolled casually amongst the rows of high fashion garments, slick-looking sales staff and display models.

Paddy came to me one day and said that a delivery was being made, but the driver insisted on seeing me personally. I followed him to the delivery bay, where a tall, casual, but expensively dressed Jewish man – unshaven I noticed – was standing alongside a big American station wagon.

'I have three hundred shifts here for you, Mr Northcott . . . Put them right on display, at thirty shillings each.'

'Invoice?'

'Don't worry about that nonsense, just get them sold.' Paddy standing listening, looked towards me, smiled, but wisely made no comment. I was beginning to realise how the wheels turned, so summonsed one of the display staff, and gave the necessary instructions. Within three hours, every shift was sold.

I was sending home to Taunton each week Barbara's housekeeping allowance, together with some of the extra commission I was earning on the stores overall takings. One week I sent an extra sixteen pounds and when next visiting the family in Taunton, enquired what use Barbara had made of the money. She said she had purchased a new lawnmower, and there in the garden shed it was . . . Great!

Barbara's parents had never really provided a stable or caring home for their children, as their service appointments necessitated much overseas travel. Both she and her twin brother had been placed in a boarding school at a very early age.

At the commencement of the war, an Australian woman guardian, a Mrs Bogden had done irreparable damage to Barbara, who, expressing a wish not to return to boarding school, had been allowed to remain at Bogden's country house in the home counties, where she provided free labour in looking after young children who were not of school age.

I remember the Brigadier taking legal action to recover monies that Mrs Bogden had been entrusted with for payment of school fees which had not been honoured. Mrs Bogden was also in the habit of entertaining young Australian air crew personnel for weekends at the country house. I gather from Barbara that she had somehow placed herself in an invidious position when Mrs Bogden insisted she assist in entertaining the young Australian guests. What had I let myself in for?

For some reason on that occasion I was not returning to Slough until the following Tuesday, and on the Monday afternoon, answered a summons at the front door. A man standing there said he had come for the first payment on the lawnmower. Apparantly Barbara had put down a one-pound note deposit, and was paying it off. I never did find out where the other money had been spent. It was the same story throughout the marriage.

At this time, I was earning well in excess of Jack's salary, but his wife Joan has always been a fantastic housekeeper. I could never understand how they were able to afford new washing machines and other appliances.

Years later, when I was staying at a hotel in Australia with a fellow company director, Graham Pilley, he opened his suitcase, and in his inimical way said, 'the silly bitch has forgotten to pack my new gold cufflinks.' Apparently his wife packed his suitcase whenever he travelled away from home. Jealous? Of course I was!

I eventually saw two managers leave the store in Slough, after heated words with the volatile Jewish directors.

When I was asked to manage a store in Hammersmith I declined, and decided to seek a situation nearer home. I applied for a manager's job with Hepworths, the mens outfitters, and on being accepted, commenced a brief course at their Tavistock Branch, starting at a reduced salary of £7-10s-0d a week whilst training. The manager at Tavistock was called Stan Youlden, who had been managing that branch throughout the war. When

I learned he was getting £6-5s-0d a week after all those years of service, I began to think.

Whilst at this branch, there was some emergency with the window display and the regular window dresser could not be contacted. Youlden was in a panic, as the new owner Norman Shuttleworth was visiting the branch for the first time. He had recently purchased some three hundred odd shops. I volunteered to put in a window display, but in my own way, and subsequently did so, with an open modern look.

When Shuttleworth arrived with the general manager and district inspector, he enquired who had put in the window display. Upon his questioning me as to whether I was interested in a display position, I replied that with two children to keep, I really couldn't afford to manage one of his shops, so certainly would be interested in an alternative proposition. The outcome – I was given a district of some twenty shops, and asked to form a display team. I promptly advertised for professional display men, and I myself soon learned the basic technique of good window dressing. After a few months, I was asked to report to Leeds, where I was appointed a senior display supervisor looking after three districts. My salary was increased to twelve pounds a week; I was given a generous travelling allowance and a regular bonus. I quite enjoyed this work, as it gave me a chance to exploit my naturally artistic talent. I enjoyed meeting people, and it got me away from an increasingly difficult situation at home. I eventually organised display studios at Exeter, Cheltenham and Cardiff, centres where I was able to get display teams together using mock windows to give them an outline, and to run down on the next season's displays.

My parents had recently purchased a lovely old house, Torr Cottage at Hartley, Plymouth, and they kindly suggested that Barbara, the children and I take over part of the house. The idea was that my mother could help Barbara come to grips with the responsibility of a young family and relieve me of much of my domestic problems. The move was never successful. On my return each weekend I had to listen to complaints and criticisms from both sides. After one such drama comforting Barbara, another child was conceived, and my second son Peter was born the following year. Talk about compounding a problem . . . I just seemed incapable of learning.

This was all contradictory in so many ways, as Barbara has always maintained that my mother was more of a real mother to her than her own, and despite the early problems between them, they remained quite close. Barbara visited Torr Cottage regularly, until my mother died at the ripe old age of eighty-nine years.

Torr Cottage – Devon

So, as my wife had criticised my parents' interference in her life, I eventually found an unfurnished maisonette, in Elliot Street, near the Hoe in Plymouth. I explained to Barbara that I would not visit, or see my parents for a year, after which, unless her behaviour as a wife and mother improved, I intended to leave her. We furnished and decorated the unit, making ourselves quite comfortable, but I was not happy and continued to worry about the conditions my children were forced to live in, especially as I was still travelling away from home, and only saw them at weekends.

I then decided to seek a situation nearer home, where I would be able to lead a normal family life.

10. Frigidaire Faculty

A Frigidaire agent was advertising for a commercial sales representative to cover part of Devon and Cornwall, vehicle supplied with the job. I applied, was successful, and shortly afterwards was sent to Hendon, the Frigidaire headquarters, to undergo a technical commercial refrigeration course. Here, all the mysteries of refrigerants, condensers, commercial evaporators, humidity and automatic controls, together with forms of heat transfer, were carefully digested. Also, the many commercial outlets using such equipment.

I soon found this to be a really satisfying job, with much variety and scope. It suited too my capability and personality. Within only twelve months, I had firmly established myself in my district. My prospective clients included nearly all retail and wholesale food outlets, the ice-cream industry, hospitals, undertakers, fishmongers, farmers, butchers, breweries and furriers; in fact, wherever there was a need, or possible need, for heavy duty, commercial refrigeration equipment.

I once required the measurements of a standard coffin for a refrigerated viewing cabinet, and visited a client of mine in the township of Saltash, just across the Tamar river from Plymouth. On querying the standard size of a coffin, the six-foot three Cornish carpenter lay down in an open coffin, feet sticking over the end, to prove that it was in fact wider than it looked. As I watched his demonstration, I thought of my next call to a frozen food manufacturer. The variety and humour the situation tickled my fancy. The farming community were beautiful, straightforward people to deal with. I have found that people who live close to the land are much less complicated and unreliable than their city counterparts . . . the rural Australian, African or Thai being no exception.

When I was staying with Jack on one occasion, and was down on my figures, he wanted me to come home early to join him on some social engagement. At seven o'clock that wet and rainy evening I skidded my car through a sea of mud into a farmyard somewhere in Cornwall. It was raining heavily. A broad-shouldered farmer stood sheltering under a shipping roof. 'Aren't you the 'deep freeze' man from Frigidaire?' I was invited into the farmhouse, where he informed me that he was getting the electricity through in about three months' time, and would then be interested in a milk cooler, and possibly a farm freezer.

I happened to mention a Devon farmer's name, a friend of mine called Joe Viggers. 'Do you know that little bastard?' He asked. I stood up. 'Mr Blunt, Viggers is a friend of mine and I object to hearing him spoken of in that fashion.' The farmer grinned. 'Sit down, son. Joe is a great friend of mine too. Get your order book out now.' I signed him up, for a Nash and Thompson milk cooler, and a large farm freezer. He insisted on formalising the sale with a healthy deposit. The electricity was still three months away. I finally got home about nine o'clock in the evening, but the day had been worth it.

Each year we had a senior technical executive and a sales executive from Hendon spend a full day on the road with each representative. There was always something to learn. On one occasion I had 'under-sold' a butcher a new cold room. I was desperate for business at the time, and had failed to work out his meat allocation correctly to assess the size of room the man required. There was trouble from this installation right from the start. Repeated visits by our local service personnel were unable to rectify the fault. I made this one of the calls when accompanied by the Hendon technical expert. He just opened the cold room door twice, closed it, and said, 'Bill, you've undersold here!' With his experience he could tell from the pressure on the door that the room was overloaded. Frigidaire replaced the installation for a larger unit. A lesson for me well learned. There are no short cuts dealing with BTUs (British Thermal Units).

The sales executive's visit proved more satisfactory. I was chasing a farmer for a milk cooling equipment order, and had rashly offered to play a game of darts with him. If I won he would immediately sign an order. So, after a few business-like calls, we arrived at the farmhouse. I knew the farmer brewed his own cider, and laced it heavily with rum. So first we had a drink 'to sharpen our eyes'.

The Hendon man was soon nicely relaxed. Despite my

reasonable prowess as a darts player, I was beaten on the last double, but it was quite apparent to the skilled salesman from Hendon that I had struck the right note, and would do future business with this prospect. Then it was on to Looe where a 'firm' butcher's cold-room order, as had previously been arranged, was just ready to finalise. I learned later that I had been given a good report . . . 'A most unorthodox representative, but one with a very high achievement level.'

Frigidaire had an annual convention in London, and the company went to great lengths to see this was a success. As we booked into the Savoy Hotel, we were given an individually addressed envelope containing the itenerary for the next few days: details of the actual convention at the La Scala Theatre, and other social engagements on the agenda.

Incidentally, the presentation of new equipment at the convention was always proceeded by a fanfare of trumpets from the Household Cavalry Band. I didn't previously realise that these musicians could be hired in Dress Uniform for private affairs.

When I went to Kenya, East Africa with the Crown Agents for the Colonies with eighteen other recruits, we were left standing at Embakasi airport in Nairobi with nobody to meet us. I couldn't help but draw obvious comparisons on that occasion. No doubt Government cannot measure up to private enterprise.

Yes, if my marriage had been a success, I would have been quite happy to stay with Frigidaire. I really enjoyed that occupation. Acceptance of clients was first class. Base salary with commission, vehicle supplied and out-of-pocket expenses. Plus of course, Devon and Cornwall was a beautiful area to be travelling in.

There was once a golden opportunity to take over a furnished guest house and café at Camelford in Cornwall, in the heart of my territory and for no more outlay than I was paying for the maisonette in Plymouth. Barbara would not consider it.

True to my promise, I had not visited Torr Cottage or my parents for twelve months. On rare occasions I would drive past my mother out shopping – a toot on the horn, and a blown kiss my only expression of love.

Though a trifle in the comedy of life, I must mention the Royal Agricultural Show. Frigidaire naturally patronised agricultural county shows and always set up a stand, including a small bar behind the exhibits. On one of these occasions, a very well dressed, good-looking young couple, attired in impeccable riding habits – very 'county looking' – visited the stand and enquired as to the capabilities of a farm freezer. As they lived on a farm near Lerryn in Cornwall, part of my territory, I invited them to have a drink, then arranged to call on them. A week or so later, imagine my surprise as I turned off the main road into a muddy little lane and approached a very run-down farmhouse. Pillows were thrust into broken windows, and there was a derelict look about the whole building. Surely this couldn't have been the place? On my summons at the door, a slatternly, unkempt looking woman answered, carrying in her arms a dirty, ragged-looking child. I recognised her with difficulty as being the same woman who had visited our stand at the show. The women had insisted on buying the freezer, on time payment to me, with no order of priorities. It takes all sorts to make up this lovely and interesting world.

Years later as a private investigator in Australia, I was to marvel at the different faces women can wear, and their fantastic ability to change style, and almost character, just as the mood dictates. Strange, but lovable creatures so much cleverer in many ways, and most certainly more devious than the average male. In my experience Siamese or Thai ladies are especially so, being made from the original mould.

Friction in the home continued between Barbara and I. Her dishonesty, especially with money, and lack of care with the children, finally wore me down. Within twelve months of leaving Torr Cottage, I moved out into a small flat in the same district. A few weeks later I was obliged to have an appendix operation and really enjoyed the relaxed spell in hospital. The only time I am hospitalised is for a surgical matter: appendix, hernia, two hip replacements now, and I must say, I have thoroughly enjoyed being fussed over, on these occasions, having the opportunity to relax and hand over my life to professional people who really care. I cannot speak highly enough of the nurses, doctors and medical staff I have met. I remember in my early days in Australia, how horrified I was to learn of the disparity between the salaries paid to nurses, and those to barmaids. But, no, I am not a 'wowser' as the Australians say, or tee-total. I still like a cleansing ale.

Whilst in the Greenbank hospital in Plymouth, just the day after my operation, I read in the Daily Telegraph that the Crown

45

Agents for the Colonies were looking for police and prison officers for service in Kenya.

Unencumbered by daily trivialities, I always seem to think and act with assurance when I am in hospital. Perhaps it is the uncertainty of life and death. My age, I saw, only qualified me for one of the latter positions, so I immediately made an application and requested an early interview. Determined now to make a complete break, I also sent a letter of resignation to Frigidaire.

As I was living on my own, I was moved from hospital to a convalescent home at Hartley. Shortly after arriving by ambulance, I received an invitation to visit the Crown Agents in London. As the Matron refused to let me travel, I asked one of the walking patients to book me a taxi for early the following morning. Leaving the home cautiously, I took the taxi to North Road station, and was soon on the Cornish Riviera to London. The interview, and medical examination in Harley Street still enabled me to return to Plymouth the same evening, arriving just as the patients were having dinner to face the Matron's accusation, 'you have been to London, Mr Northcott!' I handed her a bunch of flowers I had just picked, when coming up the drive. 'Yes Matron, to Covent Garden to buy you some flowers!' There was much laughter and I was soon forgiven.

I was accepted by the Prison Service in Kenya, commencing with the rank of Chief Officer. At this time, funnily enough, an Australian with a thriving electrical business in Plymouth, had been advised by his doctor that he must slow down. He had a bad cardiac problem.

This man had somehow heard that I had resigned from Frigidaire, and rang me up at my flat, requesting that I call in to see him. He employed several travelling representatives and badly needed someone to take over the management of his business. The package he offered me included a salary of £1,500 per annum, a new car, expenses and an overiding bonus on the business profits. I was going to Kenya on a salary of £780 a year, with the Crown Agents. Discussing the Australian's offer with my family. I had now recommenced visiting Torr Cottage. Jack, my brother said it was too good an opportunity to miss. My father, however, gave me different advice; 'Whatever money you can earn in England son, Barbara will be into it for her share. Take my advice and go to Africa.'

Sound advice I thought . . . I took it.

A new life was starting for me. A new challenge, although emotionally this was the very lowest ebb in my life, and still remains so. It was not easy, leaving the children you love very dearly, but I had explored every avenue. There was no alternative left. I was divorced now from Barbara. A Plymouth enquiry agent had assisted me in producing the necessary evidence to give her a blameless divorce. What irony! The legal costs had been paid, and Barbara had enough funds available to manage comfortably until the first monthly allotment came through from the Crown Agents. I myself, had just my thirty pounds uniform allowance. In August of 1954 my sister and her husband saw me off at Heathrow Airport.

Bettina and 'Bunty'

47

11. Africa and the Mau Mau

There were eighteen recruits on the flight to Nairobi, all destined for the Kenya prison service. I sat alongside a Scotsman, who introduced himself as Jock Ritchie. As we left the Mediterranean Sea behind us and commenced flying over North Africa, Jock started discussing the terrain we were flying over quite knowledgably. He had, it appeared, been a captain quartermaster with the Kings Africa Rifles.

When I enquired about the cost of living in Nairobi, and told him I only had the thirty pounds uniform allowance, he laughed. 'I only have thirty shillings,but what a glorious piss up we had in Sauchihall Street last night!' Jock apparently knew the score.

As I have previously mentioned, there was nobody at the airport to meet us on our arrival, but a telephone call to the prison's department produced results, and we were soon on our way to the training camp at Kamiti, near Kiambu. Cooks were soon mustered, and a scratch meal eventually served. I was now in government service. It was a completely new ball game.

We were billeted in tented accommodation: two men to a tent, and I shared with a man called Harry Mathews, a former peace-time truck driver, film stunt man and ex-captain in a parachute regiment.

I shall always be grateful to Africa. There I slowly regained my spiritual and emotional equilibrium.

I am a keen advocate of a complete change of scenery after a divorce as I have advised many of my clients when I operated as a private investigator in Australia. Move right away from a district, and if possible go abroad. Change your whole lifestyle. If a woman – even your clothes and hair style. It all helps with the new image – so necessary when regaining one's emotional stability.

So now I was learning and living a new life, trying to understand and come to grips with the origin and rationale of the terrorist organisation called. Mau Mau.

I had read such books as Last Chance in Africa by Robert Ruak, and anything else I could read about that mysterious continent. It was much as I had envisaged.

Recalling my much earlier boyhood discussions with my father, I soon realised that my conceptions of the country and the people were not far from the mark. Everything was so new and exciting: the road blocks, with the white hooded , Ku Klux Klan-type figures, pointing out Mau Mau suspects. The occasion, I soon learned, was to settle old scores and vendettas.

I also recall the seemingly endless procession of Kikuyu women detainees, dressed in white shifts, with shaven heads, streaming past our tents each morning on their way to work.

When Jomo Kenyetta returned to Kenya in 1946, after several years in the United Kingdom, he recommenced the activities of the 'Kikuyu Central Association' which he controlled from his headquarters at Githunguri. The financing, organisation, and secret arming of a revolutionary movement – which the authorities called Mau Mau soon began.

Kenyetta knew the psychology of his tribe well and a campaign of oathing was started – to wield the tribe with their local chiefs into one vibrant political party. There were many different forms of oaths – some more obscene than others but all calculated to make the recipient capable of the utmost brutality. Those who refused to take the oath were threatened, and if they still resisted were quickly murdered.

I once had a Kikuyu through my rehab centre, who alleged he was returning from his work in Nairobi (where he was employed in a medical dispensary) when he was picked up by a Kenya police inspector – an African – in a police car. They took him to an oathing ceremony where he was forced to swear a Mau Mau oath.

On October 21st 1952 a State of Emergency was declared. Kenyetta and many Kikuyu leaders arrested and government intelligence services began serious investigation of known oathing ceremonies and subversive activities. Police and prison services were expanded local Askaris being recruited from Wakamba, Jaluo and other uncontaminated tribes. Whilst white officers such as myself were recruited from the Crown Agents of the Colonies. In the UK.

We were soon fitted out with uniforms, hand-made boots, and war-time campaign ribbons were supplied. Most days were spent in the classroom studying prison rules, regulations and procedures and, of course, studying the Swahili language. This was varied , with days spent on operations with the police or army. I remember one such day quite well.

We were given command of fifty Askaris each, and given details to throw a cordon around the base of a forest hill. In theory, the army and home guard units were to sweep any terrorists from the forest and into our net. Harry, my tent mate, had the next section to me, and having placed our men in position, we met for a brief discussion on the exercise. Suddenly over the rise of the hill came a motley crowd of Africans, armed with spears, guns and bows and arrows. 'This looks interesting, Harry. Here comes our first Mau Mau!' But no, the motley throng turned out to be a home guard unit, who promptly started to cut down sugar cane which grew at the side of the valley road, and happily commenced chewing.

Suddenly a tall, well armed young European settler appeared on the scene, cut down a six-foot length of cane, and then started laying into the home guard, beating them around the head and legs, shouting 'Come on, you black bastards. Get into line!'

We approached him. 'Excuse me. isn't this the home guard?'

'Yes, that's right, but don't worry, the bastards love it!' I then saw that many of the Africans were, in fact, actually smiling and laughing. 'Gosh, Harry. What are they like when they catch the Mau Mau?'

Amongst our intake were two men who wrote and spoke quite fluent Swahili. When it came to a written language test, a crib was hastily passed around the table. As we were seated in the classroom, individual postings kept coming in, but few men volunteered, as none of us fully understood the worth of the position or location, that is, with the exception of our two Swahili-speaking comrades.

In response to a request for two men required at a certain post, to our general chagrin and consternation, these two, our only language advisors, left the room. Colonel Kylie, our instructor, had apparantly spoken to higher authority quite highly of our linguistic progress, and here we were now with a final test paper imminent – really up against it. Amazingly, though, with the skill of old soldiers, we stalled time and time again with well rehearsed excuses. We needed more time for revision. There were too many sweeps etc. Eventually, as the volunteers now readily came forward, we were finally all posted and that particular dangerous situation had passed.

An amusing character – the old Colonel. He used to get as drunk as a lord at night, say, 'goodnight chaps', and promptly walk into the nearest wall until some compassionate soul would lead him to the door. I never saw him with a firearm, but know he slept in his unprotected bungalow with a Gurkha's Kukri on his bedside table.

One of the postings that came through was for Nairobi gaol, and an ex RAF fighter pilot who accepted was detailed to officiate at one of the 'hanging sessions' then being conducted. He refused this duty, saying that he didn't come out to Kenya to hang anyone. This man subsequently paid the prison department back their air fare and returned to England. I attended one such session as an observer – on that occasion they hung ten men. The Africans impressed me with their stoic behaviour, no struggles or crys, just brave acceptance.

As I have explained to some of our so-called Christian groups who most regretfully criticise other denominations; if my lord can give me the same courage as the Kikuyu Mungu (The Kikuyu God) did for them, I will be quite happy. Yet we disparagingly call them 'pagans.'

An instance when the European duty officer came on the day of execution to transfer the condemned man to the execution cell. As the cell was unlocked, one man from about nine men would rise to his feet before any word had been spoken 'Kamau KIMATHI?' the European would say. The standing African would quietly reply 'Tiari effendi' – I am ready. The prison grapevine had already informed the inmates of the list of men to die on that day. No doubt his cell comrades had prayed with him, and prepared him well.

Such courage commands nothing but the utmost respect from me.

Government actions, throughout history, have had far too many undesirable consequences.

'Any moderate government – any government based on regular procedure and justice, ruins itself by the interruption of justice by any deviation from regularity' Humboldt

Throughout history, every so-called civilised country has at some time been responsible for the same stupidities and cruelties.

51

Whilst I am on such a macabre subject, early one morning a jeep drove up to out tented accommodation. 'Anyone for the burials?'

Harry Mathews and I, together with three other men jumped into the vehicle. We were driven some five kilometres, before pulling off the road into a large clearing, finally stopping alongside two pits that had been freshly dug, some ten feet by eight feet, and at least six-feet deep. A lorry was parked nearby, and I saw it contained a pile of naked African male bodies. Suddenly we heard the sound of womens' voices singing in Kikuyu, and soon a small column of, women detainees, with shaved heads appeared, carrying Jembies, – African digging tools. They seemed to know what was expected of them, and as they approached the open pits they stopped singing. Two of them jumped up into the lorry and started handing down the bodies to their colleagues. I then saw that each body had a name tag around the neck, which the women examined closely.

The bodies were laid in the pits, side by side covered with blankets, and the pits were then filled in with soil. Throughout this exercise the women remained completely silent.

There is no doubt that mankind pays a heavy price for the freedom that has been fought for. All so very sad. The revolutionary , terrorist or freedom fighter of today is often the hero of tomorrow. It has unfortunately always been so. It is difficult at times to keep the true meaning of life in some perspective, but we must try to find some balance, some compromise. This is where, for me, religion has some real meaning.

One night, whilst at Kamiti, a heavily armed gang attacked the PWD lines about one and a half miles from the training camp. It was quite late at night. Harry and I, in pyjamas, raced down to the armoury, loaded a truck with armed Askaris, and one each side on the running board rapidly drove down to the PWD lines, and when within range, opened fire on the attackers. The Mau Mau would fire the roofs of the huts and shoot into the burning building. This is what happened on this occasion. It was chaos – with men shouting, women and children screaming as huts went up in flames and small arms fire erupted around the quarters.

We eventually drove the gang off with rifle and pistol fire, but, being reluctant to chase into the forbidding looking bush on foot, released those villagers who had been locked in their huts, and assisted in quenching the fires.

When we finally returned to the camp, naturally somewhat black and bedraggled, we were greeted by our comrades, all properly dressed, complete with puttees and campaign medals, whilst Harry and I, standing to attention rather sheepishly, in our barely recognisable pyjamas, revolvers in hand, received a rebuke from a senior officer for leaving the camp without permission. So much for free enterprise.

Only a few months later, as a community development and rehabilitation officer I was to be labelled by many of the settlers, incorrectly, as a left winger. I wish someone , would recognise me, just once, for what I really am. A mere humble humanitarian.

Another incident I must not forget to mention: the day I visited the police stores in Nairobi. Whilst at the depot, I was asked to visit the prison next door and pick up two bods for Kamiti. Two new recruits, I thought, as I reported to the duty officer, but no, I was directed to the mortuary where two naked Africans lay, one face down on the floor and the other lying on his back on a table, his sightless eyes staring at the ceiling. As I was unable to get blankets to cover them, they were placed naked on my three-ton truck, with the rest of my load.

As I drove back to Kamiti through the heavy Nairobi traffic, I kept looking behind me at my mixed cargo, and wondering if this 'was for real!' On our arrival at Kamiti, I requested an African SGT/MAJOR to arrange an immediate burial. 'Leave them on the truck, effendi, they will be alright until tomorrow!' I looked at him increduously. 'Haven't you any respect for your own dead?' I said, thinking of the hyenas and other nocturnal predators of Africa.

I managed to unlock an adjacent office and had the two bodies placed gently on the rammed earth floor. This I saw was marked as the Accounts Office. Returning on foot to the officers mess, I asked for the accounts officer, an ex-Indian Naval Officer called Spike Sullivan. I explained the position to him.

I met Spike years later in Perth, Western Australia, when he was able to give me, as the ex-officer in charge, full details of the Hola incident in which eleven Mau Mau detainees were killed. Spike was a great humanitarian; I never saw him give out violence to anyone, yet he was to bear the full brunt of the Hola incident.

Life can be full of coincidences. In the sleepy little seaside village of Augusta in Western Australia, some thirty years later a friend gave me a present – a copy of the 'Record of proceedings and evidence in the enquiry into the deaths of eleven Mau Mau detainees at Hola camp in Kenya', which I read with the greatest interest.

Back to the Kiamiti training camp. It was still a little unreal to me after my life in sleepy Devon: drinking in the mess with the boys, or playing darts at night; windows and curtains wide open. Suddenly a loud burst of gunfire and we were greeted with the sight of a nearby village bursting into flames.

Once with a party of trainees from Kamiti, we were returning from a night out in Nairobi, travelling in an old Chevrolet. Rounding a bend, we skidded into a large tree that had been felled across the road. Fearing an ambush, we leapt out of the car, guns drawn, and flung ourselves into the bush at the side of the road. There was complete and utter silence. We remained motionless for several minutes, but there was no threatening movement. Inspecting the vehicle, we discovered the radiator was badly damaged, but the engine started, and appeared to function well. As we had all been drinking in a Nairobi club, it was not difficult to keep the radiator topped up, with enough liquid to travel some short distance. Thus we moved towards Kamiti in stages. The odour at times almost unbearable!

An interesting character with us, Taffy Jones, would enter the mess invariably with a loud cry of 'Slap it on the table – on the table!' And to much amusement from the other members would proceed to expose his virility. Why is it that service men gathered together tend to outdo each other with this sort of lewdness? An expression of manhoud maybe? Or for the same psychological reasons as an 'oathing ceremony?

It really is surprising what lengths some men will go to to emphasise their originality. No pun intended. Taffy was posted to a nearby unit, where he built a fortified rondavel, two round aluminium pre-fab huts surrounded by a concrete wall, buttressed like a castle. Before sitting down to dinner some evenings he would have a shoot out with a neighbouring Mau Mau unit, for some thirty minutes or so. This went on intermittently for several weeks. I verify the story because I saw evidence of the terrorists' marksmanship, although I never heard of any casualties. Taffy was the only other ex RAF policeman in our intake.

On another off-duty occassion, Harry and I, resplendent in

evening dress went into Nairobi 'on the town', ending up at the Ngambo Club. It was in the small wee hours of the morning that we hailed a taxi to return to camp. The route to Kamiti ran through a low swampy area where there had recently been much Mau Mau activity.

As we approached the area, the taxi driver slowed down to about five miles an hour. 'Pesi, Pesi Driver' I said, 'get a move on!.' My request was ignored, and he continued moving along at a snail's pace. Harry drew his revolver, stuck the barrel into the man's neck, and cocking it, said 'Pesi, Pesi.' The taxi shot forward at great speed, and we quickly and safely reached our destination. Such were the times.

At dances,. many men wearing evening dress carried slung sten guns with two clips taped together, and most ladies wore, quite naturally, their sometimes small pearl-handled revolvers. Amie Becker, the wife of a German friend of mine, carried a pistol in her handbag and a dangerous-looking knuckle-duster – the only woman I have ever known to do so. She had much experience in her isolated farm in the highlands, her son Peter, ran a successful combat tracking team in the Aberdeen Forest. Another comrade of mine at Kamiti was Jack Jones, an ex-foreign office man, who later worked for me in Western Australia. Jack had seen much service in government in different parts of the world.

12. Call to Arms

My training period at Kamiti was unexpectedly terminated when the Mau Mau launched an attack on Lukenia detention camp. I was sent down to Lukenia in the early hours of the morning with a reinforcement detachment of Askari prison officers. Most of Lukenia's regular African staff had fled, barefoot, over the barbed wire fence at the rear of the camp as the attack was launched at the main gate. The fence had collapsed under the weight of their bodies.

Discipline in the camp was bad. There had been a long softening-up process before the raid, which was timed to coincide with the departure of the commanding officer, a rugged Scotsman, who was getting married at the time. On hearing the Mau Mau bugle call at the commencement of the raid, the only other European officer, an Englishman called White, had remained in the officers' quarters outside the camp. He hid under the bed, leaving the camp virtually leaderless.

I closed the officers' quarters, and White and I from thence, slept in the main camp. As the regular Askaris drifted back into camp I disarmed them and locked them in a special hut. White, I remember, refused to sleep in the same room with me as I kept a box of primed grenades under my bed.

My Kamiti Askaris, built a fortified watch tower overlooking the main gate, which commanded a clear view of the countryside around the camp perimeter. One day on my return from Nairobi, I learned that White had taken a patrol up through the hill overlooking the camp. I climbed the new observation tower and saw White and the patrol silhouetted against the sky line. Borrowing an Askari's rifle, I opened fire; a few shots near the patrol, and they disappeared from view. Consternation followed and, descending to the ground, I sounded the manually operated klaxon alarm. White and the patrol came running towards the camp shouting that the Mau Mau had opened fire on them. A sergeant had lost his cap and an Askari, his sandals.

As I stood by the main gate with my Greener shotgun in hand, White saw one of my grinning Askaris. 'Was that you, Bill?' he asked. I lifted my shotgun. 'Charlie, that was definitely rifle fire!'

We received a signal one night that a heavily armed gang of two hundred men was approaching Lukenia. We hastily put out trip wires, and at the darkest time of the evening before the moon broke through, I fired the grass on two sides of the camp. The wind blew steadily the flames away from the camp – ideal. When people in Nairobi who were able to see the flames from the grass fires signalled through to ask if we were being attacked, White was quite critical, as it was not prison land that we had ignited. As I explained to him, I had no intention of allowing two hundred mad Mau Mau to gain entry to the camp, unseen. We were fortunately not attacked.

As I endeavoured to tighten discipline, it had been my practice at night to check the sentries at irregular intervals. The African happily goes to sleep whilst standing up. I was in the habit of wearing gym shoes whilst doing these security checks, and silently approaching the sleeping Askaris, would click the bolt of my sten gun, getting an immediate and startled reaction. One night, White and I, had decided to leave the security of the camp and return to the unprotected European quarters for a well cooked meal and a proper hot bath.

As the Askari fumbled with his keys to unlock the two security gates, we were left completely exposed in the bright moonlight.

'Pesi – Pesi' I said , as I automatically clicked the bolt on my sten gun. Three shots rang out, as the bolt came back too far into the firing position, and the Askari fell to the ground. Badly shaken I ordered Simama 'stand up'. The Askari immediately jumped to his feet and opened the gate. Miraculously he had not been hit.

As we approached the officers' quarters, White said, 'was that an accident, Bill?' 'Of course, it wasn't Charlie, I'll shake these Askaris into line.' White called me a ruthless bastard, a remark which I thought quite suited the occasion.

That again sounds like one of the old brigadier's stories, but again, no one was hurt. It was an accident, but I do quite agree – a stupid one! After a court of enquiry held at Lukenia into the Mau Mau raid, during which I first met Sir Vincent Glen Day of Northern Frontier District fame. I received my second posting – to the beautiful island of Lamu, north of Mombasa.

13. Lamu – The Magic Isle

I was detailed to escort a party of a hundred detainees of a special category by rail to Mombasa, and then by an East African naval vessel to, Lamu. Fortunately, I had a partly English speaking Sgt major accompanying me, which at the time was, I thought, somewhat comforting. It was still a relief when we steamed into Mombasa railway station and I handed my charges over to a local senior superintendent of prisons, Commander Fenton. An ex-navy reserve officer, Fenton had served with my father on HMS Lucia, a submarine depot ship, where he was executive officer and was aptly named Dozey Fenton. Dad was then the Chief Engineer.

After a very pleasant evening in the Mombasa club with Fenton, who remembered serving with my father and who kindly gave me some useful tips on surviving in East Africa, I retired for a good night's sleep.

The next morning it was quite a refreshing experience to watch my contingent of trainees being herded aboard the old converted English minesweeper by efficient, disciplined, well armed African naval ratings. We finally set sail – a camp bed being provided for me on the bridge of the ship.

I was able to repay the naval hospitality I enjoyed for the next two days by getting the decks of the vessel honed white by a hundred pairs of willing hands. Rumour had spread that my charges were to be drowned at sea. Once convinced otherwise, they joyfully entered into the spirit of the occasion. their very first cruise, I reflected!

My request for a theatrical burst or two from the ship's pom, poms just to impress the passengers was, unfortunately, due to lack of ammunition, not granted.

At long last we reached Lamu – that magic island mosques, minarets dhows, smugglers, palm trees, coconuts and donkeys. At that time comparatively untouched by civilisation. There were no cars on the island, only one hotel, Petleys, and the small town-ship overlooked by the old Portugese Fort, then the headquarters for the prison department and its various outlying camps. As our vessel dropped anchor, a barge drew alongside, and sitting in a camp chair at the stern I caught my first glimpse of Commander Stacy Marks, the prison's commanding officer. White uniformed, white bearded, black slouch police hat, rows of campaign medals, and, of course, wielding the inimitable cow's tail fly whisk. An impressive sight.

We commenced disembarking our human cargo; and as they streamed ashore, wading thigh-deep in mud, it looked like a shot from a Ryder Haggard film.

This was the real Africa – cut off from the world by that terrible road. Ghosts in black shrouds. glided through the streets – I found out later that these were either wives of Arabs or Muslimised Africans called Swahilis. They wore the shrouds to conceal their faces, but if you kept glancing, you could catch them unawares – wide opaque eyes would look directly and tantalisingly at you – until suddenly the veil would be parted and beetle nut juice expectorated most expertly at your feet. – just another female contradiction.

As we disembarked the commander insisted that all Europeans should be carried ashore on the shoulders of our captives. As my carrier sank almost to his waist with my weight in the thick black mud, I jumped off, and, disregarding the damage to my immaculate white uniform, staggered ashore.

As Mathews had proceeded me to Lamu, and I was soon reunited with my former tent mate. We were billeted with the local police inspector Steve Moore and his wife. My bedroom in Steve's home was the only one I have ever slept in with mud bats' nests on the ceiling. Surprisingly, I soon became quite at ease with these little creatures, wheeling and whirling overhead – their in-built radar, guiding them away from any contact with me.

Lamu had a most unusual smell: dried urine, chillies and fish. Strangely too, one soon got quite used to this most obnoxious smell. It was a fascinating place. Crumbling coral lay on the sand, evidence of decay everywhere – litter of roof thatching – cracks in whitewashed walls – once the main buildings of this great centre of coastal industry. The twenty mile deep coastal strip on which Lamu stands was originally administered by the British at the request of the local Sultan in an effort to put down the slave trade.

Prison Headquarters at Lamu

Several Europeans have spent the last years of their lives there. Percy Petley, the hotelier, Coconut Charlie, and Patterson, the African land development man, and, of course, BA Allen, one of my old friends. Coconut Charlie I understand, lived in a tent, but insisted on dressing formally in a tuxedo for the evening meal. He had passed on to happier hunting grounds before I arrived at Lamu.

Old Pat, married to Barraca, a charming Swahili lady, had at one time been an alcoholic until Barraca straightened him out. He confided to me once when I was contemplating the purchase of a Somali wife that he had never been intimate with a white woman, but had been blessed with several African 'wives'.

Baa as we called Allen, is the only white man I have known to bear scars of spear wounds on his body.

I remember quite well the first time I entered Petley's hotel wearing a crisp white uniform. Percy was sitting in his favourite chair, fingering his old fashioned hearing horn. He looked up, and said in a loud voice, 'Good God, what the devil have we got here?'

It was also quite embarrassing for strange couples booking into the hotel. If they asked for single rooms, Percy would stare at the woman, 'what's wrong, she looks OK to me!' Or, if the request was for a double room, it solicited a reply like, 'you're legally married, I hope?'

One could never win with dear old Percy.

All drinks were signed for, and Percy acted as the island's banker. If a trip to Mombasa had to be financed, a chit was signed for the two hundred pounds or whatever, and Percy paid up. It appeared as yet another item, on the next monthly statement.

When the noise in the bar late at night or in the early hours of the morning, became too offensive, as often haappened, the DC would send down a message to 'Funga the bar.' As men came in from lonely, isolated stations, though, Percy was providing them with a real service. It was their only opportunity, maybe once a month, to meet fellow Europeans and let their hair down.

Some of the Europeans became quite eccentric, like Johnnie Russell, an ex-army intelligence officer who turned up at one official function at the club, when a visiting provincial commissioner and his wife were present. John was in uniform, looking quite immaculate, with an impressive row of campaign medals, but with one side of his moustache and beard completely shaven off. Nobody, of course, batted an eyelid or made any adverse criticism. Imagine the same scenario had it been Australia!

Yes, I had some enjoyable evenings at Petleys. John Llewellyn, an ex-provincial commissioner and his wife Inger, a Swedish actress, also lived on the island at that time and were amusing company.

Allister Wistrop, a Kenya-born prison officer from Manda Island. I can visualise him now, standing on the bar, singing his Western country songs. For a hobby, Allister milked venomous snakes and sent the poison collected down south to a serum manufacturer.

Gilbert Stubbs, an artist, ex-naval commander and bomb disposal expert, another Ernie R Blown, ex-master at arms, RN both too, then Kenya prison officers. And Bardie, the fat, shrewed, Swahili customs officer, drinking his Muslim Pepsi Cola during the period of Ramadan.

I nostalgically wonder where they all are now!

14. Mkowe
– My first command

I was detailed to open a works camp at Mkowe on the mainland, some five miles by sea and six by road from the island's
headquarters. I contracted with a heavy muscled, villainous
looking but most amiable Swahili boatman to have his Dhow
'Aspro' ferry in my petrol and heavier stores. Mkowe works
camp was to be part of a rehabilitation experiment for Mau Mau
'greys' who had volunteered to take part. Mau Mau greys were
not totally committed to the cause.

At Mkowe Works Camp

My first batch of volunteers included a schoolteacher, medical dispenser, carpenters, masons and agricultural workers. It was intended to build a permanent settlement.

Harry Mathews had supervised the building earlier of a grass hut intended to be my living quarters. But when I first visited Mkowe, entering the hut through a very low doorway I saw and heard the lizards and insects, rustling through the grass walls, I decided it was not for me.

I obtained, and erected a semi-permanent officer's tent, in which I lived for some eleven months. I made myself quite comfortable on the cement floor, looking at the walls covered to some three feet with mud and wattle painted white. Over the tent I built a grass Makuti (palm frond) thatch roof to keep it cool, and I also organised an L-shaped extension that I used as a bathroom.

Mkowe was the most snake-infested area I had ever lived in: cobras, green and black mambas and puff adders were seen daily. But it's amazing how quickly one adapts.

At night, as one swept a torch through the open end of the tent a battery of eyes peering into the light made one really feel 'on stage'. The area swarmed with baboons, as the leopard, their natural enemy, had been shot out by Arab and European hunters, the balance of nature was quite upset. Lions were a menace too. Cattle had to be secured in a BOMA at night, but whether this was to deter lions or mosquitoes I forget now.

I was interested to see water buffaloes under an open shelter, recently in Thailand lying alongside burning tyres, but this was definitely to smoke off the 'mozzies'. It was all a complete change from peaceful Devon, but just what I needed after my unpleasant marriage. So I set about planning and supervising the building of quarters for my Askaris and detainees. A central kitchen had to be built, materials ordered and gathered from the surrounding bush. An office for myself, guardroom, a mess room and quarters for the Askaris and their wives. It all began to take shape and gave me time to evaluate the political and personal feelings of my settlers. Gradually, amidst the beautiful mango and baobab trees, a village started materialising. Wells were sunk – a new experience for me, and gradually the forest was pushed back and land cleared for the growing of maize and my domestic garden.

There were no fresh vegetables on Lamu island, which was just built on coral and sand, but it wasn't long before I had various vegetable boxes made, and was sending across the green harvest from my shamba to Lamus' European officers. It's amazing how a plentiful supply of labour, even in such primitive surroundings, helps. I knew at this time; like any other young, divorced man I badly needed a woman's presence. When, after my command parade on a Saturday morning, I inspected my Askaris lines, I would enter a hut, to be faced with a beautiful Somali girl lying indolently on a bed smiling at me. A red haze would envelope the scene and I would quietly leave . . . So much for my inspection. Of course, they knew how I felt – women, old chap!

Shortly after this, I arranged for my sergeant to buy me a Somali wife. He made the necessary arrangements to have a suitable woman sent down from Mogadishu . . . at the cost of fifty pounds. Patterson, the ALDEV officer, however, talked me out of this exciting opportunity, but looking back at my experiences in Australia, I still question, whether I then made the right decision. In retrospect I must admit I definitely did not!

I loved Africa, and felt at home. The Europeans I met there, of all nationalities, had come recently from Europe. We had a common bond. Not so in Australia. I always felt out of step there, in a foreign land. I am not at all ashamed of the way I feel about the country.

The Mombasa road to Mkowe was closed for almost eight months of the year. The only way out was by sea or air when the airstrip was not flooded. The rehabilitation officer in the Lamu district was a German, Dr Fredi Becker, who quickly became a close friend, and was responsible eventually for my joining the Ministry of Community Development and Rehabilitation as a CDO officer. His knuckle-duster-carrying wife Ami was writing a book called the *Island of no Return* – nice people and quite lavish hosts. When discussing the Lari massacre once with Fredi, he reminded me to keep a sense of perspective about such atrocities. As he said, when our forefathers galloped an armoured horse into battle, crushing an opponents' heads with battle-axe or mace, or a knight used a broadsword to lop off a limb the end result was just as blood-curdling and savage. Now we are able to equip our troops with machine guns or other automatic weapons. The end result is a neat, clean hole . . . but the victim was just as dead. Women and children also suffer under so-called civilised hands: from aerial bombardment and now the obscenity of nuclear weapons. Did you know, that the first atom bomb dropped on Japan, was 'blessed' by a leading church official?

The Mau Mau at this time were using simis, home-made guns, or stolen weapons. Of-course, to our eyes, the results of such raids, as at Lari, looked barbaric.

The Beckers at that time lived in a comfortable Arab-style, whitewashed house at Shella, on Lamu island, and several times on festive occasions mainly, Harry and I walked across the sand dunes dressed in tuxedos to enjoy an assignment with them.

I was happy at Mkowe – the days were busy. Apart from the settlement building, I was supervising the building of police posts in the district, and a convict camp, at Hindi, a couple of miles away; plus, of course, my normal administrative duties, made easier upon the completion of my mud/brick-built office. This had the usual makuti roof, and when the rains commenced, the roof leaked until the grass swelled, and then it could take the strongest downpour. My relationship with the Africans was good. Like the Thais they have a good sense of humour. I treated them fairly and justly, and whilst never a good linguist, eventually I had no trouble in communicating with them. There is more to belonging somewhere than learning the language.

I decided to build a guard and look-out post in one of the magnificent baobab trees which surrounded the camp site, building a platform first and then a double frame of intertwined sticks which were then filled with liquid mud. This eighteen inches thick when dried, could easily stop a .303 rifle bullet. One Somali Askari refused to work on the structure. 'I am an Askari, not a builder!'

Explaining that soldiers had built , manned and died in fortified structures, from time immemorial, I arranged for his transfer. Some week later he attempted to get a posting back to the Mkowe unit, which, of course, I refused. Many Europeans did not like, or trust the Somalis. I got on with them exceedingly well, and always felt safe with them. My final police unit when I returned to Mkowe as a district officer consisted entirely of Somalis. I respected too their fighting quality.

It was whilst I was living in my tent that I first met Padre Cheese. Past seventy years of age, he would tramp down on foot from Somalia wearing a pair of old army boots and no socks. He stayed with me at the works camp for some days, sleeping, and dining, in the tent. I had made him a wooden crucifix, and when he was conducting a church service, I would drape a sheet over a camp table with the crucifix to form a simple altar.

Sitting in the tent one day watching the old padre, preaching the word of God to some forty odd Africans, under the mango trees, I began to think. When the service was over and he returned to the tent to change his vestments, I discussed my thoughts with him. As an ex-commercial representative with Frigidaire, it was essential, that I spoke to the man who actually signed the cheque. It was of little value talking to the supervisor or manager of a business.

There were many miscarriages of justice during that period on both sides, but surely his place was in Nairobi, where the real decisions were being made, or back in England, where it would be physically easier at his age, and where he could influence the people back home. The old man looked at me. 'But Bill, my work is here!' He then explained that he was doing a translation of the Bible into the Somali language.

Truly a Christian gentleman and a saint.

It was shortly after this conversation that the old man gave a squeal, as one of my pet mongoose ran up his trouser leg. I kept two fully grown animals in the tent, for obvious reasons.

I later built a small church with a prefabricated tower, grass-roofed like the other buildings. I tried to get a bell to hang in the tower from Mombasa, but was unsuccessful. Although I was not confirmed in the Christian faith, Padre Cheese got a dispensation from the Bishop of Mombasa to give me communion in the small church.

When I re-married later however, he refused, after much soul searching, to bless my new wife's wedding ring, as I had previously been divorced.

One day – this was when I was later a DO at Mkowe – Padre Cheese occupied the small guest house for several weeks. One morning he was sitting in the lounge, as I first got out of bed, I asked him why he was up so early. Apparently, when he had retired to the guest house the previous night, he had discovered the whole building alive with Safari ants. He had slept on the cement floor in the lounge of my house rather than awaken me. I had a perfectly good spare bed upstairs. As I said before, a real Christian gentleman.

Whilst my health was always good in Africa, I once did suffer from heat exhaustion through lack of salt. I visited Lamu hospital reporting to Dr Shah the Indian in charge. I was surprised to see him on this occasion with two attractive Swahili girls, one on each knee. I had heard he was a practising homosexual, and knew he procured local ladies for the Europeans. Eventually, I got to know him quite well – a man with a good sense of humour. I liked him and was sorry to hear when I lived in Australia that he had eventually committed suicide.

There was a South African postal and telegraph technician staying in the tent with me for a while, the first South African I had met, whilst living in close contact with coloured people. He was supervising the clearing and erection of posts for a new telephone line. Elephants were in the habit of knocking the old posts down. Ted, he was called, and always wore a heavy .45 calibre automatic pistol, on his hip.

Once I was talking on one occasion to an ex Mau Mau school-teacher called Japhet Njegi, whose face was badly scarred, where a hyena had bitten him as a child.

Ted shouted across that tea was ready, which I acknowledged, but continued my conversation with Japhet. Ted walked towards us. 'Come on, Bill. You'll never learn anything from these black bastards!'

Japhet looked at me and smiled.

I questioned this detainee once as to why he had taken the second Mau Mau oath, where the men sat with their penis's through a hole, pierced in a long piece of raw meat, biting the other end of the meat each time they uttered an oath. 'Europeans put an X against a candidate's name, Bwana. We do it this way!' Some time later I had a more serious run-in with a South African police weapons training instructor called Josh. He also stayed with me. Fortunately, I was a district officer then, with a little more clout. Josh would insist on continually shouting, boy', when I had explained that my houseboy's name was Mwangi. He also objected to being called Bwana, or master, preferring the more military, effendi, or sir.

One day when I drove down to the Mkowe jetty, Josh was standing, pistol in hand, facing a Somali police driver who had a drawn knife, pointed at the South African.

'Put your gun away, Josh!'

'Place this man under close arrest, Bill,' said Josh.

I recognised the Somali as a man named Juma, and ordered him to put his knife away and return to his unit. He did so, saluted me, climbed into his truck and drove off. Josh was furious, but I had now had enough and told him so, and the next day, as instructed, he left the district.

The more intelligent Europeans by this time recognised as a

reality the political aspirations of the coloured people, and were fairly circumspect in their approach to them. As I was to realise though when I later joined the Ministry of Community Development, many of the well entrenched old-timers still found it difficult to come to terms with the new forces that were sweeping across the continent.

From Irving Spergal Street Gang Work

At a time when mankind has come to appreciate common goals and objectives, it has also become acutely aware of the deep differences which separate people. Bridges must be formed to cover the gap between rich and poor, young and old, educated and uneducated, black and white, healthy and sick, if society is to progress and the conditions of mankind be improved.

It was just the same in Africa at that time. The same questions were being asked most certainly to me. There was also, as to be expected, antagonism between prison officers and rehabilitation staff. The former were mainly interested in security aspects, with little appreciation or understanding of the aims of social workers, or rehabilitation officers. My sympathies have, on various occasions, leaned towards both sides.

This is the time to mention an amusing, but quite true incident about Wing Commander Greaves, OBE, who later relieved me at the Perkerra rehabilitation camp in the rift valley. He was at the time CDO Lamu district, and had arrived by boat one day at Manda island, I think at the Takwa camp. In any case, the camp was commanded by a prison officer called Blown. As the boat drew into the jetty, Greaves stood up, and in his somewhat pompous voice said, 'Wing Commander Greaves, Ministry of Community Development and Rehabilitation!'

Ernie Blown stood, stripped to the waist, on the jetty, six-feet tall, thick set, and muscular, the only sign of authority being his prison service uniform cap.

'Ernest R Blown, ex-master at arms of Her Majesty's Royal Navy, get off my Fugging island!'

He flatly refused the Wing Commander permission, to land. Co-operation at times between departments was at least interesting, if hardly conducive to efficiency.

I had been able to assist Dr Becker on several occasions when men have 'opened up' and given me useful information, on Mau Mau activities, names of oath administrators, location chairman, and details of actions they have taken part in.

Finding it easy to talk to people, I often openly admitted that had I been born a Kikuyu, I would have been no doubt in the same position as themselves, but I was more fortunate, having been born in Devon, that beautiful, peaceful county. This attitude of mine did not, I might add, always endear me to certain locally born white Kenyans. I have never been able to live a lie; in fact, I am almost incapable of following anything but the dictates of my own conscience. A quote by Lamennais: virtue, morality, generousity, kindness, good sense, modesty and loyalty are to be found only among the poor and humble, whose natural goodness has not been corroded and twisted by cupidity and intrigue.

To feed the settlers at Mkowe, I purchased a small herd of local cattle I had arranged to drive to Baragoni, with the Arab cattle dealer, as the herd I was interested in were being driven south from the Tana river. As we swept in the land rover around a bend in the road, I saw tottering towards us, the poorest-looking cows I had ever seen. 'Your cattle, Mr Northcott.'

'I'm not purchasing those'!

The well fed Devon Guernsey and fresian cattle grazing on the West Country farms were still fresh in my memory. But these happened to be the best on the coast and of the type I was eventually to buy.

15. A Move to the Ministry

After nearly a year serving in the prison department, I discussed with Fredi Becker the possibility of joining the Ministry of Community Development (MCD). I submitted a formal application to this effect. A few weeks later I was invited to visit the secretariat in Nairobi, and was interviewed by a board of Government officers.

Another visit to the secretariat in Nairobi and an incident involving Doctor Becker should be mentioned. Both were, in my humble opinion, instructive and amusing.

A liaison officer – no names mentioned, please – showed me a report he had just received from Doctor Becker. He was unaware at that time of my relationship with Fredi.

'I have just received a silly communication from Dr Becker, Northcott, complaining of the behaviour of a prison officer at Lamu who was chasing an Arab boy through the streets of the town with his 'credentials' in one hand, and a ten shilling note in the other.'

'This is not a community development matter and is of no interest to the ministry. Can't understand this chap, Becker.'

I looked at him, doubting his sincerity, and speculated then as to what the real policy of the ministry could be – not the first occasion I had questioned the validity of government departments.

Whilst awaiting a decision from the MCD I visited MaGeta Island detention camp in Lake Victoria and also Suyussi Island.

A West Australian, Steve Martin, Who commanded Mageta Island detention camp, had recently been drowned in the lake.

Against the wishes of the Arab skipper, he had ordered an overloaded pinnace, on loan to the prisons department, to cast off from the jetty. A few yards from the shore it had capsized and some twenty Africans were also drowned.

He had been criticised at one time for spoiling the local bride price as he entertained young Nditus (girls) taken to the island for a liberated weekend.

Eventually, I was advised that I had been accepted by the Ministry, and after a relieving officer arrived at Mkowe, I handed over my responsibilities and set out once again on the long, interesting journey to Nairobi.

As I travelled along the bush track that served as the main Mombassa road, I thought of an ex-paratrooper, Ron Belsen, who commanded Suyissi Island, whose pet hobby was keeping snakes which abounded on the island. There were cages of them surrounding his house. What made a man accept such an isolated posting. Had he too experienced a disastrous relationship in England?

There had been much unrest and trouble at the Marigat detention camp in the rift valley. I was posted to this unit, taking over the duties from an ex police superintendent – a man called Miller.

I had wished to take a Swahili language course at Jeanes School before I took up my new post, but this, I was informed, was an emergency, and my visit to Jeanes School would have to be postponed.

On my arrival at Marigat, I was pleased to find that the camp commandant was ASP Jones, with whom I had trained at Kamiti. This was to make my job so much easier, as socially we got along quite well.

The rehabilitation office proved to be a small grass building containing only a single desk, typewriter and one chair. It soon became apparent that little positive activity was taking place. Miller spoke Swahili and Kikuyu well, but he had little sympathy with his position and I am sure, no real time for the Africans.

As he pointed out to me various identities amongst the detainees, I remember him striking one tall man across the face. 'This is a real black bastard. Watch him, Bill!'

Just a few days after Miller had departed, I moved into my own mud, brick and stone-built house which Jack had prepared for me. I made this particular man a houseboy. It only took about two weeks of careful handling before his scowls and surly complexion was replaced by smiles and later laughter.

The average African is, in my humble opinion, as I have found him to be, a happy, easy-going person, responding read-ily to reasonable treatment. Exactly, in fact, as any other human being – no better and certainly, no worse.

After organising three screening teams, led by permanent

African CDOs, I commenced building an office and later an 'open' rehabilitation camp to accomomdate some eight hundred men. I was given a unit of some twenty tribal police, commanded by a Sgt Major, none of whom spoke English.

Once again I was to build sleeping and messing quarters, with a police station – handy to the new camp – but I was learning from my recent experiences.

The rehabilitation centre was located less than a mile from the main detention camp and had no perimeter fence or barbed wire of any sort. With the tribal police to maintain discipline, the next eighteen or so months I was at Marigat, we had little trouble from the inmates.

As the screening teams working in the prison detention camp interviewed men, and prepared them for preliminary selection, background checks provided by special branch officers helped to verify the information given – a lengthy process, but made easier as information was filed away and cross-referenced. Eventually, there was a final searching interview and another inmate would be released to the rehabilitation camp.

Perkerra Rehabilitation Camp

72

Upon first taking up this appointment, I had a visit myself from two special branch officers, one John Prendergast was in charge of the colonies special branch. They stayed with me overnight and I mention this only in view of what happened years later in Australia.

Another special branch man, Max Kroll, working from Nakuru, stayed with me at Marigat for two days each week, providing me with background checks on men I was interested in. In my considered opinion, special branch officers have a tendency often to pre-suppose facts, and I have sometimes questioned their conclusions.

I quote one such instance. My perfectly decent camp foreman was a man called Wilson, whom I had always found cheerful, reliable and likeable.

One day, Max informed me that someone had released General China to the open camp. Who other, he alleged, than the same man Wilson. Naturally I was annoyed to think that I had been deceived, and interrogated Wilson, on several occasions, and after carefully considering the matter, decided that the accusation was unwarranted.

Then Max started to produce damaging, documentary evidence, which was too serious to ignore. I was reluctantly obliged, to return Wilson to detention. The weeks passed, until one day an upcountry District Commissioner visited the rehab. camp, and for some reason, stayed overnight.

During the evening meal, General China's name was somehow mentioned. 'That little bastard. I knew him well – a really shifty character – was a clerk in my office for years.' As Wilson was at least six-feet tall, I began to think, and sent my police sergeant across to the prison camp with a note for Jones, the camp commandant. Eventually, Wilson , under escort, stood in the doorway of the dining room. 'Is that China?' I asked. The reply was, 'definitely not!'

I apologised to Wilson, arranged his immediate release and reinstated him to his former position. Just a coincidence had saved that man from months, or even years incarceration. Who can really tell what is in a man' mind. What motivates him and why? Certainly not every special branch officer!

Whilst at the Perkerra rehabilitation camp in July 1956, I received a letter from the Ministry advising that they were posting to me, a rehabilitation assistant, Grade 1, called Rowson Macharia. This man was a witness at the Kapenguria trials of

Jomo Kenyatta and as a result, was sent to the United Kingdom for roughly three years at the University of Manchester. He was alleged to be extremely politically minded, and had upset many European officers, since his return from England.

I was asked to give a report on him after he had been with me for one month. Actually, Rowson did not last a month. I sent him back to Nairobi, as his unco-operative attitude and his constant expectation of preferential treatment became intolerable.

He had not coped with the university course at Manchester and had been placed as a clerk in a local government office, in Torquay in Devon. Whilst in the UK he had been taken on a tour of England by the commissioner of prisons, 'Taxi Lewis,' and continually mentioned this fact. He also compared his living quarters at the rehab. camp to his beautiful flat in Torquay.

As I explained I myself came from Devon, quite near Torquay, but had lived in a tent for many months when I first came to his country.

Having recently built a large, mud brick living quarters for my senior rehabilitation staff, with their own bedrooms, central messing room, with cooks and cleaners, I considered Rowson quite unreasonable.

In my opinion he was a stool pigeon and Judas whom special branch had got hold of and used. Another blatant miscarriage of justice. At a time when his tribesmen were dying for their country, Rowson was enjoying a comfortable life in Torquay, and at the British taxpayer's expense.

The Ministry gave Rowson one month's notice on his return to Nairobi, but I also got a letter of protest from the Ministry at his sudden and rather embarrassing arrival, softened somewhat by the last paragraph. 'This mild reproof will only be of academic interest to you, in view of your much regretted transfer to the administration.'

It is stange, but inevitable, that once a course of action is commenced in life, it has to go full circle. Whether it be my foolish earlier mistakes, or Rowson Macharia's treachery, SOMEONE HAS TO PAY.

A newspaper article brought to my attention in 1959 proved that Macharia was still having problems. Regrettably, the special branch officers who first instigated his treachery are no doubt retired and living on a generous pension. We must be generous though – they were only acting under orders. C'est-la-vie!

My 'Lyons Corner House'

I decided when building the open camp that I would build a communal kitchen and dining hall. Detention camps had little charcoal stoves outside each hut on which the occupants cooked. With thousands of men housed in compounds, there were literally hundreds of these little stoves dotted around the camp. I was quite proud of my 'Lyons Corner House' as I called it, and felt that getting the Africans off the floor when eating and sleeping was a step forward. The response in the dining room was good, as I noticed men were beginning to use eating utensils in place of their fingers.

When a group of visiting settlers were being shown around the camp one day, one young chap wearing the usual side-arms, said, 'Of course, Mr Northcott, you believe in this communal living, don't you?'.

'Does that remark indicate that I may have communist leanings?' One's motives, even on basics like this, can be so easily misconstrued.

Incidentaly, when I erected a sign in the form of a flag saying 'Perkerra Rehabilitation Camp' I was often asked why the sign was so shaped.

'I have been accused of running a holiday camp for Africans, so I thought it appropriate if I made this look like one!'

Perhaps I have been a little provocative at times, but I have a short fuse with bigotry and plain stupidity.

As more Europeans began visiting the camp, I began to realise the difficulties ahead – to change the attitudes of old-time settlers was asking a lot. There was such a reluctance to give up any part of their priviledged position. Like any segment of society living with a hallowed status, giving up a larger share of the cake was just not on. There were occasional problems.

A hard-core Mau Mau element from a new intake in the main detention camp was causing problems, and I felt it necessary to quickly identify the Kiama, or committee of seven men who really controlled everything behind the barbed wire.

I discussed this with Jones, the camp commandant, and had already arranged to have two undercover men posted in as detainees. It was finally decided to cause a minor disturbance and identify men who started giving orders and taking control in the compounds. Another useful technique was to watch closely at a Christian church service, usually the Kiama members were the first to stand up and leave.

Anyway, the disturbance got under way, but soon got out of control, as detainees armed themselves with broken bed boards. It became necessary to send in the riot squad – order was soon restored. As far as I was concerned, the exercise was completely successful. The Kiama had all been identified; were segregated in a well secured hut, away from the main compounds, and would be interrogated later.

A week or so later, I was having a drink at my house with the district commissioner.

'Bill, I have had to put in my monthly defence report, an account of the recent riot at the detention camp!'

'It really wasn't a riot, John; just a mere disturbance.'

My comment raised a wry sickly smile. A week or so later Jones came across with a signal from his headquarters demanding urgent and immediate details of the recent riot.

The outcome of the incident was that I drove down to the secretariat in Nairobi, put them in the picture, and then proceeded to prison headquarters, where I gave Jack a good write-up. Quite a change for the prison departments to be so congratulated by one of our ministry officers, and it all quietened down, but a lesson was well learned.

I had in my office block a large broadcasting, or tannoy system, for addressing various compounds in the camp. On one of my official visits to Nairobi, it was also decided to equip my Willey's jeep with a mobile broadcasting and tape deck unit.

A close friend of mine, Jerry Campbell, a geologist, was working in the district, on a soil erosion study. He played in my soccer team. After a vigorous game on a Saturday afternoon, we would visit the swimming pool, throw a water polo ball around for a while to cool off, and then repair to my house for dinner, finishing the evening normally with a few drinks.

On this occasion we must have had a few too many. Jerry remembered the sound equipment in the jeep parked in the carport, adjacent to the house. It wasn't long before we were singing and recording a ribald selection of rugby and Durham University songs of questionable taste.

So to bed. The next morning when we awoke, feeling far from in top form, a group of my African rehab. staff appeared at the doorway. Could they use the new equipment? . . . Certainly. Soon there were the pleasant sounds of clear Kikuyu voices, recording in their own language a selection of recognised Christian hymns.

That wasn't the end of it.

The following week, my large static set broke down, and in response to a signal to Nairobi, a light plane flew into Marigat. An Indian Fundi, accompanied by the colonies' senior information officer, were the only passengers. The static set was soon repaired, and, as the European and his companion were staying for lunch, the latter requested that, whilst he had time, he would check out the mobile recording set which had recently been installed in the jeep. Panic Stations. The tapes had not been changed, but I was fortunately able quietly to instruct my police sergeant to intercept the vehicle, and keep it hidden until the crisis was over and the guests had left. We all make mistakes – even the Mzungu!

Jerry was a great companion, but he would insist on wearing his studded football boots when playing in our team. I can see him now, tearing down the wing, feet flashing, and barefoot Africans backing away from him . . . How they hated those boots.

The African is an excellent ball player. I once had an ex Mau Mau storekeeper, on the coast at Mkowe who had killed twenty-two men, including one European. Most respectful and diffident. It was difficult to believe such an inoffensive man had been responsible for so many killings. That is, until he became excited on the football field. I clashed with him once in mid-air. He was leaping high above me, and as I saw his face contorted with excitement and passion, I realised his true determination and potential.

Men, as most bank managers and detectives will agree, are sometimes difficult to read. I recall looking at a new arrivals special branch report, at Mkowe. The leader of a gang of two hundred men, for some three years in the forest. I thought I should possibly make this man a foreman so I sent for him. As he entered the office, I was surprised to see a slim-looking youth, of about twenty-three years of age, whereas from his record, I had anticipated a hard-bitten veteran of about forty years. It obviously pays to keep an open mind.

For relaxation, when working in the rift valley, I would sometimes visit Nairobi for a weekend and stay at the Backenhurst hotel, much frequented then by airline personnel. As Jerry, Jack and I, were sitting in the lounge one day, a visitor enquired if we were the crew of a particular airline. Jerry quickly answered, 'No, we are a submarine crew from Lake Baringo!' This was very much an inland lake. We probably looked like submariners though, with our hirsute appearance.

I sadly learned whilst I was in Thailand that Jerry died about 26 May, 1982. He was found dead in his house at Windhoek. Another good man taken. Jerry had been considerably younger than myself.

Besides my normal camp duties, I was also building and controlling a villagisation programme. Jerry had, in fact, helped me survey the sites. The houses consisted of two round mud huts joined together to create three rooms; an improvement, I thought, on the normal one-roomed dwelling. At least the adults had their own bedroom. At the time the houses were costing me in material about six pounds each. The labour was free. They were considered by some of the European settlers and the executive officer of the Perkerra irrigation scheme to be too elaborate.

As I had only about thirty men building these villages, and as an exercise at that time, counted some ninety men, land-scaping a European house, occupied by a junior agricultural officer, the inequality to me was somewhat sickening.

There was so much to do in Africa, but the priorities seemed to me quite wrong.

The Governor, Sir Evelyn Baring and his wife Lady Mary, visited the rehab. camp on another occasion, together with Robin Wainwright the provincial commissioner. Lady Mary asked me how long I had been in Kenya and how I liked it. I answered that it was a fascinating country, but added that I was also appalled sometimes at the inefficiency of the administration. My relationship with Robin Wainwright was never quite the same.

It is in the hope that my reader can learn something of me from my experiences that I mention these various incidents. I can only recount them as they actually happened; collectively they seem to have had some marked effect on my future.

Another delegation of settlers to visit the rehab. camp, was led by Will Evans, the chairman of the Kenya farmers association: Lady Pamela Scott, and accompanied by representatives of the press. Knowing by this time what was expected, I had arranged with Jones to have about a thousand men digging out an irrigation viaduct.

As we approached in a convoy of vehicles, the immense cloud of dust pinpointed our destination – most effective. Hard, dirty work was recognised and appreciated. The demonstration was nullified, however, by a visit to the pupil teachers' classroom.

These teachers would take groups of men after the day's work was completed, and teach such basics as elementary hygiene, animal husbandry, etc. However, as we were ushered into the classroom, staring at us in bold print on the blackboard were the words 'Theory of Relativity.'

My quick explanation that the pupil teachers were allowed a half hour a week of free study and this had given them the opportunity to impress the Europeans, – was hardly accepted. How did I maintain discipline was their favourite type of question. By innuendo, I managed to convince them there was no trouble on that score.

Fortunately, David WICKER, an assistant at the camp, gave me suitable support.

One of my senior African staff, Angelus Muthiki, had previously trained for seven years in a seminary to become a priest. As I introduced him to Will Evans, Angelus extended his hand in welcome. I had to look directly into Evans' eyes, almost willing him to accept the proffered handshake, which, after an uncomfortable pause, he did.

79

Angelus and Wife

One of Jones's officers, his accounts officer, was an ex-Malaysian police lieutenant called Cole. Big 'Taffy' Cole, when I knew him, was about seventeen stone in weight. He had first joined the Palestine police force, straight from the depressed Welsh coal fields. As 'Taffy' said, he had been starving then, and weighed less than ten stone.

He remembered seeing his father armed with a club with a crowd of fellow miners, marching towards the local railway station, where Winston Churchill was expected. The train did not stop at the station. Cole was a socialist at heart, as was to be expected. Several miners had been bayoneted, by troops called in to control them at his village.

David Wicker, my assistant, had been educated at one of the minor public schools in England, and had been a captain in the Indian army. I had first met him when he was a district assistant at Lamu. We had an amusing evening once; Jerry Taffy, young Wicker and myself. A heated political argument started between the socialist Welshman and the conservative ex-public schoolboy.

Jerry and I became increasingly amused as the argument became more heated. But when the antagonists had finally departed, Jerry, an ex-Grammer school boy, like myself said, 'you know Bill, Wicker is a complete and utter idiot, but he has got something. I wish I had been priviledged to go to a public school.' Coming from a Durham University trained geologist with a BSc I found that quite significant. I agreed with him.

Whilst I was at Marigat, I was requested to organise an Appeals Court for detainees. Sir Vincent Glen Day, Justice Rawling, and a Mr Mathias were to sit on this court. I had discussed with Mr Mathias that, as Marigat was considered to be in the Northern frontier district, an extra milage allowance was claimable on personal vehicle expenses. As the court sat prepared to hear the first appeal, Sir Vincent turned towards me, coughed and said, 'Oh, Northcott, this NFD car allowance – where does it actually start from?'

'Magottio, sir!'

'H'm . . . We'll bring my car tomorrow.'

I remember being amused by this incident. Even senior members of government, appreciated the little perks that could be legitimately claimed.

Eventually, a letter came from the Perkerra control committee chairman, requesting me to hand over the village building programme to the executive officer of the scheme. I now was convinced that the exercise of rehabilitation was just a facade to placate the English public. I decided to resign from the Ministry, and duly sent off my written request.

A liaison officer with the ministry flew up to Marigat and attempted to disuade me, offering me any district that I liked in Kenya to remain as a CDO. On my continued refusal, Tatton Brown advised me that Peter Lloyd, a DC I had previously served under, had suggested I might be interested in returning to the coast to run a settlement that was being considered for pseudo gangsters who were unacceptable back in their reserve. The appointment carried the temporary rank of district officer. I replied I would give it some consideration. I was still weighing up the pros and cons of my working life, after I left the Ministry, as I missed my children, a return to England had a strong appeal.

I was asked at the time by an agricultural officer if I could travel in my jeep to Nakuru, and collect a party of nurses from the War Memorial hospital. They were to be guests at a party to be held at Marigat. This is when I first met Trudy Jamieson. Driving back from Nakuru, I decided that two at least could be billeted at my house. Trudy was one of these. Max Kroll had been replaced by a new special branch officer called John Burrows, ex-Gurkha regiment, who was then doing my background checks and still spending two days each week with me.

A few days after the party, John, himself a married man, told me he had been playing tennis in Nakuru with Trudy. I felt piqued at this, being constantly alone in a bush station, and decided to drive to Nakuru and take Trudy out to dinner. She had just finished a tour of duty at the hospital, and was shortly due to fly back to the UK. Deciding now to take the job on the coast, I advised the Ministry accordingly.

As I came to realise my isolation, having already experienced nearly a year at Mkowe, and being unwilling to face this alone, within three or more visits to Nakuru I had proposed marriage to Trudy and been accepted.

In all fairness, I had explained to her that I had been married before – a disastrous experience. I had three children and was still paying maintenance.

I most certainly did not want to start another family.

So, Wing Commander Graves, OBE ex-Balloon command and his wife soon arrived to relieve me at the Perkerra camp.

He was, in his niggardly fashion, determined to find something remiss in the 'handing over' process. I had always prided myself on being a good administrator, and felt quite proud of the progress made, and how the rehab. camp was organised. A missing few gallons of lubrication oil, which the Wing Commander was badly concerned about was his only criticism and it was eventually traced to the mechanic's failure to keep the vehicle logbooks correctly written up. Graves's attitude was most marked on the day I officially handed over.

It had been the practice for the duty senior African CDO to thoroughly check the camp at 8pm each day, ascertaining from the police office that all the inmates had been accounted for. They then reported to my house 'Kilu Kitu Misouri'. Everything OK, Bwana.

I sometimes gave them a beer, as we discussed a work problem, or the next day's activities. They never took advantage. If I had a visiting European staying with me, I would not discourage them from leaving and was quite happy if they made some valid contribution to our discussion. They never drank more than one beer.

After formally handing over the duties to the new officer in command, I was invited to dinner at the Graves house. As we sat, Geaves, his wife and I, having an after dinner drink, the two duty staff duly reported to Graves, as instructed, 'Everything is OK, Bwana!'

'Alright, get out.' They stood in the doorway, and both looked towards me. I felt as embarrassed as I knew they were.

A new era was coming to the Perkerra Rehabilitation Camp.

It was whilst I was at Marigat that I shot my first crocodile. The Perkerra river was alive with them. This animal was only about seven feet long, but with beautiful underbelly buttons. I intended getting it professionally cured and tanned.

As another geologist, with whom Jerry was working was travelling to Nairobi, I gave him the hide to take to a skin curing factory. I never saw either again.

I also carried to the coast a well marked python skin, taken from a reptile that I had seen killed by a suk warrior with a bow and arrow. When I eventually unrolled it to fix to the wall of my new house, I discovered that, not having been properly cured, it had been eaten by insects and was perforated like a sieve.

One Christmas, whilst still in the rift valley, a large parcel arrived for me by post. I opened it, together with a seemingly endless series of smaller boxes, until the final box, when opened contained a human skull with Christmas greetings from Jerry and a note, 'Please rehabilitate me!' It was, Jerry told me, a Njemp tribeswoman's skull, but by this time I had learned to be wary of statements by the so-called experts.

As the African stood in awe of any European who practised witchcraft, I had the skull mounted on the wall in my lounge, wired with a pair of buffalo horns, and embellished with vulture feathers. Years later, when I unpacked my boxes in Perth, Western Australia, I was astonished to see that my houseboy had packed my Machawi. The skull is buried deep down, behind one of Alfred Sleeps' houses in City Beach.

Jerry also gave me a very young crocodile that he had found newly hatched as he worked taking soil samples. As a temporary measure I placed this in my bathroom handbasin, later transferring it to my old fashioned zinc bath, where I discovered that as I showered, it cowered at the end of the bath.

83

As with many of my stories, I am quite sure my folks in England didn't really believe that for several days I did actually take my shower with a crocodile in the bath. But perfectly true!

Whilst I remember such trivia, I must mention the occasion I wished to buy two donkeys to assist the village women in carrying water. Wishing to act strictly within my financial limits, I suggested to the DC that this item would surely would surely come under my transport vote.

'Bill, old boy, use your imagination, Call one 'bicycle and one 'wheelbarrow' and indent for them accordingly!' All a matter of experience.

16. Temporary District Officer

So, after handing over to the worthy Wing Commander Graves, OBE, I returned to the coast and presented myself to Myles North, a senior district commissioner who controlled the vast area which was administered from the headquarters on Lamu Island. He was a large friendly man, with a slow deceptive manner, that belied his astute and active mind so valuable here on the coast, where the fascinating undercurrent of intrigue was an everyday facet of Arab life.

Myles was a batchelor, had been a military governor in Somalia during the Second World War, and came from a wealthy, aristocratic family. Fortinately I hit it off with him very well right from our first meeting.

I remember when I had only been at Mkowe a week or so I had my first official visit from Myles. Having to call a guard of honour parade, often at a minute's notice, I had quickly equipped my police Askaris with two sets each of sandals and webbing etc, ready to turn out smartly whenever needed – these were always kept fully blancoed. Myles guessed that this was, just window-dressing on my part, and after carefully inspecting the immaculate turn-out, he quietly turned to me and said he would like to inspect the weapons as well.

'For inspection, port arms sergeant!'

The command was given, and, of course, the rifle barrels were filthy. Myles, an experienced old soldier, knew that I had not had time to follow through with such details. He had very delicately shown me he was fully aware of my subterfuge. I had a new respect for him. The Askaris were smartly turned out, though, considering they ironed their uniform on a mud floor with a charcoal iron.

Once when we were swimming together off Shella beach, Myles said to me, 'Bill, you are really far too intense, you know!'

'Myles, I'm a temporary contract district officer, on a comparatively low salary, but still sending maintenance payments to England, and I am, of course, thinking of my immediate and long-term future. You are a senior district commissioner on a good salary, a bachelor, and if I've been correctly informed, have just inherited a large tea estate left to you by a relative. Our financial positions and expectations are poles apart!'

Myles once informed me, that he was taking a position as registrar of Co-operatives in Kenya, and asked me if I would consider transferring as his assistant registrar. Years later, when I was in trouble and under extreme pressure in Australia, I deeply regretted not agreeing to this proposal. However, it doesn't do to look back, I have discovered, and I've always been a supreme optimist.

So now I was back on the coast, preparing for another new venture. The matter of resettling pseudo gangsters and their families naturally raised the problem of housing.

I had explained to Myles, my previous experience in the Rift Valley and I still did not wish to be associated, with the standard round grass hut.

Giving this considerable thought, I designed a bush factory producing walls, complete with standard windows and door frames, using Borritti poles cut from the mangroves, hessian and barbed wire, of which there was plenty, and cement. Once the poles had been cut on a raised jig, they were nailed together, stressed with barbed wire, and then covered with hessian. The complete wall was then lifted into a concrete bath of cement, dipped and piled up in stacks to dry.

Shortly after the first intake of pseudos had arrived, I soon had a stack of walls piling up at the 'factory'. As the corner posts were raised and the walls hammered into place, the women came in with liquid mud, plastering the interiors. The roofing squad were soon able to finish off; doors were slung and the exterior and interior painted with lime. We mixed gamaxene powder with the lime as an added hygiene precaution. Burning our own coral to make the lime.

My rough African pre-fabs were proving successful, cheap, quick and certainly a lot better in that snake infested place than grass huts.

I myself took over a shell of a house I had some two years before started to build. This had been occupied by a prison officer and his wife, and very shabbily made habitable.

I ripped the roof off, built a bedroom upstairs with large

corner windows, complete with window seats and a large L-shaped verandah. The corrugated iron roof I had completely covered by a Makuti grass roof to act as a heat insulator. A Dexion steel serving lift enabled an evening meal to be easily served upstairs, and proved invaluable.

I had noted in the regulations covering building practices, that any dwelling consisting in part of mud/brick should not be subject to a rental charge.

Great! The house was sited near a grove of huge mango trees planted in a circle long ago by some Arab dignitry – beautiful site.

At this time, the male baboons were showing marked signs of aggression. I decided to offer a five cent reward for each baboon tail. Few settlers responded to this offer.

I discovered that if I shot a baboon and hung the carcase by the tail from a tree it scared the others away for a week or so. This was by far the most effective method of control. In the present climate of environmental control and conservation, I know this sounds quite savage, but to a European living in such an area, with literally thousands of these animals rampaging through the shambas and threatening the women and children, there was no alternative.

With my house now finished to my satisfaction, I began to think of my forthcoming marriage.

Whilst working in the office one day, doing some quick costings on my current financial responsibilities, one of the new African settlers, a very fat man named Thuo Kigera requested an interview.

The long rains had as usual flooded the main Mombasa road, and as we were to be isolated for several more months, Thuo requested that, if possible, he would like to hire a plane and fly his two senior wives down to Mkowe. He had waited for them long enough. I explained that it would be possible to charter a plane, but it would be quite an expensive business.

'I have plenty of money, Bwana.' He then explained that he had a chain of shops in the reserve, his policy being to open a shop in a village, buy a local wife, train her to run the business and then move on.

I looked at this fat, ragged looking African, with his shrewd, laughing eyes, and mentally evaluated our repective financial positions. Life can be quite ridiculous, can't it?

Thuo had been the Mau Mau chairman of the Molo branch

of the KAU, but I soon realised that, like most reasonable men, all he wanted was to be left at peace, have the chance to make enough money and enjoy a comfortable life.

When his wives eventually arrived by road, I had a special pre-fab made, built with an extra room and two external doors. I was becoming quite fond of Thuo. Shortly after he was reunited with his ladies, he requested another interview during which he explained that, as there were so many single men in the settlement, he wished to seal up one of the external doors to his house.

Having gone to some trouble with the building. I refused. The following day when I saw him, I called him across.

'Thuo, I've thought of a solution to your problem. Draw a padlock from the store and when one wife is 'off duty' lock her safely in her room.'

Thuo was instantly all smiles. I had cemented our relationship for all time.

Several weeks later, with a forestry project under way, and having some thirty women working full-time planting trees, I needed a foreman to supervise the project. Who better than Thuo. He was delighted, both with the assignment and his elevation to foreman status with the extra pay involved. We planted thousands of trees.

I remember an old saying: Every man should have a son, plant a tree and build a house. I have well and truly fulfilled all three, so should feel well satisfied.

Like every community or gathering of the Kikuyu tribe, it is imperative to form a committee, consisting normally, as I have previously mentioned, of seven men. I requested that ten men be elected to negotiate with the settlement administration.

I must mention that settlers' wives were often pulled off the lorries by fathers or brothers when loading up in the reserve to come down to Mkowe when the full bride price had not been paid. It is easy to imagine the disappointment and frustration when the trucks finally arrived at the village.

As already mentioned, Mkowe settlement was for a certain category of Mau Mau freedom fighters, who on surrendering, or capture, had gone back into the forest and assisted the government in killing or capturing their former comrades. From outlaw to opportunist.

One of these, Elijah Ndere, known in the forest as Major King Kong, was a multiple murderer, but quite a reasonable man to deal with. He freely admitted that he was lucky, and should have been shot or hung by the government.

Another 'titled' personality was Ndiritu Njugi or Sir General Jesus, who was present as a Mau Mau representative at the surrender talks. He was 1/C the Rift Valley forces in 1955, in fact controlling all the gangs operating around Nakuru when Trudy was nursing at the war memorial hospital.

The general idea was to get the men out of the reserve where , for various reasons, they were unacceptable, re-unite them with their families and give them a piece of land on the coast, where they could do little further damage.

To assist me in administering the settlement, a committee of ten men was formed (elected).

MKOWE SETTLEMENT
LAMU
17 APRIL 1957

Mkowe Settlement Committee
(Elected by settlers to negotiate with settlement administration)

1. KJAGI NJOGU Ex-forest gangster and oath administrator.
2. KUNGU KINGOI Present at one killing. Has political inclinations;
   ex-forest clerk to Gen. Waruingi.
3. JOSEPH KIARIE Murderer. Seventeen killings. Forest gang doctor.
4. MAJOR KING KONG } Ex-forest leader. Murderer. Twenty killings
   ELIJAH NDARE } to credit.
5. MWANGI KOMU Ex-forest gangster. At present one known murder.
6. SIMON WAITHANJI MM committee member and assistant oath administrator.
7. KIUGU KIGUTA MM location chairman. Known to have hired thugs
   to kill off loyal Kikuyu.
8. KAHIHIA KIMANGU Oath administrator. Location Chairman.
9. CHARLES KARONGE MM secretary, Tanganyika. Forced many people to take oath.

10. JOHN KIMARU MM Chairman. Nanyuki.
Comprising:
Four murderers proved to have killed at least thirty-nine people.
2.   Mau Mau chairman.
1.   Mau Mau secretary.
3.   Oath administrators.

The committee members had between them killed some thirty-nine people. Of course, I slept with a loaded pistol under my pillow. Wouldn't you?

I was surprised one day – Christmas it was – when Jerry Campbell and a friend arrived unexpected at the settlement. Jerry's friend had just bought an old plane, and they had decided to fly up and spend the holiday with me. Great! Upon returning to the airstrip two days later ready for the return flight to Mombasa, we met a tall Australian waiting by the plane. He wanted a lift out.

Jerry's friend, an inexperienced pilot, refused this request, and despite the Australian's offer to fly the plane himself, would not change his mind. The plane, rather shakily, rolled down the rough strip and took off. The Australian left standing with me was far from happy.

One of my responsibilities at the time was checking the airstrip daily for water logging, phoning the information across to Lamu for onward transmission by radio to Mombasa. As I was checking the strip a few days later, a special branch officer I knew asked me if I had seen a tall Australian in the district. Apparently he was wanted for questioning on a drug-running matter. More of this character later.

As soon as my building team were able to operate the 'prefab' factory without constant supervision, I arranged for a spell of local leave, a relief at Mkowe, and set off in my Peugeot car for Nakuru.

My wedding to Trudy had been set for 2nd February 1957.

17. Kenya – Kismet

I had wished to invite some of my late Perkerra rehabilitation staff to the wedding, which had been set for February 1957, but as the reception was being held on a farm at Njoro, Trudy felt that some of the settlers would object to the presence of Africans. Now I realise I should have insisted, but the climate in the Kenya Highlands was then still marred by hate, suspicion and bigotry.

Fredi Baker was my best man, and the ceremony at the Dutch reformed church in Nakuru was well attended by both Trudy's and my own friends.

After the reception, held in the beautiful gardens of a well established European farm at Njoro, we left by car for Nairobi, where we had booked a sleeper to Mombasa on the night train.

I knew Trudy was a lovely person and I would never have the heartache with her that I had endured in my former marriage.

After an enjoyable trip to the coast in a very modern, comfortable sleeping compartment, we caught an aircraft from Mombasa to the Island of Zanzibar.

Whenever I see Meryl Streep in the film Out of Africa, I always remember that railway trip. It was just as beautiful, and at dawn the sight of wild game was superb. As the plane flew over the Island of Zanzibar at several thousand feet, we could plainly smell the spicy cloves – one of the island's principal exports.

Zanzibar was a fascinating place, much like Lamu in many ways, but dominated by the Sultan's Palace, magnificent gardens, and the ruins of the old palace, with huge stone pillars, baths and magnificent carved wood and metal doors.

Visiting the Sultan's Palace on one of our excursions, I duly signed the visitors book, but as Trudy automatically picked up the pen, a uniformed guard rushed across the courtyard and stopped her. Women were not entitled to perform such a sacrilege. Good for discipline and one up to the Arabs! Nice to

'District Officer: Mkowe' with Trudy

feel that somewhere, someone is looking after our masculine monocracy. I am not really a sexist, ladies. Please don't take offence.

The beaches of Zanzibar were wonderful, with excellent bathing, and after exploring the island, we were ready to dress for dinner and relax on the hotel verandah with a cool John Collins or gin and tonic. It was on one of these swimming trips, skinny dipping in a rocky cove, that Trudy, lost her new wedding ring.

The honeymoon, was over all too soon – we had a flight back to Mombasa and two nights in a hotel, whilst we collected various items of furniture and took delivery of a new three-ton Ford truck needed for the settlement. My largest purchase ever on an LPO (local purchase order).

We had also arranged to meet Jack Jones, who had finished his contract with the prisons department and was spending a few weeks with us at Lamu.

The truck finally loaded up, drums of petrol aboard for the return journey, Trudy, Jack and I, left Mombasa and headed North. We stopped at Malindi for a drink, and then the exciting part of our journey began.

There were two rivers to cross on ferries, the one at Garsen powered only by the flow of the river current, as it catches the ferry, and guided by a rope pulley arrangement slowly drifts it to the other bank.

The stretch of road from Garsen through to Malango Ya Simba*, where Harry Mathews was at one time stationed, was extremely bad.

. . . I have been bogged there on several occasions. Black cotton soil, when wet, will stop even a four-wheel drive vehicle. The four wheels spin uselessly and you could be driving on a sheet of ice.

Once past this treacherous danger, the sandy track changed course through the palm trees, as vehicles take advantage of favourable stretches, the road never seems to remain in one position.

A heavy truck or lorry is far more comfortable to travel in than a small four-wheel drive vehicle. The driving position is higher; the Dongas don't feel so deep and the dust is much less troublesome.

The sight of elephant, giraffe, ostrich, and, if lucky, rhino, helps to enliven the journey, and sometimes a pride of Somali lion come as a welcome bonus.

So I brought my bride to Mkowe, where a well trained house staff greeted us. It was good to be home . . . At least until the next day, when the mail arrived from Lamu. It included two solicitors letters from Plynouth, informing me, in the usual legal verbosity, that Barbara was taking a case to court for an increase in maintenance. She had obviously inherited her parents' heart-lessness. I had earlier, and perhaps most unwisely, written to my dear daughter Anne, informing her that I was re-marrying.

In these days of separated and de-facto wives' pensions and allowances, immediate dole for kids leaving school, I sometimes wonder how ever I have been able to survive financially. Getting re-married, I know, presented a risk, but when living in the NFD – no electricity, running water or TV – surely a man deserved some comforts.

Barbara had driven me from England in the first place

anyway. I had had a good job, in my own land, and, but for her unwarranted behaviour, would have still been with my children. Women!

Trudy was at first sceptical about the presence of lions near our house, until one day we saw a pride of five lions sleeping near the dirt road to the settlement. We would often see pug marks as big as a dinner plate within a few yards of the house, and always heard them roaring at night.

Trudy unfortunately, never really understood or liked the African. In the wards at the hospital, the sisters at that time wore revolvers. She was never able to really communicate with them as just other human beings.

18. Settling the 'Pseudos

To my story . . . After a brief settling-in period, and after making sure Trudy and my guest were comfortable, I recommenced work. I built a dispensary with hot and cold running water, improvised from forty-four gallon drums. Lamu hospital at that time had no piped water supply – hot or cold. I also built a school, church and behind the settlers' houses, detached kitchens, together with communal toilet blocks.

Trudy supervised the dispensary and school, but when I requested a higher grade teacher for the older children, I was quickly informed that the idea was not really to give a full education to the children of these ex-revolutionaries

Education by Fichte
'The anchor of salvation is in education, which in the end of the days will evolve . . . The kingdom of right, postulated by reason, the Kingdom of heaven on earth, promised by Christianity. No wonder the world is like it is!'

A local Swahili village at that time had a well which had fallen into a state of disuse , and the women were forced to travel quite a distance to draw water. The villagers thought there was an evil spirit in the well and they would not repair it. But I organised a gang of Kikuyu tradesmen, and we soon had the well cemented up and producing good clear water. On one of his visits to Mkowe, I took the DC to this village, explaining that I intended to instal a hand pump on the well. He questioned me as to where the funds were coming from.

'The settlement can easily provide a hand pump!'

'No, Bill. If the locals want a pump, let them start their own revolution!'

So these Swahili loyalists were going to be deprived of a pump. I still cannot understand his reasoning, I gave them one, anyway.

I was in the habit of taking a party of settlers in the lorry down to the sea some six miles away from the settlement for an evening swim. On the wall of my office was a map drafted from information gathered by sailors from HMS Penelope. I believe, in 1756. They had rowed along the mangrove-lined shore of Lamu, taking depth soundings.

When a newly arrived Kikuyu from the highlands was taken on one of these swimming excursions, he put his hand in the water, tasted it, and, looking towards me with surprise and said, 'Chumvi, Bwana!' Salt. I drew the attention of my clerk to the map on my return to the office and enquired why in 1756 his tribesmen 200 years earlier hadn't cut down trees and built ships in which to sail to my country. Chumvi, Indeed!

We made our own amusement. One guy used to walk around with a hang-dog expression, and I said to my Karani, Samuel, 'that man needs a good woman! Next time we go to Lamu, we should arrange that for him.'

A few days later, as the lorry prepared to leave for the jetty, the 'miserable'-looking one presented himself, smoothly attired, at the office.

'Oh, yes. Give him five shillings, Samuel from the 'goatbag' petty cash.'

Off we set, with much banter amongst the boys in the boat, as we crossed to Lamu, even more so on the return journey. A week or so elapsed, and saw our hang-dog-looking friend with his expression back to normal.'Another five shillings wasted, Samuel!

Samuel Mykarani and the boat Nyawira at Mkowe Jetty

19. Siku Moja

One day I arranged to take Trudy across to Manda Island. She had never before visited a detention camp. We motored to the jetty at Mkowe, then by boat past the mangrove trees, the waving cocoanut palms and the solitary, picturesque, white Arab house that nestled close to the water's edge.

Five miles of wonderful scenery, especially if you could catch it at the right time of day, before the sun rose fully and whilst the shadows still lurked amongst the mangroves and distant sand dunes.

At last, the roughly built coral jetty was reached, where two bronzed-looking Europeans met us. One was Allister Westrop.

They made a great show of helping Trudy ashore and over the jagged coral rocks. After all, women – white or black – were scarce on the island, and only rare visit were permitted. None were allowed officially to stay overnight.

We climbed into a battered, doorless jeep, and for nearly four tortuous miles crawled through scrub, thorn bushes and around the occasional Baobab tree, sinking at times into sand-filled hollows, or crawling for several hundred yards over huge lumps of solid coral.

After rounding a sharp bend and plowing into a bank of fine sand with the engine whining protestingly in low gear, we had our first glimpse of the camp. A towering watch-tower, built high up on a sand dune – one of six – which later appeared, overlooking the three barbed wire compounds that nestled in a hollow at the foot of four huge dunes.

This was Manda special detention camp, the present home of leading revolutionaries, a mixed bunch of primitive savage, political idealists, criminals and university-trained men.

They had two things in common – the colour of their skin and the burning conviction that the white man must give up his privileged place in Africa.

The jeep whirled past the first compound towards the

officers quarters; two aluminium rondavels joined together with a low Makuti roof, surrounded by a ten-foot high, double barbed wire fence, sandbagged chest high to form a buttress. Obviously, no chances were being taken here.

Wild-looking creatures, glared at us as we passed. Allister explained that these men refused to shave, or have their hair cut, and lost no opportunity in discrediting the European administration of the camp. New issues of clothing were immediately torn up, and the inmates deliberately looked as disreputable as possible for the benefit of the occasional camp visitor.

A tall aerial mast indicated that a VHF signals set was operated from the officers quarters. As we were served with cool drinks, one of the officers explained to Trudy about the feuds and bitter jealousies that prevailed inside the compound.

The Kiamas held absolute power with their own courts to deal with offenders, any who weakened in their resolve or were caught fraternising with the Askaris. At least one of the officers' houseboys was a Kiama member. His duty was to report back on everything the Bwanas did or said, and to pick up as much information as possible. These boys were always English-speaking, but never, of course, admitted it.

We then moved down to the beach, where the water was a great relief. The scene here more reminiscent of a secluded holiday resort.

What peculiar lives these two Europeans lived, I thought, watching them, mahogany-skinned, splashing amongst the surf. Servants galore, at no cost. A well ordered life. But did they try to really understand the Africans, sympathise with them perhaps, or did they automatically accept their superior position, maybe taking for granted that this would always be the order of things.

After some twenty minutes in the milk-warm surf, feeling clean again, we moved along the beach in search of turtle eggs.

Allister gave us a detailed account of the island's history. Well informed descriptions of wildlife, and an account of the nerve-wracking time a few months earlier, when a lion had found its way across from the mainland.

When we returned to the camp, we were greeted by a seemingly agitated group of Askaris and houseboys. A powerfully built sergeant, with a deeply scarred, tribal-marked face, stepped forward, saluted and informed Allister that a detainee had been discovered hanging dead in a cell.

'That is the chappie who wished to give me a statement this morning,' he said. ' He is being threatened with death by the Kiama. I was having breakfast at the time, and ordered him put into a cell for his own protection.'

Leaving Trudy in the officers quarters under the protection of an NCO and two armed Askaris, I accompanied Allister and his two I/C down to a small cell block. As the cell door was un-locked , we saw hanging from a beam in the badly designed cell, a detainee suspended over an up-turned latrine bucket, his gro-tesquely swollen tongue protruding from his mouth. Suicide, or staged murder? The police, I knew, would get little help in their forthcoming investigation.

The atmosphere of the party had now changed. Our lunch served by the impassive Kikuyu boys was eaten in a brooding silence. Were the Askaris really in sympathy with their fellow Africans behind the barbed wire? Was it true that the better educated Kikuyu were influencing the less advanced Askaris? Had the oathing of prison staff already started, as some well informed special branch officers alleged?

I explained to Allister that he should first have taken the man's statement. Certainly this was a higher priority than his breakfast. When a man wishes to talk, it is imperative to give him a sympathetic hearing, as soon as possible. Five minutes too late, and he could have changed his mind, been threatened, or otherwise influenced.

It was with a sense of relief that after lunch, once again covered in dust, Trudy and I stood on the rough coral jetty. Directly opposite across the wide expanse of water could be seen the host of small craft, cluttered like flies, in front of the whitewashed houses of Lamu, which, spreading for a mile or so along the sea front, tailed off into an untidy conglomeration of mud and wattle houses, which formed the newer part of the town.

As our boat forged against the wind into the middle of the channel, it was possible to recognise the one and only European Hotel, the mosque, the DC's house, where we were invited for dinner, and a few isolated figures stretched relaxed in the shade of the tall trees.

The old Portugese fort dominated the township.

This was to be the calm before the storm, for that night there was to be a Ngoma on the island, a festival of some sort which the locals held often, and for the most trivial reason. Securing the boat to the DC's jetty we made our way to the house where Myles North greeted us.

After a wonderful bath, which the boys had miraculously prepared from a seemingly inexhaustable supply of hot water, tea was served on the wide verandah overlooking the seafront. Manda Island was a brooding hazy mass in the background.

As we discussed the latest events in the district, a long canoe swept rapidly past, propelled by six muscular, ebony-coloured Swahilis standing erect one minute, then doubling forward, as they rythically moved the boat along. Without a break in their rythm, they swept under the jetty, bending almost to the gunwale of their primitive craft, causing Trudy to give a loud exclamation, which they acknowledged with wide grins, breaking then into a loud chant which could still be heard when they were well out of sight.

Later the drums started, punctuated regularly by the clash of a dustbin lid. This would continue throughout the night unless the administration decreed otherwise. After the dusty, jarring ride across Manda, it was pleasant to sit toying with a cool drink before dressing for dinner.

We watched the young men and women dressed in all their finery parade up and down, and as it grew darker, the myriad lanterns appeared. It was to be a special night as the DC had agreed to act as a judge in the fancy dress parade. Already the sounds at either end of the town from which the opposing team would march, indicated that preparations were in hand.

Dinner was lingered over, as Myles told some amusing stories of his earlier experience in the colonial service, and Trudy gave an account of her life up country, earlier in the emergency.

This was when the hospital staff were at constant war with Mau Mau sypathisers who skilfully stole drugs and equipment from the hospital wards.

An excited African suddenly appeared to inform us that the processions were now in sight of each other. Moving at a snail's pace, they shuffled forward. A thick-set Swahili, proudly sporting a full Scots outfit complete with sporran and dirk, led his group of contestants. Divided into four sections, first came several majestic figures, beautifully turned out as Knights of the Garter, carrying their helmets uniformally under their left arms.

Some comic figures followed, then the ladies of the town, dressed exotically in bright gaudy gowns, so unlike their normal black habit. Special efforts had obviously been made to present the next group to their best advantage. Here were the effeminate young men of Lamu, dressed in very short skirts, diaphanous blouses, and resplendent in earrings, with faces most carefully made up. As this erotic group slowly minced past and one caught a direct glance here or there, it was difficult to believe that they were in fact men, and not what they so obviously desired to be.

Trailing off towards the end of the procession was a miscellaneous collection of women and children, some dressed as cowboys, policemen or dancers. Bringing up the rear, making the most infernal din, was the band, lustily playing on a variety of instruments that had obviously seen better days or were designed originally for an entirely different function. The crowd meanwhile milled everywhere, screaming and shouting encouragement.

Myles and I walked slowly through the procession as it shuffled forward, Myles appearing to make notes as he examined closely, first one and then another of the contestants.

Out in front, a little ancient, ragged-looking Swahili threw out a measuring line, to see that the two processions were travelling at the same speed, and that they would arrive at the final judging point on time.

Slowly and carefully, the other parade was inspected, led by a handsome-looking African, whom I recognised as one of the normally near-naked boatmen. He was now resplendent in a naval captain's full dress uniform, complete with cocked hat, sword and epaulettes. It was soon obvious that this procession could never seriously challenge the first. Here too was a similar selection of characters, a few well turned out bandsmen, minus instruments.

Some scantily dressed dancing girls followed who, I am sure, obtained from Myles a much higher rating and attention than they deserved. Then there was the usual group of appealing young men, and as, in the other procession, a very mixed, noisy crowd providing the grand finale. After much careful deliberation and the usual lengthy and heated discussions with a myriad of officials, a necessary part of such functions, Myles made a suitable speech in his near faultless Swahili, and Trudy, to her consternation, was asked to present the prizes. Finally, as the massed bands endeavoured to play a faintly recognisable National Anthem, the crowds started to disperse into the warren like side streets. For the Europeans so ended another Ngoma.

Now, the fun would really start, as disgusted losers and jubilant victors relaxed to discuss the evening's events. As jealousies blossomed under the influence of liquor or drugs, so would a different contest take place later. A busy night was ahead for the small police force.

It was nearly two am before the tide refloated the Nyawira, and Myles helped Trudy aboard. The moon now cast its pale light across the water, clearly outlining the fleet of dhows that were then anchoring off Manda Island. The cool breeze blowing across the water was a welcome change from the close heavy atmosphere on the island.

As we cast off and motored out into the channel, I remembered thinking what a day it had been . . . A man hanging himself, or being murdered on one island, amidst an atmosphere of political hatred and barely suppressed violence.

And on the other island . . . what?

A few Europeans, judging a lot of black transvestites. Where was it all going to end? Which was the real Africa? Was it Manda Island, with its fanatical detainees, who either had some intelligence, the courage of their convictions, or both? Or was it Lamu, with its poverty, crumbling decay, yet happy-go-lucky people? Was it impossible to separate the two? Weren't they both part of the same continent? One that until recently, had defied time, and our concept of so-called progress, for centuries.

I have mentioned 'this' day's events in some detail as it illustrates not only my own feelings, but the almost desperate need for understanding and sympathy, between different people and cultures. Fortunately, modern communications, education, easier travel are bringing with them a better understanding.

MORALISING AGAIN

It is to be hoped that with the demise of the old world order with its inbred prejudices and bigotry, a saner climate will prevail. We still have a long way to go, though human nature being what it is.

Talking of bigotry, whilst the anti-Jewish feeling in England was never as violent as in Germany before the Second World War, it nevertheless existed. This was evidenced to me years later, when I took possession of my father's sword which had been handed down to him by his father, also a naval engineer. Now in Australia, as I unpacked a trunk from England, I inspected the sword closely and was intrigued to see a small piece of brown paper securely glued to the blade, near the hilt. After much effort, I removed the paper to find it was covering the engraved Star of David symbol. The sword, it appeared, had been made by a Jewish craftsman, but that fact wasn't properly accepted, or meant to be advertised by my forbears. Yet on another occasion, when visiting England on business from Australia, my dear old father quite naturally enquired 'Are there many niggers in Australia, Bill?'

I explained to the dear old boy that this was an offensive description of coloured folk, but to my father's generation this was how they thought or had been encouraged to think.

We are making some progress, but it has to be a two-way thing also. Years later, whilst sitting in a gym sauna bath, an Australian businessman was telling me how when he was in America and standing in a cafeteria queue, a coloured man tapped him on the shoulder and said, 'Whitey, get to the end of the queue.' He unsuccessfully endeavoured to get some support from two uniformed white policeman, but they just said, 'If he tells you man to get to the end of the queue, just get there!'

So it must be made to work, but also both ways.

I did think whilst in Africa, that perhaps the white man was superior in many ways to the African. That is, until I reached Australia, where in my work as a private investigator I met depraved, degenerate whites, who behaved far worse than any so-called primitive African.

Enough moralising – it's the Sleep side of the family coming out again: judgemental attitudes, hypocrisy and all the other weaknesses we have. But still there is a lesson to be learned somewhere on history, experience, and how we look at life.

My dear brother Jack told me that on one of his visits to Spain he was asked by a Spaniard, where he lived in England.

'Plymouth . . . the home of . . . el Drako!' he replied,

It transpired that the Spaniard had never even heard of Sir Francis Drake and knew little of the Armada period – that part of history of which most Devonians are so proud. History too, it seems,is recorded in so many different ways, to suit, no doubt, the pride and ego of individual countries, who like their people, must have a good perception of their own image.

But back in the settlement at Mkowe; once the settlers were

all housed, we commenced laying out five acre strips of land, for the settlers' use and as part of an agricultural experiment. We continued by burning off some blocks, building wind breaks on others with different methods of soil preparation and cultivation. All the information collected was sent to the provincial agricultural officer in Mombasa. With the tree-planting programme, cattle herd to look after, dispensary and school to supervise, plus police drills, weapon training and the normal settlement administration, Trudy and I were kept pretty busy. There was also the financial side to control: payments to settlers and police, votes to prepare, for housing, transport, police, messing, wages, etc. But I was never short of money for worthwhile projects.

I remember once when I visited the secretariat in Nairobi to solicit the sum of five hundred pounds to build a rehabilitation staff mess at Maragat. I saw one of the treasury people I knew quite well and gave him as requested my various votes. After disappearing for a while, he returned to the office, and I saw that he had increased the votes – by a total of a thousand pounds.

'Bill, I like you. I know you'll make good use of the other five hundred pounds'

This sort of confidence I found inspiring, but what turbulent times lay for me ahead.

I had been called to the cattle boma several times to see a sick or allegedly dying animal. They all looked pretty sick to my eyes. I was informed a few days later, that the beast had just died. It took me several months to realise that the settlers were killing the animals with a sharpened stick driven into the rectum, then using the carcase to supplement their normal meat ration.

Once I had learned of this chicanery, I called the store-keeper, Albert, who distributed the rations, and told him to record the weight of the next carcase, and list it as a normal meat issue. Not surprisingly, I never lost another sick animal.

Albert Simba was a meticulous storekeeper; his bookwork and handwriting would have done credit to any European clerk. Once a month he would present his store ledgers to the office for my inspection, and I generally complimented him on his high standard of work. That is until one day, something about his attitude, a little overconfident smugness, prompted me to take a closer, more searching look at his work. Then I found it!

His figures were completely correct, but when turning a

page in the ledger, I saw his 'carried forward' total did not correspond with his 'brought forward' figure on the preceeding page. This is where Albert was hiding his discrepancies. The food, timber and other stores he had been selling to augment his income.

When I eventually handed over the settlement to a Kenya-born district officer, named Peter Elms, I did a physical check of all the stores, even measuring with a tape the running feet of building timber held in the wood store. As I expected, there was a considerable shortfall. Albert admitted he had been selling timber for the making of furniture. Explaining to him on this occasion that, as I had enjoyed the little mental exercises he had presented me with, I would write off the missing timber.

I predicted that within a few months of my departure he would again abuse the privileges of his position; would get caught and duly punished. Naturally, I had warned Peter Elms, my relieving officer, as to Albert's activities. I had been advised on several occasions that Kenya-born officers were much more casual than the officers recruited from England, and Albert certainly didn't need any encouragement was this the bias that I objected to in other people.

I was not surprised whilst on leave in England to learn that Albert had been caught stealing government property, and had been put back in detention.

Jones was at one time in charge of C camp at Manyani, where some 27,000 Kikuyu were detained. He amusingly told me, when first posted to Manyani, and when the camp was controlled by local Kenya-born men of the difficulties they had in getting correct 'lock-up' figures. The count of numbers of detainees held in each compound. It had been the practice to count heads, write the figures on a piece of paper, or cigarette packet, and report to the duty officer. A running total from the different compounds would reveal 150 men short.

A recount showed there were now ninety-seven men missing. Eventually, after several more recounts, patience began to wear thin.

'Back to the mess for a drink boys. Can't do much better than that!'

The figures, according to Jack, were rarely correct.

Trudy was contacted at Mkowe one day by a local Swahili man who reported that his wife was dying. Visiting the woman, it was discovered that she had aborted a child, and was suffering from Septicaemia and was very ill and weak. After giving her an injection, Trudy arranged for a boat to take the patient across to the district hospital. The woman died enroute in the boat. Trudy was very upset. Asking the husband, why he hadn't notified us earlier, he replied that he thought the medical facilities at Mkowe were only for the Kikuyu ex-terrorists. How terrible!

Another settler admitted to Trudy's dispensary had been bitten by a large Nyoka (snake), and, despite an injection of serum, remained in a coma for twenty-four hours. Inspecting his leg, I noticed a large bite mark on the left foot. It looked like a python bite. As I had never seen a python whilst at the coast, I questioned my tribal police sergeant. Yes, he had seen a large python a few days earlier, crossing the road, as he patrolled on his rounds by bicycle.

'What did you do, sergeant?'

'I dropped the bicycle and ran!'

The reasoning process of the ordinary African tribesman did cause much merriment at times.

One day we had boarded the boat at the Mkowe jetty and prepared to set off for Lamu. A strong tide was sweeping the boat back against the jetty. I ordered a tribal police corporal to push the boat away from the jetty. Grasping the gunwale firmly with both hands, he started pulling towards himself 'Harder, corporal!' The muscles bulged as he strained valiantly.

A party of Swahili boatmen standing on the jetty watched this performance, with much amusement.

In all fairness, the corporal was an up-country African, had probably never seen the sea before, and was certainly not acquainted with boats. It is silly to generalise . . . Why mention it then?

I have seen university BA correspondence papers completed by detainees held at Manda Island, which proves that not all Mau Mau adherents were primitive savages. These papers were written by men like JK Cege, living in long grass huts, sleeping like animals on the floor surrounded by barbed wire and guarded quite often by primitive Askaris. Their companions were a mixture of hard-core terrorists, criminals and prospective political leaders. They did well to turn out such academic work under these conditions.

We had some interesting guests at Mkowe too. An old settler friend of Trudy's was writing a book, and stayed with us for several weeks. When he had first arrived in Mombasa, forty years earlier, he had just enough money to buy a rifle and some ammunition. He earned his first money shooting buffalo and selling the hides to Jaluo tribesmen for making shields.

Another interesting guest, a lady journalist, had arrived alone at night in a battered old Volkswagen. The road was still not officially opened. She had driven alone on the terrible road from Garsen through elephant and lion-infested country. At the time she was writing for the Mombasa Times, but had travelled extensively throughout the world, often hitching lifts in military air transport.

It was whilst she was staying with us that I killed my first cobra, which was lurking coiled outside the toilet that Trudy was occupying. I remember hoping it was not the spitting variety. My first blow hit the wall and broke the stick, leaving me with only about eighteen inches of wood. I didn't make any more mistakes – I couldn't afford to. Its hood was inflated with venemous-looking eyes searching mine, and it too was getting angry! However, it was speedily dispatched.

Whilst BA Allen was staying with me we became close friends. When he first told me he had been married four times I was a bit shaken. I had never met one of his breed before. Now, with two broken marriages and numerous liaisons behind me, I feel more in sympathy with him. He was at that time also, a CDO. We would swim together off Mkowe jetty and spend hours afterwards philosophying about life, as we sat and watched the sun go down over the Island, and the Arab dhows sweep gracefully past the usual drummer in the stern beating away. Yes, I felt very close to BAA.

He had commanded a force of irregulars at the beginning of the war, and later served as a Colonel in the intelligence corps at the court of Heili Selassi in Ethiopia. He was a boxer of some repute, when he was a regular in the Kenya police, but a self-effacing sort of character.

When placing numerous cups and trophies around the top of the rough mud wall surrounding his bedroom, he informed me they were trophies from the days when he did a bit of 'pugging for the Kenya police!'

We were discussing the violence that was an almost everyday occurrence then, and he recollected that on one occasion as he lay back on cushions at the Emperor's Court and the girls fed him grapes, he could hear the cries of the tortured coming from the dungeons below.

'Different then, Bill, old boy, but not the done thing these days.'

He had married a lady of the court in Ethiopia and had a daughter whom he visited whenever possible. Like many expatriate Englishmen, myself included, he loved England and its people, but could not settle down in the UK permanently. At least, not whilst alive.

He was finally killed in a traffic accident in London whilst on leave in England. I am sure he would have died quite happy.

BAA never mentioned to me that he had worked in Australia for a short while, until I said I had lived in Perth, and received a letter from him saying that he had 'humped wheat' in a place called Benjaberring in Western Australia. I can well imagine what sort of reception he would have had with his upper-crust public school accent. No wonder he didn't mention it!

Before we leave Mkowe, I must mention another incident that I feel is of interest . . . I was placed in a position where I had to cancel a number of detention orders, and finding no help from the government regulations, I drew up a rather detailed and specific document, submitting it later for the DC's approval.

'Far too detailed, Bill, old boy. All you need is a simple document with plenty of . . . 'Whereas, wherefore and wheretos in it . . . Whereas, I, William D Northcott. etc.' under the power conferred, etc, etc.'

'Just get their thumb prints on it. Anything you don't want them to do is wrong. Anything you do want them to do is right!' Shades of the old Brigadier! All very simple if you look at it from one point of view. But I was learning, even if I didn't like it.

When 'BA' first came to stay with us at Mkowe, he would usually join us, in the evening for dinner. Occasionally though, he would have his evening meal alone in front of the guest house on a camp table set alongside a camp fire. Invariably it would be sardines on toast, one of his favourites, the table set correctly with place mats, silver, serviettes and the inevitable bottle of Chianti.

I remember commenting on him once to Trudy as we overlooked the solitary figure dining alone. When his meal was finished he drank his glass of wine, silhouetted against the blackness of the nearby forest by the dying embers of his fire.

'What an unusual man BA is!'

When I visited him at his home in Maidenhead, I had to enquire from the police as to his correct address.

'Mr BA Allen, sorry can't help you, but Colonel Allen, lives at the manor house, at so and so!'

That was BA. And as we motored up the dark overgrown driveway and stopped outside an imposing granite arched doorway, the house looked like BA's home would be. A pull on the large old-fashioned door bell was eventually answered by BA in person.

'Bill, old boy, Trudy, darling, come in!'

We were ushered into a large comfortably furnished darkened lounge, lit only by a small single-bar electric fire. A small TV was also switched on. I looked around the lounge, festooned with trophies from abroad; elephant tusks, spears, animal heads and other souvenirs barely recognisable in the very dim light.

I saw in my mind's eye, BA sitting around his small camp fire in Africa. He had created the same familiar atmosphere that was obviously so dear to him. Yes, I have known some fantastic characters. I am lucky.

Peter Elms, on his arrival at Mkowe was a young six-foot, fit-looking chap. He unloaded his vehicle, taking out a heavy ammunition box. 'Grenades Bill. Never be without them, living alone with these black bastards!'

When I eventually officially handed over the settlement to Peter, It was almost a replay of the Wing Commander Graves exercise.

Trudy and I were waiting for a plane to fly out to Mombasa, as a batch of settlers, their wives and children, were returning to the reserve. The lorry was parked outside the settlement office, and as usual with the African, every-thing they possessed was being loaded aboard, including crates of live chickens.

Peter suddenly jumped up on the lorry and started hurling the chicken crates off. They naturally broke open and birds were cackling and flying everywhere. 'When I say no fugging chickens on the truck, I mean no fugging chickens!' The Africans returning settlers, and well-wishers seeing them off all turned towards me. I saw again the mute appeal in their eyes.

So many conflicting emotions existed for me in Africa at that time, but my nerves were getting frazzled, and I badly needed a change of scenery.

Some of the settlers were genuinely trying to rehabilitate themselves, but the difficulties of a strange climate, different type of agricultural land, inadequate rewards and the shortage of women, plus the feeling of indefinite exile was too great to ever expect the scheme to be a success with the conservative Kikuyu.

The formidable task from my point of view was also getting men who had been living, and fighting for years in the forest, to settle down to a regular job of work.

We even tried to stop female circumcision, but without success. Money again – it lowered the bride price.

Trudy and I had discussed our future. I would have liked to have continued serving in Africa and I still regret that I was influenced to leave.

A new post opening up on the Somali border was of great interest to me. Trudy, however, wished to return to England first, and then go on to Canada where I had been advised that a position was waiting for me with Frigidaire.

I had already arranged the necessary details and letter of introduction. On a local leave in Nairobi I had also, as a back stop, been interviewed and accepted for the position of colony sales manager with a firm called Equipment Limited, who had just taken over a Frigidaire franchise. There were several options open to me when we finally boarded a plane for England. I had a year's accumulated leave.

So much for Africa. I have unfortunately never been back.

20. On leave in England

Here we were then, back in England, and just before Christmas. I bought a big, second-hand MG Coupé, and we started visiting old and new relatives, spending a few weeks here and there, until eventually, tiring of living out of suitcases, we rented a small furnished cottage at Poundsgate, near Ashburton in Devon on the edge of Dartmoor, all for the magnificent sum of thirty shillings per week.

Duffle-coated and rubber booted, we would trudge up the hill through the heavy snow to the local pub. It was such a pleasure to talk to the locals, play an enjoyable game of darts and sup a good old-fashioned pint of Devonshire 'Scrumpie'.

We had my children to stay with us for two weeks. It was such a joy to see them again and listen to their happy chatter.

Taking a picnic lunch, we would hike up to the moor and select a suitable tor, climb to a point of vantage and look out across the broad stretch of rugged countryside before sitting down to our picnic lunch. So little time seems to have been allowed me with my children.

When I returned the children back to their home, I was invited in by them. Going to their bedroom, I noticed the beds were still unmade yet the children had been with me for fourteen days. Barbara had not changed.

Whilst on leave I was invited to a boxing match at David's school and felt terrible as I saw my slim, undeweight son – to my mind obviously undernourished and not well looked after – climb into the ring and fight like a lion against a heavier boy. With David covered in blood, the fight was stopped, the decision going against him. He looked appealing at me, as much as to say, 'Dad, I've done my best.' For me it was a self-accusing moment, I shall never forget. He had as a baby shown all the courage in the world just to survive in that oxygen tent in Greenwich Hospital.

REFLECTIONS

State authorities aren't by any means always to blame, but do tend to make difficulties for so many millions of less advantaged parents to spend time free from worry with the children.

Often the state machinery, tax collectors, magistrates, civil servants etc, who exist to protect society from excesses and abuse, are in fact the instruments of much inhumanity. This is further aggravated by the competitive spirit of the Western world that breeds discontent, disrupts the tranquility of the family and often leads to its complete fragmentation.

Democracy and capitalism by no means pursue similar aims, and to me, both words are used too loosely by many politicians.

It is strange to see here in Thailand, a country that is just starting to pay lip service to democracy, so many fathers walking happily home hand in hand with their young children or the whole family out riding on a single motorcycle.

The Buddhist influence of true asceticism, where men cease to be an irritation to their fellow men through any kind of struggle and competition, for privilege, profit or fame, has no doubt helped a lot. The Thai people have lived with their faith for centuries. They know self-restraint, humility, self-effacement and renunciation, virtues which are not always present in the so-called civilised, industrialised countries of the west. But this life style is slowly deteriorating here in Thailand, as old cultural habits are being replaced by western values.

I recall I once had my name taken and a caution given in Perth by a surly police sergeant for walking on the wrong side of the footpath in Hay Street; now, incidentally, a pedestrian mall. Western society to me does seem so heavy and ponderous, or am I only judging it by Australian standards where perhaps my experiences were unnatural. Certainly immoral, when the important family unit appears to be of the least concern to the authorities, despite their flowery electioneering promises.

Corruption, as I have already stated is rife in Thailand, but it is at all levels, an open across-the-board species, not the selective, often licensed persuasion we seem to tolerate in the West. Even at seventy-two years of age, I still find myself trying to unravel so many riddles, and still seek answers to so many questions.

As my story unfolds perhaps you may well have asked yourselves some of the same questions. If so I would be delighted, if still alive, to open with my readers correspondence for the discussion of mutual points of interest. Not too much abuse please! I still do have quite a few Australian friends.

The mysteries and priorities of life have always intrigued me. We are certainly going wrong somewhere. I am really amazed too at how little we now seem to value the good old basic virtue of honesty. No man in public office should be tolerated if even the slightest indication of dishonesty is uncovered. This applies even more so to our legal services, for whom, most certainly the Western Australian species, I now have nothing but the greatest contempt. This is only my own personal opinion. Bear with me and let me finish my story. For now it is an end to the Sleep moralising. Back to my tale.

THAI SONKRAN,

As I write at the moment the water-splashing festival of Songkran is taking place, marking up the traditional Thai New Year. To our western eyes throwing water at moving vehicles and motor cycles is a dangerous game, but there are few accidents. The police too get splashed, but a carefree air of gaiety and humour prevails. I note, however, the glad-wrap type covering that the police use to protect their side arms. The whole family gets into the act as parents cheerfully fill water containers for the children's use. Lorries and utilities carrying drums of water vie with each other, as laughing passengers, drenched to the skin, throw water at all and sundry.

But what is life all about? Rules and regulations or freedom and happiness?

STILL ON LEAVE

Whilst on leave in London, I met a friend who flew at one time as a pilot with the East African Airways. He had recently returned from Canada and informed me that there was a deep recession in that country, making it difficult to find work. He could not even get a ground job – never mind one flying. I then decided to forego any further attempts to migrate to Canada.

When staying at Enfield with Trudy's mother, we had dinner one night with an aunt of mine, Beatrice – my mother's youngest sister and her husband Vernon, who had a very successful wholesale furriers business.

It was with much sadness, years later, that I heard shortly after Vernon's death that Beatrice had taken her own life. She had left a note saying that she couldn't go through another winter without him. They had had a wonderful marriage and had rarely been separated. A touch of insanity in the family? Possibly – but also a lot of moral courage.

Anyway, discussing our future plans at this dinner, Beatrice suggested I write to her brother Alfred in Australia.

'Isn't he a barrister, Beatrice?'

With all the contempt and dignity that the Sleep women could so easily muster, she replied,

'Bill, Alfred is a common inquiry agent.'

Equipment Limited in Nairobi had wired me requesting a firm starting date, but Trudy had objected to being left in Nairobi whilst I was travelling throughout the colony. The salary package included a nice house outside the City and a new car, but I remember I was also influenced in my decision by my inability to get an air-conditioning course anywhere in the UK at that time. I telegraphed Equipment Ltd that I regretted I was now unable to accept the Nairobi position.

In retrospect, I realise this was a big mistake. I should have returned to Africa, preferably remaining in government.

I never seem to change. I know deep in my heart that when I listen to a woman's advice I am in trouble. But with the lovely ladies I am unfortunately, as men have been throughout history, Just a born loser. This weakness though, has cost me dearly.

Anyway, I wrote to Alfred Sleep in Australia. Yes, he was delighted to assist me, and sent me an introductory letter for the West Australian agent General in London, who had at one time been one of his parishioners. I followed this up, and after the normal time-consuming formalities, we said farewell to our respective families and set sail on a ten pound-assisted passage to Australia. The third biggest mistake I have ever made in my life . . . But how does one foresee the future?

114

21. Down under

The trip out on the P&O Strathnaver was uneventful. We met some nice people and Trudy made a life-long friend, a lively ex-WAAF named Muriel, a game spinster, who at the age of sixty, had decided to seek a new life down under.

As we came in sight of the Australian shore, we saw the white sands of the coast stretching for mile after mile. Nearer Fremantle we had all the preparations of packing souvenirs and now the mounting excitement of really seeing our new country for the first time. Very slowly the boat was manoeuvred into the harbour.

Everything on shore seemed so small, a lot more old fashioned than I had imagined. The buildings too, seemed built very low. There was a crowd of casually dressed people on the dockside. The children, some in night attire, rather amazed me.

As the ship moved in closer and finally moored at the wharf, I looked down and endeavoured to identify my uncle. I imagined I could recognise him quite easily because of the family likeness, and a photograph I had viewed for many years on my Mother's bedroom mantlepiece, of a good looking young cleric with a mop of curly hair. We walked up and down the ship, looking towards the wharf, scanning the upturned faces. Suddenly, a shabby-looking, short, stoutly-built man, in the company of two ladies and a couple of children, looked up and shouted out, 'Bill Northcott!'

I yelled back, 'You must be Alfred?'

So this is what the celebrated private investigator looked like. I carefully searched the unexpected face and recognised the Sleep penetrating eyes. Eventually we were allowed ashore and the introductions followed – my aunt, cousin and her two daughters, the usual animated period of greetings.

Then came our clearance through Customs, very casual; nothing was checked or inspected; so different to years later, when at Perth Airport on repeated occasions, I was thoroughly gone through, with a fine-tooth comb, the formalities were completed, and out to the car park.

My first impression of the trip to Claremont was that the houses seemed very small, bungalow types, but with well kept, very nice gardens. Our destination, Taylor Road, Nedlands, was apparently also a small dwelling, but beautifully kept, with an impressive-looking rose garden at the front. The interior of the house was very clean, and the kitchen well equipped with domestic appliances.

Almost as soon as we arrived, my uncle, without removing his raincoat, suggested he and I go down to the hotel, where he had arranged accommodation. We drove to the Highway Hotel, a very bare-looking place, devoid of any character, where I duly registered. As we entered the bar, I studied my uncle's face closely, and noticed that his hands were shaking. He ordered a brandy for himself and as requested I was given a ridiculously small glass of beer. Before I had taken my first sip, Alfred had downed his brandy and ordered another.

'Cripes, it was cold on that wharf. I was expecting to get a drink on board. I would have brought some grog with me had I known you were going to be so long getting ashore!'

The beer, to me very cold and slightly bitter, was, Alfred assured me, the best beer in the world. A claim I have heard made in so many countries. After he had downed several brandies, it was quite obvious to me that my dear old uncle was an alcoholic.

'You aren't a bloody wowser, are you?'

'What's that, Alfred?'

'You take a drink!'

I realised then, that I had a new vocabulary to learn even when speaking with my English relatives. The profanity of his language and suggestive talk to the barmaid led me to realise that he was a vastly different type to what I had expected. After purchasing a few bottles of beer, which were placed discreetly in the boot of the car, we returned to Taylor Park. A well prepared meal followed, and a general discussion on our various life styles, and then we drank our way through the rest of the day.

I soon learned that Alfred was a self-taught man who, as a rivet boy in Devonport dockyard in England, had first educated himself by reading the classics, when, according to his story, he should have been counting rivets.

116

Trudy and I were then driven back to the Highway Hotel. There was no morning tea or newspapers provided, but there was a good cooked breakfast, after which we went to the office to pay the bill. I was assured that this had been taken care of by my uncle, but I insisted on paying. As the bill was about twice as much as I had ever paid for bed and breakfast anywhere, it made me slightly apprehensive as to our financial future.

That day we moved into one of Alfred's houses at City Beach, a clean, two-bedroomed, timber and asbestos beach house. At a nominal rent of £4.10s.0d per week. I was at this time sending home twenty pounds a week maintenance for Barbara and the children, but still had two months paid leave left.

On our way to City Beach, we were driven through the centre of Perth, which impressed me as being a well laid out city. I was not particularly impressed with the old-fashioned looking shops, window displays, primitive buses and the very indifferent looking and casual bearing of the policemen. The cleanliness of everything, however, was beyond reproach. I do admit that when I first ran along the city beach, the relaxed lifestyle appeared to be everything we could have wished for. Geographically and from the material point of view, Australia would be a hard country to beat. I feel nevertheless, on the spiritual plane that something has always been missing.

When I saw a dead moth lying for several days on the floor of the outside toilet, I remember remarking to Trudy how different the country was from Africa. There, predators roamed everywhere. Life at all levels was so temporary. I had run over a puff adder, in my three-ton truck once on the way to Mkowe jetty. Returning some twenty minutes later, I stopped and inspected the completely dry vertebra. Not an once of flesh was left. That moth in Africa would never even have settled on the floor.

During our first few days in Australia my uncle entertained us with some ribald, lewd stories of his life as a private investigator. I had secretly formed an impression of dear Alfred, but was still continuously embarrassed for Trudy, as I had never heard a man behave in such a fashion in front of a lady. All his stories were complemented by flamboyant, often rude gestures and much laughter.

The most I saw of our new country in the first few weeks were the fantastic beaches where I swam daily and the

Claremont hotels and yacht club, where I appeared to spend an awful lot of money. I was introduced to many people, Alf's mates, as he called them all, who appeared to have a deep love of Australia. These, despite their somewhat diverse appearances and obviously poor physical and in some instances questionable, mental condition, alleged that they were earning fantastic amounts of money. This gave me hope for the future as my leave would soon run out.

Upon occasionally mentioning that I had to seek employment soon to augment my dwindling resources, I was told by Alfred that there was plenty of time, and 'let's have another drink!'

We did have several enjoyable evenings with the Sleeps, who organised a barbecue on our behalf, which, in such a beautiful climate, helped convince me that we had made a wise choice in coming to this country. We had met a cross section of people: milkmen, policemen, doctors, mechanics and lawyers, but no Indian chiefs, everyone seemed friendly. No evidence of any formality.

I had a letter of introduction to the Frigidaire commercial sales manager in Sydney, but Western Australia appealed to me, and I had no desire to settle in a big city.

Various exploratory calls and visits to the native affairs and native welfare departments, the Commonwealth bank migration services etc, met with the usual platitudes, but no constructive help. The native welfare department could start me as a patrol officer at the equivalent of £750 per annum – less than I had gone out to Kenya with several years before. Bearing in mind my twenty pounds a week maintenance, this was completely unacceptable. But, I had to start somewhere. The average wage would have been less than twenty pounds a week. I was facing a formidable task.

The local Frigidaire people had nothing immediately available to offer, but enquired some four days later if I would be interested in managing an electrical business in Barrack Street. Yes, I was, and after a short interview I was accepted commencing, if I remember correctly, at the princely sum of twenty-four pounds a week and commission.

I was in a new country though, and had so much to learn, even at thirty-nine years of age. In the Royal Hotel, William Street once, drinking with a party of five or six men, it was my turn to 'shout' a round. As I considered that I had drunk quite

118

sufficient myself, I bought the 'round' but left myself out. When we finally left the hotel, Alfred advised me to, 'never do that again.!'

'Do what, Alfred?'

'Refuse to drink a "round".'

'I didn't refuse anything Alf. I am thirty-nine years of age and if I don't feel like another drink, I'm not having one!'

This was my first experience of the Australian macho self-image.

When I started my new job I presented myself on a Monday morning at the store entrance. An Englishman asked me who I was, to which I replied, 'The new manager'.

This was the man I was replacing but it was the first he had heard of it. Hardly a polished start . . .

The business, I soon saw, was very run-down – no proper stock control system, sales training, or even incentive commissions were paid to anyone other than the manager. My predecessor remained with the company. I was able to purchase a second-hand van and put him on the road as an outside representative. When he was hanging around the store one morning, I asked him when he was going to start work.

'I'm hungry Mr Northcott, and I cannot get my commissions.' I could hardly believe this at the time, although I have since met several hungry Australians. I offered him five pounds from my wallet and he quickly disappeared. He returned about midday, and I enquired where he had been.

'Home, Mr Northcott. I gave my wife the money and we went shopping. Our boss isn't too liberal with his payments, wages or commissions.'

As he alleged, the store did owe him commissions he had earned as a manager. I visited a director's office in Murray Street and informed him of the situation. The director looked at me rather vacantly over his glasses.

'What should we do, Bill?' I summed up this situation very quickly and already a picture was emerging.

'Pay him'.

The business had a cycle department, and when I questioned the man in charge as to how many units he had sold the previous week, he answered, 'I don't know.' He had been with the company ten years and just wasn't interested. I remained with the company for just three months, which was long enough.

119

One day I enquired from Alfred how much money he had taken that week. 'Not good, son, only ninety-four pounds!' Knowing he had been out each night drinking, I began to think

Alfred had recently sold the business to his assistant, a man named Stuart Leckie, who had been with Alfred some fifteen years. The arrangement was that Stuart would pay Alf twenty pounds a week for the business, whilst the latter was alive, and would then pay auntie a thousand pounds when Alf died. The business then belonged solely to Leckie.

With rent coming in regularly from his houses and other investments, Alf thought he would be quite well provided for.

A few weeks before I arrived in Perth, Leckie had visited Alf, thrown the office keys on the table and said he was unable to run the business. His inability to handle money had soon confirmed that he was unable to pay the secretary or meet the other costs of the business.

The office was closed, and both investigators then advertised and operated individually from their respective homes. Leckie, although a good field man as I was given to understand, like Alfred, drank quite heavily, lived in a small rented apartment and ran, I remember, a very battered Ford Zephyr car.

Discussing our economic situation with Trudy, I decided to apply for an inquiry agent's licence. I inspected the vacant rooms in McLaren chambers, William Street that Alfred had occupied since 1928. These consisted of two, dingy and dirty rooms with a shared row of outside toilets. The suite being on the first floor.

When I mentioned to the Sleeps, that I intended applying for a licence, auntie Edith, a lovely lady, with a dry Australian sense of humour, attempted to dissuade me. I should have listened to her more carefully.

Previously, Alfred had suggested I work with him, but on evaluating their different financial status and living conditions, I had correctly assessed that Stuart did not have much to show for his fifteen years work with my shrewd old uncle. Once the decision was made, I gave a months' notice to my employer and made the necessary application for a licence.

22. Private Investigator 'Soon Soon Jet'

Having experienced for myself the shattering emotional trauma of a divorce, with the very painful separation from my children, I felt I was mature enough to cope with the thankless task of a private investigator and build up a reliable and trustworthy agency. This was certainly my intention when I applied for a licence, second only, of course, to my urgent need to augment my financial position.

I knew Alfred handled only divorce enquiries or matrimonial problems. I intended to handle any investigation of a private, legitimate nature. So I set about cleaning and painting up the office and selecting basic items of furniture.

During the waiting period of several weeks for the processing of the licence, I set up an easel in the office and commenced an oil painting. This was a hobby I had always been interested in. I was working on this painting, when a Sergeant Burrows and a colleague from the CIB came to interview me. The painting was a large abstract of a Mchawi (witch doctor) dancing over Perth. No doubt they thought I was an unusual applicant. This was, incidentally, the only picture I have ever sold.

Eventually the licence was granted. I started advertising for business and visited solicitors in an effort to endeavour to obtain work.

Much later, a lawyer informed me, 'Bill, we wouldn't have touched you then with a barge pole. An ex-colonial officer, in a strange country, far too English, and we all knew it wasn't a case of knocking politely on the front door. We didn't expect you to last.'

The first month I recall I took exactly twenty-two pounds, which really set me worrying. I could not last long like this.

As Alfred had kindly promised to pass on the odd client that he could not, or did not wish to handle, I was a little disappointed. A couple of test calls to Taylor Road confirmed my suspicion. I would in fact get no help from Alfred.

Some few days after I had confirmed these suspicions, Alfred walked into the office, and in quite a dictatorial manner said he wished to use my desk to interview a client. Realising he was probing my reaction, I told him politely to get lost.

'If this is war, son, your rent is up two pounds a week.'

'Take a week's notice, Alf, as from today.'

The female client arrived, and she was interviewed in the waiting room by Alfred.

My dear uncle, I knew, was now ready for a drink. We walked across the road to the Royal Hotel, which gave me the opportunity to explain that I was no Stuart Leckie and had no intention of being used like he had been. I was getting a bit fed up with Alfred. His mostly sexually orientated behaviour, I was finding rather embarrassing by this time.

Trudy and I vacated the house at City Beach the same week, and moved into a flat in Outram Street, West Perth. Lady luck then smiled and I had two clients in one week, one being a farmer and his daughter.

As I listened to their story and asked a few pertinent questions, I sensed I was somehow not on the same wavelength. Something was missing!

The hard-bitten Australian then made some facetious remarks, to which I replied 'What sort of stupid bastard do you think I am?' Whereupon he looked at his daughter and grinned.

'He's OK! How much did you say, Mr Northcott, eighty pounds?'

After they left the office I looked at the money and reflected. You don't say to a burly Australian lumper from the waterfront. 'Take a seat sir, I will be with you in a minute.'

I had to change my entire approach – I did.

When Alfred's lady client, arrived at the office to pay her fee, I telephoned him at home. He requested that I take the cash and give her a receipt. That evening I visited Taylor Road, gave him the money, and was invited to stay for the inevitable beer. This gave me the opportunity to explain that, although Leckie was unable to pay him twenty pounds a week for the business, it would be more profitable for him to send me a client or two and get more than the twenty pounds. Everyone would then be happy. He would receive his beer money, Barbara her maintenance and Trudy and I could start eating properly. As it was, we would buy a mutton flap at the weekend for one shilling and make an Indian curry – our weekend joint.

So the clients finally started drifting in . . . An unknown solicitor sent me a client. Quick evidence was obtained, a well presented statement forwarded, and I received in reply a request to visit his office. He then frankly explained that for some reason his regular investigator was unavailable and in desperation, he had sought my services. Our quick results impressed this lawyer and in the future we handled most of his enquiries.

One day Stuart Leckie came into the office and requested working for me as he had done for Alfred. As I had by no means consolidated my position, had no cash reserves for emergencies and was still very much feeling my way with the Australians, I declined his offer.

I knew Stuart drank heavily and his nerves were shot. He had been 'peppered' once in the buttocks by shotgun fire, and his experience in New Guinea, where during the war he served in a machine-gun unit, hadn't helped.

Rather amusingly, on that occasion, when a police sergeant telephoned Alf and informed him that Stuart had been shot and was in hospital Alfred had laughed.

'What's funny, Alf?'

'Only that I was going to do that job myself!'

I was still very unhappy though, when I heard that Stuart had committed suicide sitting in his battered Zephyr one night whilst on a job, fortified by a bottle of whisky. He had secured a hosepipe to his exhaust, closed the windows and given his life away. So very, very sad. Would he still be alive If I had employed him?

Alfred knew Stuart very well, and a few weeks earlier when I had asked him why he was always reading the obituary column in the paper, he replied 'Just seeing if Stuart has done it yet!'

There is always a lot of intrigue crime, corruption and manipulation going on in any city. When Alfred first confided in me, and told me some unbelievable stories about the real Perth establishment, legal procedures and activities, together with some of his own experiences as an enquiry agent. I thought the old boy was really 'talking in his cups!' I now realise, of course, that he was being completely honest. Was this perhaps why he drank? Was he as disgusted with himself as with the system that had provided him with his material wealth?' The reputation he had built up, both before and during the war, was most certainly well earned. I only knew him, remember, when he was on the 'way out'. He always wore his RSL (Returned Soldiers League) badge proudly. He had been a warrant officer padre in the First World War serving with the Australians in France.

I did find it somewhat obscene that in such a business he had made a lot of money during the Second World War whilst our family was being bombed in England, or serving elsewhere, abroad in the services. From a naive Methodist minister of God, he had degenerated to a cunning survivor in a difficult and dirty business. My Mother would have been very sad and disgusted had she visited Australia and met him.

He told me a story once in his early days in the business when a lawyer sent for him and offered him three hundred pounds to alter one of his statements. Looking out of the window, Alfred pointed across the street to a parked Oldsmobile car . . . 'See that car . . . If ever anyone could do with three hundred pounds, it's Alfred R Sleep. My equity in that car is only sixty pounds, but if you think I'm going to sell my soul to the devil for a measly three hundred pounds you're wrong!'

A few weeks later that lawyer was made a supreme court judge. It is doubtful if he would ever question Alfred's honesty.

In retrospect, I realise now I did too much for my clients. I was disgusted in the early days by the way the public had obviously been treated. The name of the game was just money. There were a hundred and one valid excuses why you could not get results. I decided to ignore them and build my business on a solid basis of achievement. Before any investigation was commenced the client was obliged to pay an up-front fee. 'Have you ever heard a TV private investigator ask the client for money? Yet on the screen they get in such life-threatening situations, all for free!

Whilst my business had now started growing, it wasn't quite fast enough for Barbara. She had somewhat embarrassingly had the English court order transferred to the jurisdiction of the West Australian courts. Fortunately, I was able to get free legal assistance, and the matter was speedily dealt with.

Our financial position now began to improve. I was able t o employ a typist/receptionist, being extremely lucky in engaging an Anglo-Indian lass called Winifred Hinton. She was well educated, an excellent typist, with the right type of presence and personality for our unusual type of business.

Winifred's father had been a senior driver on the Indian railway. I really admired the way he had managed to migrate to Australia with his many children. He was a small wizened man, not unlike Mahatma Gandhi in appearance. In Australia he worked as a boiler attendant at Welshpool. Despite the heat and the humble job, I never heard him complain.

So there I was working daytime in the office, interviewing clients, preparing statements or appearing in court to give evidence. I was out in the evenings, doing field work, often until the early hours of the morning. When the office was quiet during the day I would sleep on the floor until I could afford a suitable reclining chair. Winifred would wake me if a client visited us.

At least seventy per cent of enquiries at that time were for the securing of evidence to be used in divorce proceedings under the old matrimonial act. Fortunately, this has now been changed to a much more civilised and humane arrangement – a given period of separation with sufficient proof of the marriage breakdown. Divorce evidence under the old act was purely the evidence of association, affection and opportunity. Nothing particularly difficult, but necessitating much time spent waiting and watching. Each case, because of its people-orientated nature, was different. Once the evidence had been collected and evaluated, there was, of course, the final confrontation, or raid.

In a hedonistic society like Australia, collusive divorces, whilst illegal, were not unknown. A solicitor friend of mine, later a family court judge, once accused me of handling such cases. When I vehemently denied this accusation.'But, Bill, you have, I've sent them to you!'

He was the criminal, not me. Naturally he would have carefully rehearsed the clients before they contacted me. What a charade!

It is rather ironic because he is enjoying a magnificent salary, with many perks and privileges, whilst I am living in Thailand on a humble Veterans Affairs pension. But then again, I feel quite clean, and that is important to me. Sacrifices have to be made.

The same man defended me once on a minor wilful damage case in the local court. He knew the facts of the case quite well, and knew that I was completely innocent, despite the verdict going against me.

Months later, referring to the case, he said, 'But , Bill, you were guilty!'

'I was what?'

'Guilty, Bill. The judge said you were.'

Not quite my idea of British justice, but then, we were playing Aussie rules.

On another occasion at the Esplanade Hotel in Perth, I was drinking with a group of lawyers, one of whom had just returned from the north of the state, where he had been defending an Aboriginal man on a murder charge. One of the lawyers turning towards me said 'He was definitely guilty, Bill. He must have been. He was black.' Hardly believing what I was hearing, I put my glass on the bar.

'You blokes give me the S . . .ts, ' and I walked out of the hotel.

I can appreciate why sometimes I have not been too popular!

In an endeavour to give some idea of the life style I was now leading, I will recount a selection of cases, matrimonial and others, that we accepted.

Whilst I have only my memory to rely on, I will only deal with a few of these enquiries that have left a deep impression on me. The minor details I will endeavour not to colour or fabricate, but the essence of each case is completely and irrevocably true. After all, at seventy-two years of age, do I honestly need to exaggerate or indulge in flights of fancy? I have no need or desire to impress anyone. Most of these cases too, ended up in one court or another. There are records somewhere

I do not agree, as one Australian lawyer said to me as he was attempting to justify perjury, that 'it is only words, Bill!'

To me, the truth is still the truth.

23. Wrong Place, Wrong Time

First I will tell the Jimmy X story, one of my earliest cases.

One evening on the 6th January 1960, I received a telephone call from a man identifying himself as Noel 'Y', requesting that I travel to Albany with him as he had heard that his wife was staying at the Premier Hotel with a man called Jim.

As Albany is some four hundred miles from Perth and I was scheduled to give evidence in the supreme court on the following day, I agreed, provided we could travel in Y's car and return to Perth the same night. A fee was agreed upon. At about 8 pm I met Noel Y at his home in Como, collected my fee, and then set out in Noel's car for Albany. As we drove away from Perth in the comfortable Ford Fairlane, I was given an account of the recent domestic events. Noel informed me that Stuart Leckie had previously been engaged to conduct an investigation into his wife's activities, but he, Noel, had been unsuccessful in contacting him earlier the same day. Leckie, he had recently learned, was a friend of Jim's, and had in fact been the best man at his wedding. This was information he was unaware of, when first engaging Stuart.

Noel, a butcher by trade, had been notified by a friend who had telephoned and told him that Jimmy and Mrs 'Y', were booked into the hotel. He had also given him the registration number of an Austin Westminster sedan that Jim was driving.

As Noel talked to me on that journey, he told me that he had been one of the principal witnesses in a recent Royal Commission into illegal betting. Thus I formed a fair impression of my client's character. He was mentally quite sharp and rather amusing.

We eventually reached Albany, sometime about 1 am, and checking the car park of the Premier Hotel, indentified the Austin Westminster, parked as expected. The hotel was in darkness; the front door was open, but the reception counter closed. I had noticed that the licencee was a man named Francis Joseph Lynch.

A guest suddenly appeared, and I requested where the Lynch's room was located. Receiving directions, we went upstairs and knocked on the appropriate door. Mr Lynch answered my summons and I enquired which room was occupied by a Mr Jimmy 'X', the driver of the Westminster sedan parked below. Lynch asked me if we were the police, to which I replied that I was investi-gating a case involving that particular vehicle.

Putting on his dressing gown, Lynch first directed me to a wrong room, then led me back upstairs and along a corridor.

Suddenly a tall, heavily-built young man, wearing a maroon-coloured dressing gown, left a toilet and proceeded down the corridor. Lynch pointed to him and indicated that this man was Jimmy. We followed and saw him enter a room, but before he could close the door, I moved forward, and, pushing it open, followed him into the room.

Lying in a double bed was a woman whom I recognised from a photograph as being Mrs 'Y'. Noel also identified his wife and after the necessary formalities, we left the room. Lynch then said, 'you're a divorce detective.'

I replied 'Yes, Mr Lynch, I am a licensed investigator.'

Driving back towards Perth, almost half way home, a car came racing up behind us – Yes, the Austin Westminster.

'Y; accelerated to nearly a hundred miles per hour, and driving onto the edge of the road, endeavoured to spray gravel chippings at the approaching car. The Austin overtook us, much to my surprise. I didn't realise it was capable of such speed.

As I quietened 'Y' down, I explained to him, that we had first-class evidence, and there was no need for further risk taking.

The next morning, very tired, I was in the office early, preparing myself for the supreme court opening at 10 am.

Jimmy 'X' walked into my office, unnanounced. He offered me a considerable sum of money to drop the case and became very abusive when I refused. I knew by this time that he was an insurance executive, married to a very nice lady, but was a well known playboy. I also learned, much to my cost, that he was a firm drinking companion to some of the senior CIB police detectives. Two or three weeks passed, and my statement had been forwarded to 'Y''s solicitor and I now had other cases to think about.

I was a little disturbed though, when two CIB officers

visited my office and started questioning me as to the events that had taken place in Albany. It transpired that Jimmy 'X' had conferred with some of his police mates, visited Albany at least twice to see Mr Lynch, and was beginning to cause me trouble. I showed the two police visitors a copy of my statement, and after reading this, they accused me of lying, saying that I had definitely stated to Lynch that I was a policeman.

A week later I received another visit from the police and was formally charged with 'stating that I was a police officer.'

The outcome was a foregone conclusion; I appeared some time later at the local district court where the charge had been amended to 'pretending to be a police officer'. Lynch gave evidence and I was duly found guilty and fined ten pounds. When the police magistrate, the notorious AG Smith asked me if I was quite happy to let Lynch 'assume' I was a policeman, I somewhat indiscreetly but honestly, replied that I was 'quite happy to let Lynch 'assume' I was the Archangel Gabriel'.

Hardly the diplomatic reply to a question from a staunch Roman Catholic . . . But how was I to know?

Some months later in the supreme court, Jimmy 'X' put up an expensive, four-day defence. I was asked by his solicitors in the first cross-examination whether it was a fact that I had been found guilty of 'pretending to be a police officer.'

I agreed, 'Yes, that is so, sir.'

The Chief Justice, Sir Bertie Wolfe, who was hearing the case, asked Council about the relevancy of the question. 'The credibility of the Witness, your Honour'. To which the Chief Justice replied, 'because one man disbelieves Mr Northcott, it doesn't mean we all do. Discontinue that line of questioning.' Jimmy 'X' lost his case, despite every trick he could muster. One of the first, but no means the last time, that I heard witnesses perjure themselves in court.

'After all, it's only words . . .' I have never heard of a perjury case being successfully prosecuted in Australia. I was discussing this facet of the law with Leo Woods, one of Perth's most experienced criminal lawyers, when he said, 'Bill, you can't expect people to tell the truth if it's to their detriment, can you?'

The 'X' case was my very first run-in with the WA police force at that time, though I still had some respect for the boys in blue which unfortunately took several years to completely erode.

The sequel to the 'X' story was told to me some years later.

Jimmy was serving a prison sentence for embezzlement. He was charged with a second offence, but whilst awaiting trial in the supreme court cells, he committed suicide by poison, unable to face a further term of imprisonment.

I had long since ceased operating as a private investigator when I lived in a unit directly opposite 'X''s house. As I stood on my balcony looking down, I thought of the irony of life. God certainly does 'move in a mysterious way his wonders to perform.'

Throughout my life, I have always felt supported by some outside influence. I am quite sure that if one tries hard enough and keeps faith with God and himself, one must win out.

I was quite childishly pleased years later when I passed AG Smith, the then retired police magistrate, in Murray Street in Perth. We recognised each other almost simultaneously, then he lowered his eyes to the footpath as he drew near me. We each knew, deep in our hearts, what we were really worth.

24. The Pressure Continues

There were a series of murders in Perth early in the 1960s, and a man who visited me one day alleged he had recently had an attempt made on his life in Melbourne. He gave me some detailed information which I thought was most definitely a police matter. I walked across to the CIB office, then located in William Street at the central police station. I asked to see Sgt Burroughs, who was later promoted to the chief of the CIB.

'What do you want him for?' I was gruffly asked by a plain-clothes man.

As I replied that I had some information to give him, a very tall, heavily built man entered the reception area, and in an aggressive manner said, 'come on then, spill it!'

'Don't bother old boy, I'll wait for Sgt Burroughs.'

'Less of the fugging old boy' was the parting remark to me as I left the station. Obviously, there was some form of culture clash! I understand better now, but certainly didn't then. The last sort of an address to an Australian Civil Servant was, at that time, to call him 'old boy'. It has an unacceptable colonial ring to it. If pulled up by an Australian police patrol man it was then better to call him 'mate' than 'officer' – thus immediately identifying yourself as a fellow Australian. I had never met such bigotry in Africa and certainly not here in Thailand.

As I successfully finalised a few cases, I was able to improve the office conditions with an air-conditioner and reclining chair. I also invested in an expensive Miniphon tape recorder. As fast as I moved one step forward though, I was driven two steps back.

I had engaged CP Birds, one of the largest accountants at that time in Perth. In those days, no income tax relief was given on money that was sent out of the country on maintenance payments, so my twenty pounds a week to Barbara earned me no tax relief at all. Imagine my feelings when CP Birds' man walked into the office one day and said, 'I have your tax assessment here, Mr Northcott'. I owed nine hundred and seventy pounds. My bank balance at the time was just a hundred and twenty pounds.

Upon my requesting an explanation from him, he said, 'This was worked out from the figures you gave me,' which was an obvious implication. Was I again being too honest?

Years later, at a Director's' meeting in Sydney, New South Wales, we were given three sets of balance sheets to choose from. They were the same figures, but differently presented. I realise now how terribly naive I had been. I will never, ever, believe in a set of accountant's figures again.

Just imagine what it must be like with a 'Country's' budget! No wonder we are in the present global economic mess. Nobody believes anybody else. The pigeons must come home to roost eventually. I believe like Lang Hancock, the mining entrepreneur, that a 'country's' treasurer should balance the budget properly and not rely on these fantastic deficits that all countries have learned to live with. It must breed dishonesty.

Anyway, back to Sleep & Northcott investigations.

I had no alternative but to request time to pay. For months afterwards, added to my maintenance problems, were the tax man's spoils to be considered. Life obviously wasn't meant to be easy.

When Trudy and I first arrived in Australia, an article had been written for the *Weekend Mail* headed, 'they lived with Mau Mau', giving a brief, if not valid description of our life in Kenya. An Englishman who saw the article came to visit our flat in Outram Street. He was an articulate man, dressed in a shabby sports coat, and appeared not to be very well off. It transpired he had been a Sgt Major in an English regiment, stationed in Kenya during the war, training the Kings African Rifles. By trade he was a plumber, but was at this time employed sweeping out cattle trucks at the Midland railway junction. Because of local union rules, he had never been allowed to practise as a plumber in Australia.

His purpose in visiting me was to solicit my assistance in helping him to return to England with his wife and daughter. I explained my position, but was able to pay him for a few simple enquiries he made in the district. He appeared very grateful.

Visiting his state rented house at Midland once, I was shocked to see the conditions under which the family lived. He had sold most of his furniture towards the fare home, and was virtually sitting and eating on packing cases and sleeping on the floor. His last items of furniture for sale, were a gas stove and a refrigerator.

I purchased these, enabling him to finalise his departure from Australia. Some weeks later I received a happy letter from England where he had obtained employment as some sort of laboratory assistant. The only possessions, apart from clothes that he returned with, were his complete set of plumbers tools, which he had never been allowed to use. I found this at the time, very sad. In those early years, I saw many potentially good migrants leave Australia.

John Shelton, an ex-mines administrator from Rhodesia, on being told he was unsuitable for a bread carter's job because of lack of experience immediately booked his fare back to Africa.

'Topper' and Hilda Brown – He was an ex-superintendent of police in Tripolitania and lasted in Australia about four months. Topper used to visit the 'House of Degradation', as he called the social security office, once a week, where he spent an hour or so interpreting for some of the Italian migrants. He kept all his social security cheques and gave them back to the department. He said he wanted nothing from Australia. When I invited them to a picnic once at Yanchep, Hilda said, 'No thanks, Bill, we've already seen enough of this country!'

Pat and Peter Campbell were another couple. He was an ex RAF equipment officer, working in Fremantle as a shipping clerk. On their return to South Africa, they wrote me several happy letters, and had settled down in their new house, which was a great improvement, they said, on the weatherboard house they had been buying in Bayswater in Perth. I know if I had been able to afford it, I too would have gladly left Australia, but it was many years before I was able to do so. Rather worth mentioning is a letter I received from one of my former African staff, enclosing a cutting from the Daily Nation, together with a comment. How true it was he didn't really appreciate, 'that I had apparently jumped out of the frying pan into the fire'. The article was written by John Bates, giving rather a lurid account of the terrible times he had experienced in Australia: Heat, flies, no work, etc. It is truly a small world.

Bob Fletcher who worked at Sleep & Northcott investigations as an office manager, was at one time a police prosecuting officer in Nairobi. An excellent man, who after twelve months in our employ, also decided that Australia was not for him. I was really sorry to see Bob return to South Africa.

When I once visited the Marita service station on the Stirling Highway in Perth I recognised Max Kroll, the ex-special branch man who used to stay at my house in Marigot, serving on the pumps. He was managing the service station, but later told me he was considered by the oil company executives to be too independent. They were looking for ex-mechanics who were more easily handled. Then he moved to Port Moresby where he worked with the special branch of the Australian Federal police. He came to see me a few years later, also on his way back to Africa.

I must now mention Bob Service, an Englishman with a very Pukka public school accent. When I first met him socially he was selling cemetary headstones in Perth. Successfully too, I assumed, with his solemn dignified demeanour and always impeccably attired in dark suits.

Bob had owned a boarding house in Melbourne, which he had leased out as he wished to take an extended holiday and see a little more of Australia. On his return to Melbourne he found the house shut up. All the furnishings had been stolen and he was now completely without an income.

When I discovered that he had worked for a large, London-based firm of private investigators, I gave him a weekly retainer, engaging his services on a temporary basis. Bob had travelled extensively throughout Europe on private and commercial enquiries, and also held a current racing driver's licence. Unquestionably he was a good man. Suddenly, he too decided to leave Australia, but even whilst many miles away in England, managed to give me a spirited boost when I most needed one.

I was now getting trouble with the police about once a year, and on this occasion, had a charge levelled against me of 'wilful damage. A client had broken a window in the course of a divorce investigation. A quite normal procedure, but as I was considered in charge of the raid, I was held responsible. Normally in a case such as this the client was held responsible for immediately securing the services of a glazier and replacing the glass. The police had never previously taken action over such an incident. Alfred had been doing it for years.

Naturally on the day of my court appearance I was not feeling exactly exhilarated or at peace with myself. Until the mail arrived, Bob was with a film unit in my home town Plymouth and had sent me a magazine portraying the new rebuilt city. On the rear cover was an outline of the city almost completely covered with black dots, each representing a high expolsive bomb that had been dropped during the wartime Blitz. Looking at the picture now I thought that this was something to worry about, my mind cleared almost immediately and I felt at peace . . . Thank you, Lord!

As I entered the courtroom, a newspaper reporter I knew approached me.

'You look pretty cheerful, Mr Northcott.'

'Yes. I'm not interested what you bastards think of me. What I think of myself though, is important.' Everytime in my life when I have been up against it something has come along to boost my spirits. Yes, of course, I have always prayed. Again, thank you too, Bob.

I mention these odd little incidents purely to indicate how events were shaping up in my life. Many people from East Africa, migrants and prospective migrants at that time, seemed to find their way to my office. I listened to many stories, some quite heart-breaking. Most of these people were hard-working types who had held responsible positions overseas, yet they couldn't seem to get started in Australia.

One such was Jack Jones, the ex-commandant of the Marigat detention camp. When Jack left Kenya he first joined the justice department in New Zealand, and later moved to Fiji as a senior stores officer when they were building the new Nandi airport. Having come to Perth originally on holiday with his wife, he subsequently moved across permanently.

I had recently been offered, at a very good price, the purchase of an employment agency located in the same building as Sleep & Northcott.

Knowing that Jack was returning to Perth and had a ggod reputation for handling men, I thought he might be interested in running such a business. I bought it on the condition that the present manageress was able to continue working until Jack arrived. When he finally arrived in Perth and had settled down, I offered him the management of the new business on a salaried/share basis, which he accepted.

The venture was never successful. The type of people seeking employment didn't offer Jack the inspiration he needed, and after a few months, barely covering expenses, I sold the business. I took Jack into the investigating business until he eventually moved back to New Zealand, taking up a position as

135

a publications officer with the government printers.

We had been friends for a long time, but my faith in human nature was now becoming a little shattered. One evening, only a few days after he had arrived from New Zealand, I took him out with me on an evening assignment.

On my return to the house, he alleged that he had lost his wallet containing some eight hundred pounds Australian and $300 in Fijian currency. We retraced our steps but were unsuccessful in finding it.

Nearly two years later, when the police telephoned that the wallet had been found on the the the roof of a west Perth factory, I realised that my suspicions had been without foundation. Jack reported to the police station to identify the wallet. As the sergeant counted out the Fijian notes, which was all the wallet contained, he stopped after some time, and looked enquiringly at Jack, who pretended to be unaware of the unspoken question. After a further similar pause, the whole three hundred was counted out, Jack gave the sergeant twenty pounds which he thought was adequate. The sergeant grabbed the note, put it in his pocket, but said nothing.

Many years previously, as a young man, Jack had served in the London Metropolitan Police.

On his return to the office, he mentioned the incident and recounted how in London a policeman would have first thanked the benefactor, recorded the donation in the police welfare fund book and issued a receipt. But this was Perth, Western Australia, not London – truly a different world.

One evening when I returned to my flat in Outram Street for a coffee at about 9 pm, I was annoyed on my return to the car to see that I had been issued with a police infringement notice for parking without lights. Mine was the only vehicle in the street to receive a ticket though all were without lights. The next day in the office I wrote a carefully worded complaint to the commissioner of police. I received no acknowledgement, but was obliged to report for a police traffic lesson – a complete waste of time. I learned nothing new, but it was an unnecessary humiliation. I could tell that pressure was now being applied. This was to be the name of the game, and much worse was yet to come.

Trudy, when she on a long Christmas vacation from the kindergarten, where she had found employment and when I was particularly busy and working flat out, kept badgering me, saying she wanted a child. I reminded her of our earlier agreement, before we were married and of the financial pressures we were still under, the fact that I was still paying maintenance and would be for some time. She became quite demanding however; my resistance weakened and eventually, to her great happiness and my discomfort, she became pregnant. My beloved son William was born on the 17 October 1962 at the St John of Gods Hospital, Subiaco.

25. The Gouldham Case

Some time in late 1962, at the time William was being born, I now notice – A Yorkshire man, Bernard Kenneth Gouldham, visited the office. He had just come out of prison after serving some forty-seven weeks. His solicitor had recommended our services.

The story he told me was that he had been convicted of 'having intended to deceive his principal by giving him an account which ommitted to state explicitely that eight hundred dollars had been deducted for his own use. Gouldham was a real estate agent and the alleged offence involved the building and sale of a house. As he was completely broke, he stated he was unable at the time to pay me a fee. I listened to his story and believed him when he said he was completely innocent.

It appeared that one Sunday, six months after he had started serving his sentence and was being held at a prison farm near Perth he was visited by his wife, who was accompanied by a plain-clothes police detective sergeant. The sergeant produced an already typed statement which he requested Gouldham sign, saying that if he did so he could secure his immediate release. Mrs Gouldham tearfully pleaded with her husband to sign the statement and come home. As the statement was in fact an admission of guilt, I admired Gouldham's grit when he refused, reiterating that he was not guilty. Having questioned him closely and fully believing his story, I decided to help him.

As a first step I fitted him with my Miniphon tape recorder and asked him to visit his principal, on whose evidence he had been convicted. I naturally, cannot now recall, after so many years, the exact conversation, but it was alleged on the tape that the police had made repeated visits to the principal stating quite clearly that they were out to 'Get Gouldham'.

Those were the actual words used. Even after they had received the principal's first truthful statement which exonerated Gouldham from all blame, they persistently came back, until eventually they wheedled an amended statement from him. This led to Gouldham's arrest, charge and later conviction.

It was a start. Some months later I appeared as a witness in the local court on Gouldham's behalf and was cross-examined by the Crown Counsel.

'Mr Northcott, I suggest you cannot tell me the first three words that appear on this tape?'

'No sir, this is not a piece of poetry that I have memorised by heart, but the enormity of the accusation on the tape has left an indelible impression on my mind.'

Gouldham's appeal was nevertheless dismissed. Actually, it took him eight years to clear his name. Ken later visited my office and told me he was taking his appeal to the supreme court. What were my thoughts? I had always been treated most fairly by this court where I was constantly giving evidence. I told him so.

Weeks later he visited me again and showed me a seventeen-page document of inspired semantics as to why he was still considered guilty. So much for my faith in the supreme court.

Yes, for sheer grit and determination Gouldham really impressed me. He wouldn't let go. A credit to Yorkshire, he was a shrewd businessman, a professional real estate man, with a well earned, comfortable lifestyle. Whilst in prison he lost everything – business, house, car and reputation. On his release he sold cigarettes for a living, until slowly he rehabilitated himself and became the state manager for the Fire and All Risks Insurance Company.

The Crown Prosecutor, Alan J Dodd, who conducted the original case against Ken, had meanwhile left government service and commenced private practice as a lawyer. Ken befriended Dodd, helped him organise the administration of his practice, and eventually the original statement which had been held in the Crown Law Department was located. This completely exonerated Gouldham, and he eventually received $12,000 compensation from the government.

Small compensation for the terrible ordeal he had been through.

When preparing a financial statement for his claim against the government, he showed me a letter written by Alan Bond, the ex-millionaire entrepeneur. 'Had Ken Gouldham been operating in the real estate field in WA between the years of 1961-1969, there is no doubt he would have become a millionaire.' It

139

obviously did not carry much weight. Strangely enough, Ken, who is now deceased, and his long-suffering wife, to the best of my knowledge never left Australia. Looking back, I am still amazed at the double standards that applied in Perth, at that time.

26. Justice – Aussie Style Intimidation

This was another case that disgusted me. The client's name I honestly cannot remember. I have no reference material here in Thailand.

I had received a telephone message from the office to meet a new client in Forrest Place. Name and description were given to me. Hurrying round to Forrest Place, I saw an old man alighting from a taxi who fitted the description given, and so I approached him. After I introduced myself, the old man gave me brief details of his predicament.

A solicitor, a friend of his son, was holding several pieces of expensive jewellery in safe custody and now refused to hand them over, despite the old man's claim to being the legal owner. We walked up to the lawyer's office in Padbury Building, and the old man entered first. Suddenly I heard a man's loud voice. 'I told you to fug off out of here .Get out!' Entering the office, I introduced myself to this very irate, florid-faced individual, and informed him I was a private investigator acting for the old gentleman.

'What do you expect to get out of this old bastard? A fat fee?' He used to be a millionaire until we ripped everything off him. Now he's got nothing!' An admission was made, however, that he was holding various pieces of valuable jewellery, including a platinum and diamond-studded watch. The lawyer said he had no intention of releasing them.

After an unsuccessful visit a few days later to see his partner, I was obliged to write a letter to the barristers board. Eventually, I received a telephone call to collect the jewellery and my fee was paid with a diamond encrusted tiepin. The irony of this affair was, that shortly afterwards, the same lawyer was appointed a local court magistrate.

I would read in the newspapers on several later occasions that Mr . . ., sentencing the accused, said, 'Society cannot tolerate this sort of behaviour.'

I felt like vomiting.

That there is criminality in high office in Australia has been borne out by the Costigan and Fitzgerald reports, and whilst I was battling for an existence as an enquiry agent, paying heavy maintenance and tax payment arrears, a certain Crown Law officer and his wife were actually running a call-girl racket from the Crown Law offices in Perth.

THE COSTIGAN REPORT

In his analysis of the problem Costigan said the issues 'Reflect upon the office of the crown solicitor'.

His report documented the history of the **Bottom of the Harbour** test case, being handled in the Perth branch of the Deputy Crown Solicitor Office. The case identified by the Tax Department in 1973. He claimed there was dishonesty in the Perth office and incompetence in the Canberra office of the Crown Solicitor. He alleged false statements had been made by the Perth office in Canberra which further delayed action.

An officer in the Perth branch along with his wife began a prostitution business under the name **Kim Introductions,** through which he tried to avoid tax. His wife became involved in the bottom of the harbour tax schemes.

Three officers of whom Costigan was particularly critical were the Perth Deputy Crown Solicitor, Mr R Massie – Principal Legal Officer Mr S O'Sullivan who left the instructions in the bottom drawer and senior legal adviser Mr A Bercove whose wife was involved in the Tax evasion schemes

If you knew the drill you telephoned when requiring a service girl for sexual purposes. Even Thailand, with its open, tourist-orientated service industry, does not operate with such blatant high-level exclusiveness. Amazingly too, when asked to resign, the man had the effrontery to appeal against the decision.

My dear old alcoholic uncle had told me that all major prosecutions in WA were handled through the Crown Law department, where it was the practice to prepare two briefs – one 'guilty', the other 'not guilty' – then the powers that be decided which brief was the more political to pursue. The element of justice was a secondary consideration. To me, it is still of vital importance. That's what this book is all about!

IMTIMIDATION

A Dutch client once engaged our services to investigate the

continual theft of expensive wooden crates, which had been causing him a financial problem for some months. He had reported the matter to the police but without any positive results.

In the early hours of one morning, I was on surveillance at his business premises when a shadowy figure suddenly appeared and commenced throwing the cases into an adjoining property. I jumped over a dividing wall and confronted the thief, who immediately struck out and commenced grappling with me.

'Pack this nonsense up. I'm a private detective!'

The man shouted at me in a foreign language; finally broke away and ran into a shop next door. I identified him as the owner of the shop, a Maltese, second-hand furniture dealer.

Returning to my flat at about 5.30 am I had just made a cup of tea when I heard heavy footsteps approaching the front door. Answering the summons on the bell, I was greeted by two men who identified themselves as police detectives. They had already been advised of the results of my investigation, and said that unless I dropped the case they intended charging me with 'pretending to be a policeman'.

I quietly explained that the evidence I had obtained was for my client's use and it was up to him what he did with it. There was no further police action in this matter, but I learned later that the Maltese furniture dealer liaised with the bailiff's department and disposed of re-possessed furniture. Of course not! I assumed the police had been so promptly notified of the incident from this source.

I also recall meeting a prostitute contact of mine over on William Street horseshoe bridge. She was holding the hand of a young child and crying. I knew the girl was a first-class mother, who had been financially forced into her profession. Upon enquiring what was troubling her, she informed me that the bailiff had just visited her home and taken all the furniture, including the blankets from the baby's cot. As I had just received a generous fee for a successfully completed case I was able to give her some money to purchase new blankets.

I understand that these days the system is more humane. The Bailiff is required to leave a minimum amount of furniture, including beds and bedding. This is the association of ideas working again.

Bernadette Mathews, an Irish prostitute, was telling me in

my office how the vice squad, when organising a stag party, would request the services of individually selected demi mondaines. These poor creatures had to report as ordered and accommodate the officers – for free, of course. Months later, when facing my almost yearly police charge of 'impersonating the police' their official idea of my modus operandi, and an easy one to perjure.

My solicitor asked me what I was prepared to pay to get a 'not guilty' verdict.

'Oh . . . one hundred pounds?'

'No, Bill. Give me the Bernadette Mathews tape. That will do.'

I did get acquitted, and gave him a copy. I was learning slowly. Each profession must engender some statistics, as mine did . . .

My face was smacked once a week by irate women clients. I had developed a sickly grin technique, whilst my head was ringing, and a warning comment 'that it was a good job 'he' had not done that.' I went through this together with a good fist fight once a month. Then, most dangerous of all, there was my annual conflict with the police department.

Whilst talking to a private investigator in Adelaide,once, a lightly built, quiet man, I asked him if he ever had such trouble. Of course, he had had exactly the same experiences as myself, but had an arrangement with the courts that any offer of violence was quickly followed by a civil action and damage of three hundred pounds always awarded against the offender.

He was lucky not to be operating in West Australia, but his surname was, for a PI in Australia, rather risqué – Gardener Fluck.

What a ridiculous way this was to earn a living. Why hadn't I stuck to the display business or the comparative safety of government Service in Africa?

144

27. A New Recruit

About this time I first met John Dowson, who had just arrived from Kenya. His wife Rosaline had nursed with Trudy at the Royal Memorial Hospital in Nakuru, and had been a guest at our wedding. John was an ex-metropolitan and Kenya policeman and his father had a big law practice in London. John had the necessary experience I now needed, and a few weeks after the first meeting, he joined the firm.

Trudy and I had moved from the flat in Outram Street to a house in Altona Street in West Perth, which was divided into two completely separate units. John and Rosaline moved into one of these self-contained apartments.

I had also by this time equipped my vehicle with a two-way radio station, the base and ariel tower being installed at the apartment site. Trudy had the telephone where clients could reach her and now the radio with which she could easily contact me. Things were definitely improving and the business becoming more efficient. It was my ambition at the time to build the business up and gradually withdraw from the field work, directing operations from home. I had no desire to emulate Alfred, at sixty years of age, still going out at night, and running into all sorts of problems. We were, I realise now, far too ahead of our time. West Australia was still operating at a different pace.

When Dowson had been with me for a short while, he came to give evidence in the married womens' court which then existed, where maintenance matters were assessed. As I gave corroborating evidence, the opposing solicitor questioned me as to why an inexperienced man like John had been allowed to handle this case. 'Inexperienced, sir? with eighteen years in the metroploitan police in London, A chief inspector of police in charge of a murder investigation squad in Africa – I would have thought him quite capable of handling a simple divorce investigation in Australia!'

The Simba Club was operating in Perth at this time for the social benefit of African expatriates, mainly those from Kenya. One evening, John and I called in for a social drink at one of these gatherings, mingling separately with club members we each knew. Suddenly I heard John's very distinctive voice raised in anger. I moved across to where he stood, confronting a tall Australian man.

'You know nothing about Kenya. You're bullshitting!'

Looking at John's antagonist, I thought I vaguely recognised him from somewhere. After posing a few questions, I realised he was the same man who had stood on the Mkowe airstrip some years before requesting a lift out to Mombasa with Jerry Campbell and his friend. It is truly a small world. The Australian was a mining engineer, and, like many in his profession, well travelled.

When dear Winifred left to get married, I had a stream of inept girls in the office. Some talked too much about their work and the others were just... just frustrating! One, on the very first day she started work, had her boyfriend in the office and when I returned from a brief visit to a solicitor, I confronted a heavy passion session in progress upon opening an office door.

Obviously, this was not one of my better selections. The boyfriend seemed quite surprised and angry when I asked them both to leave.

I was acting for a lady named Betty Z at the time. She was a lovely person who ran a modelling academy in Perth. Confiding in her as to my staff problems, she, said that she might be able to assist me. Two or three weeks later, Betty telephoned to make an appointment for a prospective applicant by the name of Patricia Serve.

Pat duly reported to the office and was interviewed. She was married to a local wool buyer, but had been out of the workforce, looking after her two children, for some ten years.

We were extremely busy the week that Pat started work and it was soon apparent that her typing speeds were incapable of dealing with the volume of paper work then being handled. As Pat had all the other qualities – namely intelligence and presence – I was looking for, I felt rather disappointed. When she mentioned she was prepared to undergo a crash refresher course at her own expense, I decided to hold my impatience in check. Within two weeks, Pat was able to handle everything we gave her efficiently. She mentioned then that, having been a housewife at home for some years, it was refreshing to be back in the mainstream of life again. From then on, Pat was always the first one into the office in the morning, always anxious to read the activity reports and see what had happened the previous night. It was good to have the office running smoothly.

By this time we were exceptionally busy: clients came from our own advertisements, solicitors, personal recommendation and from having seen press cuttings of our troubles with the police. Any advertising is good advertising, and people knew we were able to get results.

One man, working on a mining site up north, read from a newspaper whilst sitting on the toilet that we were having some minor trouble with the ploice. He promptly stopped work and drove hundreds of miles down to Perth to engage our services. Several of our clients in a row, however, ran into near or fatal trouble.

As I listened to the news one evening, I heard that a man had been flown down from Kalgoorlie to the Royal Perth Hospital. I recognised his name as that of one of my clients. He had been found badly beaten up at the 300-foot level in a mine shaft and was lucky to be alive. The next day I visited the Royal Perth Hospital, to be informed he was in a certain ward. As I entered the ward, I saw it was occupied by two strangers and an Aboriginal. The latter turned out to be my client. He was absolutely covered in one big black bruise. He had been jumped and savagely beaten by a man wielding an iron crowbar. I visited him some weeks later at a flat in Gildercliffe street, South Perth. He was seated in a wheel chair, and it appeared he would never be able to walk or work again. He had recognised his assailant, but would not admit it to the police.

'We take care of these things in Kalgoorlie in our own way, Mr Northcott!'

The second case was big George, a Yugoslav client of mine, who had just received a heavy maintenance order. 'I not pay that bitch a penny!' he told his mate.

'George, this is Australia. If you don't pay up, you might as well go and hang yourself.' George left the room shortly afterwards and did just that.

With my own experience of maintenance payments, I sympathised with him, but on checking his file, was still pleased to see that he had finalised our account before taking such drastic action.

147

Another country client whom I arranged to meet in Perth never arrived. Driving too fast in a bad emotional frame of mind, he slammed his car into a huge karri tree as he took a bend too fast.

Then a burly lumper from Fremantle Wharf came into our office and asked us to locate his wife, who had been away from home for several weeks. We did so and duly gave him the address.

'That is my son's address. She is not there. Give me back my fee.'

I explained that private investigators never made refunds. Several days later he re-visited the office and gave us a car registration number, the owner of which he suspected had some relationship with his wife. No problem – whilst he waited we checked the car off and found it belonged to a man who resided at the same address as his son. What were we prepared to do about it? Nothing, unless he paid another fee to engage our services for a further investigation – a hard game.

He duly re-engaged us, and one night at about midnight one of our men visited the son's house at Cottesloe. The wife was not at home. At 3 am one of our spotters, Drew, a real night owl, had checked the Cottesloe house and found the subject's car parked in the driveway. I instructed him to collect the client from Hamilton Hill and meet me at the Ocean Beach Hotel in Cottesloe. The three of us then visited the house.

It was a bright moonlight night, and as I watched my burly client walk nervously up and down in the garden, I must have somehow smiled at my thoughts.

'What are you grinning at?'

'You. First of all, you didn't believe your wife was living here, but now you're like a nervous cat, and don't know what to do next.'

'What would you do?'

I gave him my opinion, but advised the utmost caution, and explained again, the type of evidence acceptable to the court and the risks involved.

It was obvious the client was in a very angry and emotional mood, but this had happened many times before. It was an emotional business.

Eventually, we followed the client through a rear door into the house. As we entered what appeared to be a kitchen, a man wearing only a pair of jockey shorts appeared in a hallway. My client, recognising him as the owner of the vehicle we had checked, immediately rushed at the man and commenced punching him around the body and head. Simultaneously, a woman ran out of an adjoining room, and as she looked like my client's wife, in an endeavour to identify her properly, I ran after her. Suddenly, I felt a terrific blow on the back of my neck, staggered against the wall and recovering my balance, saw several men appearing from various rooms. I beat a retreat to the kitchen, and realising that the raid had to be aborted, attempted to cool the situation.

Explaining who I was and why we were there, I gave one of the men my business card, listening at the same time to a lurid account of the 'bastard' we were acting for.

We finally left the house, and after a few words with the client explaining how he had nullified the raid by indulging in a bout of fisticuffs when he should have quietly looked for solid evidence as I had instructed.

I ordered Drew to drive him home. At 5.30 am I was fast asleep when the bedside telephone rang. It was Drew. He had taken the client home and had been invited in for a cup of tea.

A summons on the front door of the client's house a few minutes later had revealed the man's son, accompanied by another man. Drew then gave me a graphic account of the savage fight that followed. Our client's ear was torn off and unfortunately he died in hospital in the early hours of the morning. The son, rang me at the office the same morning and said his mother wished to see me. I suggested she call at the office. She never did.

I heard nothing further about this case. There appeared to be no inquest, and no charges levelled against the son.

After all . . . he wasn't an English enquiry agent!

28. What a Way to Earn a Living

Another client, Bill Q (it actually does begin with a Q), went missing for several days, until he was traced to the repatriation hospital at Shenton Park, where much later, I was to have my first hip replacement. He had, it appeared, been found in his Perth lodging house, lying in a pool of blood, with a big gash in his groin. Rather unsympathetically, I reminded him that he had no right to attempt 'hari-kari' whist he still owed me fifty pounds. Some of my male clients were hopeless creatures. No wonder their wives sought solace elsewhere.

The night we finally raided a house in Leederville, where Q's wife was sleeping with a man called LJ rather bears this out. This co-respondent, on hearing that he was in the presence of Bill Q, sat up in bed, held his hand out and said, "We've never met Bill, have we?" Q looked at me. "Is it alright if I shake his hand, Mr Northcott?"

I would not, on reflection. like to see my reply in black and white – but you've guessed! I was thinking how very matey it all was, yet looking around at the filthy room – all so very sordid.

No wonder Alfred and Leckie drank and so much for European superiority.

I had a certain grudging respect for the revolutionary in Africa, but these people – white people – were just degrading. The tribal African had some code of behaviour, some discipline, but these people had none.

As regards the raid I have just mentioned, Mrs Q took no part in the proceedings. She lay on the bed insensible, sporting a huge black eye. Whether she was drunk or drugged, I have no idea.

A Geoff M, came into the office one Saturday morning and asked if I would travel to Midland Junction where his wife was living with another man. I assessed this correctly as a statement job. A brief written confession of guilt, and I quoted him thirty pounds. Could he return to the office at 1 pm, I asked. He returned promptly on time accompanied by another man whom he introduced as Jimmy Mason, an ex-WA middle-weight boxing champion.

As we drove towards Midland, my two passengers occupied the rear seat of the car. Geoff M suddenly asked me if I was an Englishman. I replied in the affirmative, and as I did so, glanced in the rear-vision mirror, seeing them exchange a derisive look, which I interpreted, no doubt correctly, as slightly contemptuous. Waiting for a break in the traffic, I turned the car around and headed back towards Perth. When I was asked why I did this, I explained that I had absolutely no intention of working for bigoted clients.

They apologised profusely – 'M' saying his solicitor had highly recommended me. Thinking of the thirty pounds, my maintenance money for a week and a half, I headed once more back to Midland.

As we entered the town, I was invited to join my clients for a drink at a hotel. I refused the drink, but accompanied them into the hotel where they each drank a whiskey and milk.

'M' opened his chequebook. 'How much do you want, Mr Northcott?'

'Forty pounds, please.' I received a cheque for this amount.

As anticipated, we obtained the necessary signed statement easily and after dropping my client and his friend off, I headed for home.

The following Monday proved that 'M' had no account at that bank and that the cheque was worthless. I personally served the summons, demanding forty pounds plus costs.

A few days later, an old lady struggled up the stairs to the office breathing heavily and introduced herself as 'M's mother. As her son was out of work and battling, – Weren't we all – would I take two pounds a week until the debt was paid? Yes, providing not a single instalment was missed. So I agreed to this arrangement. A few weeks later 'M', obviously under the influence of alcohol, visited the office. He wished to discuss with me the wonderful job the English had done during the war.

'Have you paid your two pounds, 'M'? If so, bugger off.' I was gradually getting acclimatised.

Eventually, the account was finalised and the client asked for his statement. I slowly searched for it in the filing cabinet, extracted it, looked at 'M' and just as slowly tore it into little pieces, letting them fall to the floor.

'So, what do I get for my money?' 'M' asked.

'Nothing – but next time you meet an Englishman who acts like a gentleman, don't think he's wet between the ears. Pick up the pieces and get out!'

Yes, this was a hard game – not conducive to any sensitivity or refinement.

I had been threatened with all sorts of violence, but was now able to assess the real threat from the bluff. As glasses came off, false teeth came out, and belts were significantly tightened, I could remain quite calm and unaffected while I quickly assessed the real intentions.

29. After the Ball

I trust I am not boring you with my reminiscences, but I must mention the Butchers Ball case.

We were acting for a young butcher and had obtained first-class evidence of his wife's misbehaviour, on this occasion also recorded on film.

Yes, I do agree this is a terrible way to earn a living, but my peculiar talents have been somewhat difficult to market. Incidentally, the ex-shop manager from my early days was now working for us as a photographer. Anyway, my client was quite pleased as his wife had led him a merry dance for a long time. The following morning after the successful raid, the young wife, looking pale, demure and rather childlike, visited the office. I gave her an envelope containing the negatives of the film – our usual practice – with one print, on the back of which one of our more imaginative staff had printed 'after the ball'. She thanked me and enquired shyly what the next step was in the legal proceedings. I explained the procedure and advised her not to worry. The sequel was that my client was in a hotel one evening drinking shortly afterwards when in walked the co-respondent. They had worked together at one time. He was also a butcher. They shared a drink together and began to talk.

'Ken, you never really loved your wife, did you?'

'Do you?'

'Oh, yes. We intend getting married just as soon as all this business is over.'

'Have another drink – are you expected down there tonight?'

'No, not until Friday!'

The outcome – when the hotel closed my client and his love-lorn companion, nicely primed up with alcohol, raided the wife's house for the second time. They found the demure little damsel in bed with two other strange men.

Women can be tricky – ask my son, Peter!

The fairer, weaker sex are much more ingenious and cunning than men; have a greater sensitivity and imagination too, in most cases. It runs through all social classes.

I received a call one day from a lawyer requesting my presence in his office. A new client – please excuse me – but she was a veritable bitch of a woman, wanted her husband's activities investigated. She was, of course, unable to lower her dignity by visiting a common enquiry agent's office. Thank you Auntie Beatrice!

The target, was in the medical profession and it was one of the first cases we finalised with the aid of the two-way radio. I recall, we radioed Trudy to telephone the client and get her down to the husband's surgery, where he was receiving esoteric, but no doubt therapeutic treatment from one of his nursing staff.

Jack Jones was with me at the time. As we were filling her in with the facts, she looked at Jack, and in an imperious, arrogant manner, said, 'We don't want him here!'

I quietly asked Jack to watch the rear of the premises, and then proceeded to justify the fat fee I intended this woman to pay. On securing the evidence, we returned to my car.

'I don't want a divorce, you know!'

Of course, she didn't. The old man had to pay for the rest of his life. She would see to that.

The following week, a call from her solicitor requested our statement. 'When your client settles the balance of her account – no problem. The statement is already prepared.'

An hour or so later, one very irate lady rang stating that we had received ninety pounds and that was all we were getting.

'Don't worry Mrs S, a summons will be issued and served on Friday if you don't pay us a further ninety pounds.'

On Friday morning, there was another call, but in a much more conciliatory tone.

'You didn't really mean that Mr Northcott, did you?'

'Yes, Mrs S, my secretary is typing the summons now. An extra thirty pounds for me to visit your solicitor's office, thirty pounds to Mr Jones for loss of face – you can't speak to an ex-Foreign Office man like that – and thirty pounds for being such an unpleasant lady!'

'Oh, alright. I'll send you a cheque.'

'No, Mrs S, I can't accept your cheque. You bring the ninety pounds in cash to my office, within an hour, if you want the summons stopped.'

She came within the hour and I struck another blow for mankind. I told her what I really thought.

There seemed to be so many neurotic folks in the lonely, wide open spaces of WA. Some clients could not, or would not accept or face up to the truth. We were asked to keep investigating cases without any real justification, and paid good money for nothing. No wonder this type of work attracts the con men. Some people will believe anything they want to.

30. It Takes All Sorts

One wealthy homosexual who engaged our services to find out who was persecuting him, kept a woman friend in a house, paying her a generous monthly stipend. I was curious as to their relationship, and went to call on her. She proved to be an intelligent, attractive person. Admitted, she was enjoying the several privileges that our client provided, but much to her chagrin, had never been able to coax him into her bed.

I remembered the many lonely nights I had spent in my tent at Mkowe. It's a strange world, but no, I didn't take advantage of the situation . . . Honestly!

Some clients, men and women, could be downright dangerous.

A lawyer's wife asked us to act for her, saying her husband was mixed up in illicit gold transactions in a large country town. Bob Service visited this town to make the initial enquiries.

One evening, about 11 pm I received a call to visit the client at a suburban hotel. She wanted to see me immediately. I drove to the hotel where I saw her standing at the entrance, wearing an 'after five' dress.

She instructed me to park my car at the rear of the premises. I did so, and later she led the way upstairs to a private suite. As it was an extremely hot night, I accepted her offer of a cold beer and proceeded to brief her on the investigation.

I soon became aware that she was not a little bit interested in my dialogue. She appeared somewhat remote, and sensing approaching trouble, decided a quick exit was the order of the moment.

As I walked with her back down the stairs, I deliberately caught hold of her hand and told her not to worry. Immediately I touched her I knew my suspicions were correct. She was most certainly not one little bit interested in the investigation.

The following morning a call was put through to my desk and a man's voice asked if I usually visited women clients late at night.

The speaker identified himself when asked as a partner in a St Georges Terrace firm of auditors. I naturally made no admissions, but informed the caller that in my work as a private investigator I found myself in all sorts of peculiar circumstances. I was then informed that my client was an alcoholic, and a very dangerous woman. Replying that I was not a fool I thanked him for his interest, but still did not admit I was acting for the person he was talking about. I most certainly did, however, get the message.

Almost a year later one Sunday night, the same woman rang up again and wanted me to visit her immediately with a view to re-opening the former enquiry. To my reply that it hadn't exactly been successful previously for either of us, she replied, "Oh, that was that fool you sent up to . . .!". She was referring to Bob. I asked her to visit me in the office, but, as suspected I never heard from her again.

Alfred Sleep had mentioned on several occasions that it was possible for a private investigator to strike up a sexual relationship with at least sixty per cent of his clients. I now agree with him.

John Dowson alleged too that I had upset numerous female clients by not making overtures to them. As I then explained to him, we were in business to make money. That was the only name of the game for me. I wanted no more problems. I was still paying too dearly for my earlier mistakes.

A few comparatively peaceful months passed – the normal face-smacking and early morning physical activities were all par for the course.

Until we once again became involved with the boys in blue.

31. More Trouble

A Polish man had engaged our services and we had followed a couple back to a Cottesloe flat. At 3 am or thereabouts – no union rules in this game – we approached the door of the now darkened street-level flat. I knocked on the door, and when questioned as to who I was, answered truthfully, "Northcott, of Sleep & Northcott Investigations." A woman's voice told me to fug off! in no uncertain terms, Twenty minutes later, the flat door was opened and a woman I recognised left the flat.

We submitted our evidence, together with previous incidents, to the solicitor involved. Remember . . . association . . . opportunity . . . and . . . affection.

He was quite happy. Our evidence would be quite sufficient to pursue a successful case through court. A week or so later, two smiling police detectives visited the office. They questioned me about that particular case and accused me of saying "open up, police here." Was I really supposed to be that stupid? To add insult to injury, one then said . . . 'oh yes, don't forget the assault.'

When the woman had left the flat, the police had conjured up an alleged assault on her. What would I want to stick my neck out like that for? Facts were right out of the window now. It was all pure fiction. I ordered them to leave the office. Inevitably they returned and I was formally charged with 'saying I was a policeman'.

What an insult in Australia to my self-esteem, but when a private investigator is standing in a court charged with such an offence, it is really most disconcerting to see an articulate, smartly dressed woman, timidly giving evidence against him. Apart from feeling pretty vulnerable, one also feels disadvantaged and handicapped. After all, the magistrate has eyes, ears and presumably also, some sexual awareness. Despite my calm exterior, I was aware of all this, and most certainly felt intimidated . . . That is, until my defence counsel asked the woman, 'When this man's voice identified himself as the police and you told them to go away, what did you actually say?'

The sweet, young innocent, dropping her guard, replied, 'I told him to fug off. They have their bullies too.' Saved by the bell. I won that one. Nice girls don't talk like that!

By this time we realised the pressure was really on. The outcome of these various police charges could only result eventually in the loss of my licence. Nothing is new in life and these games had been played in Australia for a hundred and fifty years. It was all a matter of control. The technique was well rehearsed.

Discussing the situation with my solicitor, it was decided that we should form a limited company; create a third entity that would not be so vulnerable. More expense, I thought, but it had to be done. We desperately needed a life-line. When discussing our problems once with Frank Corser, the senior partner of Corser & Corser, John Dowson asked Frank, 'What is the real trouble, Frank, with Bill's relationship with the police?'

Frank replied 'Bill is too dinkum to be a private investigator in Western Australia. He's too honest!'

After this discussion, John and I walked together up Howard Street. My companion was very quiet. 'What are you thinking, John?'

'Bill, my father, as you know, has a law practice in London and I have been mixed up with the law most of my life, but when I hear a lawyer say, that a person associated with the profession can be 'too honest', there is something very wrong.'

Apart from John's military service as a captain in an airborne regiment, he had always served in a police force somewhere.

32. A Limited Company

Shortly after we had set the wheels in motion to form a limited company, we were conducting a matrimonial enquiry in Broun Avenue, at the end of beaufort Street. John had undertaken the initial survey.

One night, after we had obtained some good evidence on this case, he and I were doing surveillance on the same matter. John was driving a company car, a small Ford Anglia, and I was in the passenger seat. We were watching a parked car in East Perth; the time was about 10 pm. As the vehicle pulled away, I glanced at the nearby house and saw a man peering from the porch. I was sure I identified him as the man who should have been driving the car we had commenced following. Mentioning this to John, he disagreed, saying I must have been mistaken. I had an uneasy feeling. Something didn't feel right.

We followed the car carefully through an indirect route to the house in Broun Avenue. It came to a stop as expected outside the subject's house, but nobody left the vehicle.

Parking the Anglia well away from our quarry, we crossed the road, jumped a fence, and took up a position of concealment directly opposite the parked car. As we re-evaluated the evidence we had already built up, John wished to approach the car, confront the occupants and finalise the case.

I decided, however, that caution was indicated; something still didn't 'feel' quite right. The couple remained, seated in the parked vehicle. Unusual! Why? They should have entered the house.

Suddenly a car drove down Broun Avenue with two men in the front seat. I thought I recognised it as a police vehicle, and decided then to call off the night's activities.

Telling John to leave the Anglia where it stood and to make his way back home on foot, I myself crossed the road well away from the subject's house. As I approached the junction of Beaufort Street and Broun Avenue a car came from the direction of the city, travelling very fast. I flung myself down into some long grass,losing my expanding wrist watch as I did so. The speeding car spun round. I felt the rush of air as it stopped just beside me. I lay completely still, expecting any minute to hear a gruff voice say, 'Alright, Northcott, get up!'

I realise now that I was lying very close to the car in fact under the beam of the headlights. A few minutes later the vehicle drove away. Getting to my feet, I ran towards the houses in Broun Avenue. As I jumped over a wall, I saw a uniformed policeman in the back yard of the house we were interested in. Avoiding the row of houses, I ran behind them, and eventually came out at the top of Broun Avenue. A marked police car was parked under the shadows of some trees and two uniformed men were sitting inside.

My fears were confirmed. It was an entrapment exercise.

Walking a long way home via the Guildford Road, I eventually arrived at my apartment in West Perth by 5.30 am thoroughly dispirited,.

In the office the next morning we were having a conference regarding the night's events, when my solicitor telephoned.

The company Sleep & Norhcott Investigations Pty Ltd was now a reality.

I learned later that the police had enquired how they could stop the company being formed. Only a Criminal charge against me could stop its formation.

It was quite apparent that, had we approached that vehicle with its police decoys, all hell would have been let loose. My ESP had saved the day. Well, at least for a short time.

This is when I finally decided to sell the business. I had well and truly had enough. I just wanted to earn an honest living and not get mixed up in such ridiculous fun and games. At, of course, the poor old taxpayer's expense.

33. A Pommy Bastard

Shortly afterwards we were briefed by a Tasmanian solicitor to trace a woman who had left Launceston and her husband. She was last heard of in WA. Tracing the Lady, we discovered she was living with a man in Fremantle and was known in the district as his wife. Our statement, with corrobarative evidence was sent over to Tasmania, but we were later informed that their supreme court would not accept just an affidavit. My presence, or a signed confession from the couple concerned, was required. I approached the errant parties to be met by a hot denial of identity.

As I was extremely busy and could ill afford a trip east, I reapproached these people one Sunday morning to see if once again I could solicit a signed confession from them. The de-facto husband was drinking on the verandah with three other men as I approached.

'What the hell do you want now, you Pommie, bastard?'

I explained that eventually he would have to pay all costs for the impending court action. I was busy and could ill afford the time to travel east. Would he reconsider his decision.

'Stop bullshitting, do you think I'm stupid?'

So, I had to travel to Tasmania and personally give evidence in the supreme court. I often felt like paying another call to see if they had got the 'bill of costs'. At least they had had a chance!

A short time after I had returned from Tasmania – a trip that had given me the opportunity to meet Harold Sleep in Adelaide, a Perth lawyer, requested I call and see him.

It transpired that a client's father had reported that one of the S & N Investigators had tried to sexually harass his daughter.

It could only have been John . . .

Questioning him about this, he admitted he was on an enquiry with this woman at 3 am one morning.

'Bill, the atmosphere in the car was so tense, I thought she welcomed my advances!'

Asking him for the keys of the company car he was using, I told him he was fired, and I would give him a week's notice, but did not want him to work anymore.

I did not intend to tolerate this sort of behaviour.

His increased drinking had worried me for some time and on one occasion, he had been arrested for drunken driving. I recall going down to the central police station to bail him out. After a night spent in the company of such derelicts, I must admit, John had retained some semblance of dignity.

It has always puzzled me how men like John, with so many advantages – a public school education, father a wealthy lawyer, an ex-airborne captain, and with all his police experience – can act so irresponsibly. I had suspected for some time that he was having clandestine liaisons with one or two clients. As long as it did not affect the company, I was not too perturbed.

Before temporarily retiring John from my story, I must mention an interesting incident that happened to him as a policeman in Kenya – at least,John's version. He was then a police inspector at a post in Masai territory. A Masai Morani had just returned from a hunting trip, and found his brother intimately entertaining his young wife. Losing his temper, he speared his brother and killed him. The tribal elders, ordered the Morani to report the killing to the police.

Walking quite a distance to the police post where John was then on duty, the dusty warrior stuck his long bladed spear into the ground, and as ordered, gave John a detailed account of the killing.

John listened to the man's story, but did not put pen to paper. He evaluated the motive and circumstances surrounding the killing. Dismissing the morani, John thanked him for coming, and as the Elders had ordered, reporting the matter.

'I would have done just the same Bill, under the circumstances.'

Summary Justice . . . but now we weren't in Africa and here, from the earliest days, lying and cheating had been just a matter of survival.

Before I finish this chapter of my life – a few more cases. After all, it's not often you can read factual reports from the life and problems of a private eye, albeit in the rather unusual circumstances then existing in Western Australia.

34. Deutschland Über Alles

We were briefed by Mrs D to get evidence of her husband's misbehaviour. He was a lecturer at the University of WA, once serving in a crack Hungarian cavalry regiment during the Second World War fighting with the Germans. Imagine the scene - Mrs D, Vic Cross the photographer and myself sitting on a log at the back of a house in Maylands. We were endeavouring to shelter from the heavily falling rain.

Mrs D was telling us how she had been a member of the Hitler JUGEND and how she had cried when she first heard that her Fuehrer had died. That would have been at the time when I too was serving in Germany.

Suddenly, the back door of the house was flung open and her husband went to visit an outside toilet, whistling quite melodiously Deutschland Åber alles!. Vic, a chief petty officer in the Royal Navy, had been torpedoed whilst serving on a Russian convoy escort cruiser. He looked across at me in the light reflected from the kitchen window. Knowing what we each were thinking, we both grinned simultaneously. Vic was always quite cool on these raids, and his sense of humour helped keep things in the right perspective.

The night ended in a hectic fist-fight between Mr D and myself. As we beat a strategic withdrawal, we had all the evidence we needed. Running back out, through the garden, Vic ran into an outside garden water tap which caught him just above the scrotum. Being right behind him protecting our exit, I stumbled into his back, driving the tap harder into him. Regaining my balance, the hefty correspondent, an English lass, came threateningly towards me, wielding an empty magnum bottle. I just had time to draw breath when the bottle bounced off my chest and shattered on the ground.

The next morning, a police sergeant rang the office and said he was investigating a trespassing complaint. We had trampled a neighbour's vegetable garden in the dark as we gained entry to the back of 'D''s house. The sergeant mentioned a fight and said someone had been hit by a bottle. I then laughed and said it was me.

On this occasion, the very rare occasion, the police were very good about it and nothing further was heard. The raid had been completely successful.

I had commenced seriously, advertising the business for sale, but without success. I realised it wasn't going to be an easy assignment. Meanwhile I had my final case where the police were involved.

35. Fair Go, Mate

The 'A' Case. Mrs 'A' my client was a beautiful person and I am not just talking physically. Sometimes you soon become aware that you are representing the wrong party. In this case – not so. The slow build-up of evidence began. 'Association' was easy, but the other two requirements were a little more difficult. One night, following a call at the South Perth Civic Centre, Mrs 'A' and I followed her husband and his partner back to a house in Inglewood. We watched and waited until all the lights were finally extinguished. Approaching the house silently on foot, we listened at a front window and plainly heard a man and woman speaking from the darkened room. Mrs 'A' identified the male voice as that of her husband. We checked the rear of the house. It was securely locked. A window was open further along the front of the house and Mrs 'A' volunteered to climb into the house and open the front door. I had just helped her over the windowsill and she had dropped to the floor when 'A' appeared, wearing a dress shirt and bow tie but no jacket.

He grabbed his wife by the throat and shouted 'Burglars, we're being raided!.' I stood back from the window, and, using his Christian name, said . . . 'pack it up. You know it's your wife.'

Mrs 'A' then broke away, opened the front door saying, 'quick Bill, come in.' 'A' immediately slammed the door shut. The glass panel fell out and pieces of glass scattered across the verandah. A shrill woman's voice, from inside the house said,'I have rung the police.'

Charming, I thought . . . Here we go again. I walked up the steps to the front door where 'A' stood.

'If you come across that threshold, you Pommy bastard, I'll got you as well, for trespass!'

As I stood amongst the glass on the porch, the police arrived – four detectives in civilian clothes. One grinned at me as they entered the house. None of them spoke to me. Ten minutes or so later they reappeared, said they did not wish to take a statement from me, and, getting into their vehicle, drove off. I took Mrs 'A' home.

My readers need no imagination to understand the coming sequence of events. In the course of time, I was formally charged with 'wilfully breaking one glass door'.

When I appeared in the local court, I was surprised to see that the assistant Crown Prosecutor, Nixon, was handling the case and not the usual police inspector. When we recessed for lunch I asked Frank Corser, my solicitor, why Nixon was prosecuting.

'Apparently, Bill, you have stepped on someone's toes, well above detective inspector level.'

Interesting! Why was the system working against me? I may never know.

Summing up after lunch, the notorious AG Smith observed that during the lunch recess he had re-read the transcript of evidence.

Whilst he was impressed with Mrs 'A's contribution, he felt that in the heat of the raid with all the shouting she had been mistaken.

There had been no shouting and he paid scant regard to the position of the broken glass, preferring to take 'A's word against Mrs 'A's and my own. He found the accused guilty of the charge and fined me ten pounds.

As I stood at the cashiers desk to pay the money, 'A' stood grinning alongside me.

> For this is the law of the jungle,
> as old and as clear as the sky,
> and the wolf who keeps it may prosper,
> but the wolf that breaks it must die'
> As the creeper encircles the tree trunk,
> so the law it goes forward and back.
> For the strength of the pack is the wolf,
> and the strength of the wolf is the pack.

RUDYARD KIPLING

167

36. Towards the End
(An Error of Judgement, Giving Evidence)

At long last I had two prospective buyers interested in the business. One of these was a German who had been living in China for many years. I gave them both copies of my balance sheet etc and awaited events.

One of the commercial enquiries we executed will give you some reason or clue for our deteriorating relationship with the WA police. We were briefed by a businessman whose accountant had drawn his attention to an unusually large inconsistency in the returns from a self-service delicatessen he owned in Belmont. The business was managed by a manageress, with a staff of three assistants. The matter had been reported to the police, but without success. We decided to feed a series of marked notes through the till at various times through the day and later in the evening. There was apparently no attempt to tamper with the till.

One Sunday night, as I was watching an indifferent film on the TV, I began to think about this particular case and decided, very much on the spur of the moment, to visit Belmont. I had no sooner taken up a position of surveillance than I saw a station wagon, a vehicle I knew was driven by the manageress, pull up on a side path at the rear of the shop. She entered the premises and began loading the wagon with a considerable number of boxes.

After closing the shop, she got into the vehicle and drove towards a house where I knew one of her staff resided. She parked her car near the side entrance and went into the house.

I alerted Trudy on the radio and asked her to arrange for John Dowson, who was still then in our employ, to rendezvous with me as quickly as possible. Fortunately, it was some ten minutes before she reappeared, accompanied by a girl whom I recognised as one of the shop assistants. They had started to unload the car when John suddenly pulled his car in behind mine. Together we walked up the hill and confronted the two women. They were naturally shattered.

We loaded some of the boxes in the boot of my vehicle and the remainder in John's, and drove to the central CIB office, where charges were laid. The police were not particularly impressed.

A week later in the early hours of the morning, I walked past the Gilt Dragon, a night spot in Wellington Street. A solicitor I knew was standing outside talking to another man. The lawyer gave me a smile as I acknowledged his greeting. He informed me later that the man he was with was a detective police sergeant and the following comments were made.

'Isn't that that bastard Northcott?'

'What have you got against, Bill?'

'Nothing, as long as he keeps his nose out of police business.'

Fair enough, I suppose. But we all have to live.

I can now appreciate, to some extent, their point of view. A detective sergeant at the time was getting thirty to thirty-five pounds a week, and subject to all sorts of petty rules and regulations. Here was a Pommy riding around in a new, two-way radio equipped car, employing recently arrived migrants, from, of all places, Africa. Probably a lot of nigger-kickers to boot! And he must be making a lot of money. I knew too, they must have wasted a lot of time watching me.

Several times, as I have returned to West Perth in the wee hours of the morning, a large Chrysler Royal sedan, with at least six detectives in, would cruise up the lane behind my house. As I closed the garage doors – 'goodnight, Bill', 'Goodnight boys,' I would reply. They must have been waiting a long time, to say 'goodnight!' Funny, I never got to know any socially – perhaps, though, it was just as well. I saw that Chrysler Royal prowling around a number of times at night on its roving patrol.

Actually, there is nothing particularly difficult about any regular routine private investigation. it is important, though, to understand human nature, and the normal reactions of people under different circumstances.

I remember a flight sergeant in the RAF police, an older man than myself, and an experienced investigator. When I asked what his peacetime job had been, he replied that he had been a barman in a cocktail lounge at a central Leeds hotel.

Obviously, listening to all sorts of different characters, talking freely in a relaxed atmosphere had given him the ability to form a fairly accurate assessment of human beings. There are so many ways to get information.

On one occasion, we wanted some information, from an eastern states criminal, living in Perth, with some local men. I had thought about various approaches to the particular problem. Suddenly, it came to me.

We got hold of an old car, drained the radiator and ran the engine until it was nicely hot and steaming, with suitable side effects. Then Pat, attractively dressed with a very lovely companion, drove it around the corner, parked on the lawn of the subject's address and switched off the engine. After lifting the bonnet, looking suitably distressed, our two ladies, approached the house for water. They were advised as anticipated, that it was dangerous to put cold water into a boiling radiator.

'Really? How lucky we are!'

They were invited into the house; had a drink, cigarette and the usual overtures and conversation, and got exactly the information we had been hoping for. All too easy.

To a man's friend – 'do you know the bastard?' or saying of an enemy, 'What a nice guy, so and so is!' will usually solicit some useful reaction. That wandering wife from Tasmania happily signed her *de facto* name when informed she had just won a 'cake mix' competition. A good private investigator can play many roles, but without that knowledge of human nature he would be useless.

We were trying a man out once as to his suitability for a permanent job with us, and had given him a simple survey job to do. He reported back to the office with most impressive information, and the layout of a house we were interested in. Imagine our chagrin when the client telephoned to say he had just received a telegram from his wife to 'call off that blond Dutch investigator'. He had misassessed her gullibility. We often had difficulty in evaluating the personalities of the people we were involved with.

AN ERROR OF JUDGEMENT

Those terrible divorce triangles could easily be overcome with just a brief written statement. But how can one tell, what a person has in mind or at what voltage they operate at.

I misjudged such a situation once when I openly approached a man at his lover's address.

I was in company with the wife, and was invited into the house to watch TV as the three people directly concerned had a private discussion in another room. After twenty minutes, becoming restless, I broke up the discussion.

'Thank you, Mr Northcott. You have been very understanding. I'm going back to my wife and will take her home.'

A reconciliation – in some cases – was great. Who honestly wants to see any marriage break up?

The next morning, however, the client came crying into the office. After I had left the house the husband had said 'you bitch. Putting a PI onto me! Did that stupid pommy bastard Northcott think that I was going to give him a statement, just like that?'

We pacified the client, but now knew who we were dealing with. Two weeks later, a well planned raid brought different results. As I explained to the now very subdued husband that we, unlike solicitors, were not governed by any set of fees and could charge as we thought fit. Naturally, my account would take into consideration his biased views of my intelligence and heritage so he would definitely be lumbered with the costs eventually.

As we returned to the car the jubilant client said that half the vehicle, parked in the driveway, was in her name. I suggested she take immediate possession and sell it. Saying she was too excited to drive, she gave me the keys. Asking my associate to drive my car away with the client. I opened the door of the parked vehicle in the driveway and switched on the engine.

It really is extremely difficult to find the light switch in a strange car, the correct gear; to secure the locks on the door; watch the rear vision mirror and still find time to dodge wild punches as you struggle to close the drivers side window. I know . . . I've tried it!

Far more dangerous to steal a man's car, in fact, than interfere with his love life. The vehicle was duly sold at a good price; a receipt procured for far less and half of this reduced amount duly found its way to the husband. Naturally, my client was highly satisfied. I cannot, unfortunately, at my age now remember whether she paid us a bonus. Surely she would have done?

GIVING EVIDENCE

These matrimonial cases – How I began to loathe them. They would come to court some three or four months later. It was often difficult to remember, and sometimes even identify the client. I would quite often have five or six different cases in court on one day, and to refresh my memory I began taking photographs with me.

Once, as I was sitting in the supreme court to give evidence, and waiting for his Worship to appear, I saw a man glowering at me from a bench on the other side of the court. I checked my photographs. He was the man I had confronted one night as he had been seated in the back of his car with his paramour, parked down a dark lonely road at about 3 am. His case was duly heard; my evidence accepted and a decree nisi granted to become absolute in three months time.

As the court recessed for lunch, I walked through the supreme court gardens, towards the city.

A loud voice shouted 'Mr Northcott, how does it feel to be a perjurer?'

I looked behind me as this newly divorced man and a male companion moved toward me. I waited for them, then explained the fact that the evidence I had given was true. Evidence of his 'association' and 'affection' for the co-respondent, and, of course, the 'opportunity.'

'You heard the evidence' I continued, 'and I remember you told me that night to 'bugger off digger or I'll do you over'. You'd been drinking solidly for some seven hours and were in no condition to do anyone over!'

He looked at me, grinned and said, 'come and have a drink, Mr Northcott.'

I declined his offer, but shook hands and continued on my way.

Most men were pretty good about things but I have found a bit of humour and a laugh can cool some potentially dangerous situations.

I had raided a room once at the Broken Hill Hotel in Perth. This was a daylight exercise when I was acting for a clean-cut, strapping young Australian man. We had found his wife in a delicate situation, with a very good-looking, lightly built Englishman. He wasn't a Devonian, so it wasn't a very delicate situation. The young Aussie was trembling beside me. I knew it wasn't with fear, and grasped his arm to quieten him down. When the formalities had been completed, I invited him to cool off and have a drink downstairs. As I ordered a beer, he pleaded to be allowed back upstairs to give the Englishman a thrashing. I advised him to get his decree absolute first and not complicate things.

Suddenly we heard a man's voice, 'have a drink with me, Mr Northcott!'

'Do I know you?'

'You should do, you put the torch on me last week.' Funny old world.

Yes, I really do agree, it was a 'orrible way to earn a crust.

Women aren't only a weakness, they are damn expensive.

37. The Final Humiliation (Philosophies)

Back to business. Eventually only one prospective buyer was left – the German man called Feldman. He was still giving the matter serious consideration. Rosaline Dowson telephoned the office one day and asked if I could visit Kalamunda to see her. I did so and she explained that John was sick in bed, unable to get work and could I help him. Going into the bedroom where John was lying I explained that I was definitely getting out of the investigating business and already had a serious prospect to take it over. I then suddenly thought having a working manager would make the business a much more attractive business proposition, and would possibly also, broaden the field of prospective buyers to include those with no experience, but money to invest. Discussing this thought with John, I told him that if I was staying no-way would I re-employ him, but he was a good field and office man and knew the business.

I asked him why he hadn't started his own agency. 'Bill, I know I couldn't!' A strange admission from such a man. So, as we could be useful to each other, I agreed to start him immediately on a salary of forty pounds a week as the manager of the business. I'm sure he was genuinely grateful – I know Rosaline was.

As I had long anticipated, I was eventually summoned to appear once again in the local court, where AG Smith had the greatest pleasure in finding I was 'not a suitable person to hold an enquiry agent's licence in WA.'

I fully agreed with him, but for different reasons. He was only acting, anyway, as he had been instructed.

I can think quite calmly about this period in my life now, but at the time, whilst quite expected, it was still something of a trauma. Parting from my kids to go to Africa . . . and now this. I certainly feel no sense of shame, and, as the chickens in Australia are now coming home to roost, I realise more than ever that I was, and am, answerable to a far greater power.

A Queen's Counsel advised me that as the licence only applied to matrimonial cases I was still able to conduct other investigations. We did have a section at one time dealing solely with missing persons.

My acute ESP saved me from running into trouble once again.

Two men came to my house one evening and asked me to undertake a matrimonial enquiry. They said they were quite happy to pay me immediately, and one of them placed several large denomination notes on the lounge room table. As he did so, I sensed in them both a feeling of excitement and expectancy.

'Pick it up boys, do you think I'm silly?'

As they smiled at me, I felt their anger quite plainly.

'What do you mean, Mr Northcott?' I tactfully showed them the door.

This sort of entrapment was childish, but who motivated it, and why? The two men – so obviously plain clothes police detectives, were endeavouring to entrap me into taking a matrimonial enquiry when they knew I was not licensed to handle such an enquiry.

Was it still a throw-back from the anti-Vietnam protests that I first participated in? The police had taken photographs, I know. Or, did it stem somehow from my service in Kenya? Was Colonel Spry, the officer commanding ASIO, (Australian Security and Intelligence Organisation) an ex-Indian army man, or an old friend of Brigadier Armstring? Had dear old Wing Commander Graves, given me an unwarranted label? Or was I just becoming paranoid?

PHILOSOPHIES

Political pholosophies encourage strange bedfellows. When I was marching in one anti-Vietnam war protest in pouring rain, I remember many pro-Vietnam right-wingers were standing jeering at the marchers from the pavement – safely of course under the shelter of the shop canopies. I recognised the Crown Law man of 'call-girl' fame – one of the more vocal antagonists – as he stood shouting and fist-waving hysterically. The same man was running a high-class, call girl racket with his wife. Imagine it – from the Crown Law department offices in Perth of all places.

When an enquiry was instigated into this criminal behaviour, he was fired, but had the effrontery to appeal. Quite amazing to me, when at that time I was under such iniquitous pressures.

My dear son David, a recent migrant to the country, was also amongst the opposition. An ex-British soldier, then very right wing, watching his dear old dad, soaked to the skin, marching with the Commie rabble. What a load of intelligence-inspired . . . Hogwash!

There is no greater 'freedom lover' than me. That is why I am now in Thailand – which means 'the land of the free'.

England, with its ridiculous Victorian conventions and hypocrisy, had let me down and was I really expected mildly to accept the pressures and difficulties that I had experienced in Australia. Of course not, and it was all so unnecessary! But, once out of an intolerably despicable and archaic environment, you soon recover.

> The right of the individual to contract out of a state, which no longer commands his assent, must therefore be conceded.
>
> FICHE

> 'We never had more laws, more lawmakers or more officials, but each year the country becomes more lawless. There is growing contempt for authority which invites contempt when it is misused.'
>
> RUSHDOMIE

I don't know where the quote came from, but it all sounds very familiar to me! Do you know, Even at seventy-two years of age, I still find life, interesting and exciting. It isn't always easy being true to one's self. That's why we all need prayer.

> To thine own self be true, and it must follow, as the night, the day, thou can'st not then be false to any man.
>
> HAMLET,
> WILLIAM SHAKESPEARE

So, with John Dowson managing the business, the problem for me when the sale was finalised was where did I go from there? The German buyer was now keen to move in.

176

38. Facing Forward

A Jewish manufacturers' agent called David Wise, a friend of Pat Serve's husband, had been in the habit of cashing cheques from our office. One day he invited Pat and myself down to the Palace Hotel from where he was showing a range of Italian knitwear. He had about eighteen sample garments in his room – high-class merchandise, commanding a good wholesale price. These he showed to Perth store buyers.

I questioned him about the economics of his business, whereupon he proudly showed me his order books and explained his commission percentage. On a cursory check of the order books I ascertained that he had already written up many thousand dollars' worth of business. No physical risks, or the myriad problems that faced a private investigator. It made me think.

As we walked back up William Street towards the office car park, I talked with Pat, who at one time had been a model.

I expressed my thoughts about leaving Australia, which I should obviously have done, but did not wish to do so in an atmosphere of defeatism, or self-recrimination.

If I considered starting a similar business to David's, would she be interested in coming in with me on some form of partnership basis, or did she wish to continue, with Sleep & Northcott? I knew she enjoyed the job. I suggested she talk it over with her husband, as there was no immediate hurry.

Pat had always conducted herself well in the office with the many different types of people we inevitably had to associate with. I also valued her business acumen, and realised her knowledge of the fashion trade would be invaluable.

The German buyer finally signed up, and took over the business, with John Dowson as general manager. Pat's husband had visited the office, and discussed my offer. He proved quite agreeable, and it was with a great sense of relief that I closed this difficult and unrewarding chapter of my life as a private investigator.

During the years I had then been in Australia, I had never had a proper holiday. I had been to the Eastern States several times on investigations, or to give evidence in the Tasmanian supreme court. My only leisure time had been snatched at weekends, or during the few trips to Rottnest Island. I swam at the beach, as often as I could do. But no experience can be all bad; I had learned a lot and had many amusing incidents to look back on. At least I had been a good investigator; given value for money, and, as I had been told, acted with a certain aplomb. I was still a super optimist, confident of my own ability and sure that something better lay ahead.

But I had a long way to go yet!

Trudy had not been the type of person who is worldly wise or quick thinking enough to offer me much assistance in my late sordid business. It had not been much of a life for her either.

I was in the office all day and out in the evenings, often until the early hours of the morning. She couldn't even watch a film on TV without some disturbance. I well remember one evening, returning home about 9 pm. and asking her to make me a coffee . . .

'Can't you see I am in the middle of a good film?' No problem. I made my own coffee! A far cry from our life together at Mkowe.

Sunday was one day of the week, however, I did try to keep clear for the family, but even that was not always possible . . . I needed the money.

I arranged a meeting when David Wise next visited Perth and told him of my intentions, asking him to list the names of any manufacturers who might have been seeking representation in the West. As it was apparently necessary to travel to Melbourne, I also explained my personal position to David, and how, for so many difficult years, I had been a faithful husband. Did he know any suitable female playmate for me in Melbourne? In his business, of course he did.

So, for the first time for many years, I felt free of immediate problems, as Pat and I boarded an Ansett flight to Victoria, little realising what heartaches lay ahead.

It was unusually hot when we arrived in Melbourne and caught a taxi to the Parkville Motel, where we had arranged a booking. Being a Sunday and impossible to get a cold alcoholic drink under their archaic liquor laws, I was always amazed that the public tolerated the 'six o'clock swill' for so long. We showered and and changed in our separate rooms, and I visited Pat next door, where she had made a cup of tea . . . We sat chatting. I knew little of her personal life. Trudy and I had visited her home, in Mount Pleasant once at a party she had hosted. As far as I knew, she was happily married.

Are you clairvoyant too? Suddenly it all came out.

Garry, the husband, had been a playboy for years, away from home most of the weeks buying wool in the country. The inevitable happened. We had respected each other for a long time but now there was a new electricity in the air.

The story of her marriage unfolded. She knew the pressures I had been living with for several years. I was, only too human, to my great shame. I did not sleep in my own room for the remainder of our time in Melbourne.

But David Wise had worked hard on our behalf. Within a few days we were negotiating with several manufacturers that he had selected as worthy of our attention. We needed, he explained, a variety of merchandise. Day, evening wear,sports and swim wear. Suits, Coats, and miscellaneous ranges like handbags, plus, of course, budget ranges of less expensive merchandise. Manufacturers naturally preferred well established agents, but Pat and I presented ourselves well, and my early tailoring experience gave me some basic grounding in the rag trade.

We had soon made firm arrangements with 'Exmoor Creations.' These were suits mainly, but excellent, well finished garments, with a tailored look. 'Leading Fashions' a budget sportswear range, was also confirmed,together with knitwear, swimwear and after five manufacturers. We were beginning to get a business together. Rothmere coats were interested, and a day or two later we finalised their representation.

In this type of agency business you actually get paid only on the merchandise, that is invoiced into store. So, if you are showing summer ranges in the winter season, you have to wait several months before commission became available. The average commission at the time was only five per cent. Vastly different to my former business when you received cash first before you even moved out of the office.

So, with a new love affair blooming, we continued to work hard in Melbourne. Moving around, meeting new people, visiting factories, inspecting merchandise and the inevitable socialising. Soon, however, the picnic was over, and with our thanks to David, and to his good wishes for our future, we boarded a flight for the return journey to Perth.

Now the difficulties and the terrible heartache began. I had been a faithful husband throughout those terrible years and despite the many temptations. But now I had really blotted my copybook. To make matters even worse, Trudy had wanted a playmate for William, and had just told me she was pregnant. What a dilemma!

This is the only period of my life I still feel genuinely ashamed of. Trudy was a good woman and did deserve better. The fact that for so many months I had been under extreme pressure was really no excuse. It says much for Trudy's generous disposition that we have always remained good friends.

39. Simba Agencies

Fred Curran, an old lawyer friend of mine, had offered me premises in Forrest Place, the heart then of Perth's business centre. So, whilst we were awaiting the arrival of our first ranges, we opened a showroom in Padbury Buildings, on the first floor and Simba Agencies was born. Pat and I did a lot of the work ourselves, but at last we were quite satisfied. Our new showroom projected an excellent fashion image.

Now, unable to continue living a lie, I had told Trudy of the despicable way I had behaved. I was nearly torn apart. Pat had also confronted Garry. After several weeks of uncertainty and soul searching we moved out of our respective homes and together took a furnished flat belonging to a Greek friend in South Perth. Pat's two children, Debbie and Tony, came with us. This flat in Mill Point Road was quite near the Perth Zoo, and when I awoke several mornings and heard a lion roar, in my troubled mind I was back at Mkowe. At least there I had been certain of my role in life. Now I was for the first time beginning to doubt even myself and the direction I was taking. To any man considering such a move as I had just made, I would advise the utmost caution. Living with two strange children who associate you with the break-up of their family, can in the early days be soul-destroying. Especially when you yourself are riddled with guilt. Yes, at first this was so, until we slowly began to understand each other, but it really was difficult. We had such different backgrounds too.

Garry was Jewish. His father was a Polish migrant who had worked hard collecting bottles in the early days, but eventually had made a lot of money. Being determined, as so many of his generation, that his boys would have a better chance, the old man gave them a good education and almost anything else they wanted. He could then afford to.

So living, as Pat's children had done, in a free and easy Australian environment some friction was inevitable, considering my very frugal and disciplined childhood in England. I remember being annoyed one morning when Tony ate sixteen, large Weetabix biscuits for breakfast. No restraint had been applied to the children in any way. It was a difficult learning period for us all.

We were invited on one occasion to a party, given by Athena, our landlady and friend. I had never attended such a party. They were mainly Greek guests, where people so spectacularly and brilliantly danced across the furniture and so unreservedly enjoyed themselves.

Pat really introduced me to the world of music. I soon appreciated the necessity for such periods of relaxation. I realised then that I had been missing a lot. Gradually, however, the family integrated and settled down, as with humour and tolerance we began to appreciate each others' point of view. Any inter-personal relationship is most certainly enhanced too when there is some respect on each side.

When our first range of merchandise arrived, I remember how disappointed we both felt. In style, finish, colours and quality, something was lacking. We decided to wait before approaching the larger stores with such a mediocre selection. Soon, the Exmoor suit range became available. Here we were most impressed by the professionalism of the finish, presentation of colours, fabrics and the cut of the garments. As a tailoring man from way back, I really appreciated the range, and Exmoor most certainly started us off on the right track. The fashion business, though, is much like the female species itself. Somewhat fickle and unpredictable. At this time, however, suits with the tailored look, were fashionable, and our first sales presentation to the larger stores was well received. We started writing up some excellent figures.

When opening with a new season range, the routine was first to book the services of one or two good models who could do justice to the type of garments being shown. Then we made firm appointments with the buyers, each of whom was responsible for their own class of merchandise in a large store. Many manufacturers often came across from the Eastern States themselves at a showing to assess the acceptance of their range and assist in sales. Neville Baker of Exmoor Creations was one such manufacturer. He came across to Perth regularly at least twice a year.

Neville was a gentleman, of Russian-Jewish descent and he

182

had the advantage that his brother Richard ran the firm Richard Baker Creations in London. He was able to give Neville much help in forward planning on new seasons' ranges.

As we began entertaining Neville and mixing with him socially on his visits to Perth, he soon became our closest ally and friend. Throughout our six years in this industry, we never had any problems with Exmoor commissions; what was ordered was invariably what was delivered to the store months later. So many manufacturers had material supply problems, steming possibly from financial short-falls. These defects in the system, though, always affected our commission payments. We had written up the business – at least manufacturers could deliver the merchandise. After months of belt-tightening, and now my paying maintenance to Trudy, commission was slowly starting to come through.

Fortunately, Anne, my daughter, was nursing in England, David was in the British Army and Peter at a Royal Naval training establishment. At least, the English section of my family was now becoming self-supporting.

After several months of operating the new business, often being obliged to show two ranges simultaneously, it became apparent that we needed much more floor space. Shortly after Fred Curran, my old lawyer friend died, we moved into second floor premises in King Street.

Mentioning Fred reminds me how his law firm was finally closed down. Fred's wife, a Catholic, had always been hostile to his position, as one of Perths leading matrimonial and criminal lawyers. The very same week he died, she walked into his office, gave immediate notice to the staff, and just closed and locked the Chambers door. Several times clients came into our adjoining showroom, and poured out their tale of woe . . . They had paid Fred, so much money – but now what?

I referred them to his son-in-law, a solicitor working in St Georges's terrace, but I did feel that more consideration could have been shown to these clients with unfinished business.

Before we say goodbye to Fred, God Bless Him, I must tell you of one of his clients Snowy Rowles, a multiple murderer in WA, who was eventually found guilty, and committed to hang. Fred defended him and on his conviction, put in various appeals – the final appeal being rejected. He visited Fremantle gaol to inform Snowy. Upon entering the cell, he saw Rowles stretched out on the prison bed.

Naturally, Fred looked suitably sombre of countenance, but Snowy, looked up, grinned and said . . . 'Cheer up, Fred, its me thats hanging tomorrow, not you!' The white man too can die bravely, even if sometimes not for such lofty principles.

Back to the fashion business. The premises in King Street consisted of a large showroom, a nice office, and at the rear of the premises we had about 1,500 square feet of stock room space. We were also serviced with private modern toilets and workroom facilities and wide doors at the rear of the premises to expedite parcel deliveries. As the building had recently been redesigned and renovated, it was a simple matter to lay out the showroom. 'Front' in such a business, is most important.

Shortly after this move to King Street, we somehow met Beatrice Faust and became involved in the Civil Liberties Movement. For a while, evening meetings were held in the showroom. Both Pat and I knew there was something wrong with society's values – too much stupidity, bigotry and ignorance and far too many injustices. But, what to do about it? We were groping, but more, important still thinking.

In retrospect, of course, we achieved very little other than publicising our feelings and focusing attention on the movement. Like the Ministry of Community Development in Kenya, it was really just a façade.

Still . . . we had tried.

Fortunately Pat was able to do some modelling herself – Mainly suits and coats. I had been pleasantly surprised at the quality of the girls we engaged from some of the Perth agencies. Modelling is a hard game and the girls who do manufacturing agency work earn every penny they get. They have to change garments throughout the 'showing' period, yet still retain the calm, smiling demeanour so essential to the professional girl.

I take my hat off to them. One Canadian lass, we had met socially, a schoolteacher by profession, had done some modelling work in Canada. A very relaxed, intelligent lady, she worked for us continuously for six weeks one season. She was well received by most buyers and did a really proficient job.

Some of the manufacturers, unlike Neville Baker, were hopeless. One was a fast-talking, ex-East end Londoner, called Phillip – Jewish like so many men in the rag trade. He was a hard, unrealistic salesman. A small suburban buyer would come in with a total budget of some $20,000 and Phillip would start his act. As she placed an order for one or two garments, he would say, 'But this colour is a must this year. You had better have a few in this . . .' So it would go on. I used to get quite embarrassed knowing the client's inability to sell,or pay for the garments she was being coerced into buying. On one such occasion, I left the showroom in disgust and walked down to the American Health Studios, where I was a life member. I gave myself at least an hour's hard work-out.

On my return . . .

'Where have you been, Bill? Pat and I have been flat-out for the past couple of hours.'

'Phillip, I just couldn't stand listening to any more of your heavy sales pitch!' The same man, when discussing business overheads, was telling me what a magnificent showroom he had in Sydney – a factory employing three hundred odd girls, obviously a big show compared to our small Perth business.

Rather amusingly, Pat and I once arrived unannounced at his business address in Sydney. We were greeted at a small, dingy reception desk by an unshaven, unkempt looking youth of about eighteen years of age. Phillip was not in the factory or showroom. We were told he was probably down at his wife's restaurant. We duly presented ourselves at this very ordinary, lower middle-range cafe to see Phillip seated on a stool, behind tha cash register. He did have the good grace to blush and we naturally accepted his offer of an indifferent three-course meal.

The methodology he employed was to get a range designed of about thirty garments and then offer them to his various unsuspecting agents to see what business they were able to generate. Depending on the reception and volume of orders, he would 'job' them out to wherever he could and get them made up cheaply. Not a reliable method, as far as we were concerned, and no wonder deliveries were unreliable and so many orders unfulfilled.

We soon discontinued representing this plausable pseudo manufacturer.

40. Hardly Specialised Selling

Rothmere coats was one of our better ranges – well cut, well finished garments, trimmed with excellent furs, minks, fitch, sable etc. It was a pleasure to show these coats which Pat enjoyed modelling. We wrote up some excellent figures.

Jack Lew, the proprietor of Rothmere, was also a Polish Jew, whose family had migrated to Australia in the pre-war years. He was a very short, very fat, bald-headed man, always smiling, and with a terrific sense of humour. He was a fantastic dancer, very light on his feet, like so many corpulent people. By trade he was a master cutter.

I recall that as Jack and I were wandering around one of the stores in the city, inspecting coats made by various opposition manufacturers, he said, 'Bill, we will have to buy our way in here. All these coats are made by manufacturers who only do business that way!'

Then he explained the technique. The coat buyer was quite innocently offered a monthly advertising budget. It was completely up to her discretion where or if she placed the adverts. One manufacturer he alleged, to ensure healthy orders, had actually parked a brand new Mini Minor car in the staff car park and personally given the keys to the buyer, thanking her for past efforts on his behalf.

I am still learning, but what an education!!

There must be more to life than this. I had been taught how to discipline, detain, shoot and hang men, discreetly follow them and commit perjury, and now to manipulate and bribe them. Of course, I had long ago learned to live with lies. Is it any wonder I now turn to God? I must believe in something!

Shortly after we had moved into the new showroom, we had become acquainted with a Yugoslav lass called Vera Stock.

She was initially a dressmaker, but had designed some quite interesting 'after five' dresses.

41. Legassic

After our experience with Phillip, the Sydney manufacturer, I suggested to Vera that she make up a small range of about eighteen model dresses. I asked her to let us market them for her under a distinctive label and hopefully build up a worthwhile manufacturing business. Some weeks later, Vera brought in a range of dresses which had an originality about them that appealed to both Pat and myself. We decided to market them under the name of 'Legassic', the name of my mother's grandparents.

As a point of interest, my dear sister used this psuedonym when she was also a successful model in London years ago.

So, after the Legassic labels were printed and the stage set, we booked the usual appointments with the buyers and went to much trouble in preparing a suitable background for Vera's range. When the experienced buyers saw the Legassic range, it soon became apparent that they too agreed with our judgement. The orders snowballed. Vera was naturally ecstatic. She was a tall, statuesque woman, with heavy, but finely cut Slav features. She had a delightful sense of humour and at one time had been an interpreter with the British Embassy in Hong Kong, or was it Singapore?

I can see her in retrospect, dancing with Jack Lew – an 'incongruous' looking couple; Vera bending low down frequently to kiss Jack on his bald pate. She had too, some interesting contacts in many walks of life, many gathered in her duties as an interpreter in the Far East.

But, unfortunately, we had got carried away in our promotion of the Legassic range and had planned a showing, more of a social affair, on an Italian Liner, the Flotta Laura, that was then berthed in Fremantle. This proved to be disastrous in one way, but no doubt avoided a lot of future problems. We had invited the larger store buyers to the showing, and as they were seated, in comfortable chairs, a steward served a civilised selection of drinks and the models appeared on the catwalk.

The ship's lighting, so much more penetrating than the lights in our showroom, immediately picked up the puckered, faulty hem lines and several other defects. I glanced across. Yes, the buyers had noticed. We had been trying too hard again.

The next few days inevitably saw the cancellations come in.

Poor Vera was distraught, and broke down crying in our showroom. She too had been working hard for weeks and had been relying on other people too much. It was then I thought that perhaps I had previously maligned Phillip in Sydney. It wasn't so easy after all!

At this time I was carrying a lot of stock in the business and had thought of opening a retail outlet to clear it. Perhaps this was the opportunity. When Vera had composed herself, I discussed my thoughts. Vera could set up a small workroom behind the shop and make bespoke garments for individual customers, while I could clear my stock. We rented a shop in Rokeby Road, Subiaco; named it Legassic Fashions, and commenced decorating and furnishing the shop. I opened a joint banking account with Vera.

Before we officially opened, I personally dressed the windows, featuring the colours of the Subiaco Football Team. The night before the opening we had a small celebration in the shop to launch the new venture.

The guests included some well connected business friends – bank manager and unfortunately, to our later distress, Arthur and Mrs Brooking, members of an old WA family. They ran the National Tailoring Company, situated directly below our showroom in King Street.

Everyone congratulated us on the way we had laid out the shop. One very experienced lady who ran a very high class boutique in London Court, said it was very much a Sydney presentation.

42. Troubles Ahead

The following day, Arthur Brooking visited me at the office and asked me if I would be interested in helping him face lift his tailoring business.

I declined, despite his assurance that he could easily get a government grant to defray any costs incurred. He was quite obviously impressed with the way both Simba agencies and the new retail outlet were shaping up, and wished to stimulate his own tailoring business, which was then in a state of decline.

During the following weeks, Arthur Brooking, repeatedly confronted me with his proposition. His wife too spoke to Pat on several occasions. As our business was located directly above the National Tailoring Company, it was almost impossible to avoid a meeting with the Brookings.

Eventually, with their persistent invitations, my own greed, and the thought of an increased income, I was influenced in drawing up a formal agreement, regarding my commitment to the tailoring firm. Briefly speaking, for a fee of one dollar on any single garment sold by the National Tailoring Company, I would provide the expertise to revitalise the business. I would not be responsible for any expenses incurred or be responsible in any way for the signing of cheques or disposal of monies earned.

The Tailoring Company had a factory in East Perth, off William Street, with a workshop and retail business in King Street under our premises.

So I drew up a plan of campaign, submitting it to Arthur Brooking. He was keen for me to implement it as son as possible. I myself then, had no idea of the soul-destroying difficulties of installing, in a short period of time, even the basic requirements needed to make a run-down tailoring business tick. I only thought I did.

There was little, if any, appreciation by the management of the small points that make the difference between success and failure, I had always felt at least ten years ahead of myself in Australia. That was in the late 1950s and early 1960s.

The old-fashioned store displays, crude advertising techniques and the low level of sales practices then in vogue offering a variety of merchandise on a brazen no deposit basis.

As I said, I had on my arrival in Australia an introductory letter to the General Manager of the Frigidaire Commercial Refrigeration Division in New South Wales. I should have used it more effectively and visited Sydney, but took the easy way out, and unwisely, decided to stay in Western Australia.

Back to the National Tailoring exercise. After cleaning up a showroom in East Perth, modernising the shop and display in King Street, I concentrated on getting some new, modern-style books illustrated. I also engaged a couple of bright, young professional salesmen. I felt things were now moving. But Brooking's attitude then began to worry me. The pedantic posture to his business made me realise that we were on diverging courses.

Then the salesmen informed me that they were having difficulty getting their basic salaries. This was serious.

When Jack Lew of Rothmere next visited Perth, I requested that he visit the National Tailoring factory with me and give me his opinion of their operation. I knew Jack was an astute businessman, with many successful years' experience in the Australian wholesale clothing field.

We visited the Brookings set-up in East Perth with Jack spending some time in discussion with Arthur and his factory manager. When we were walking back to King Street, my companion was deep in thought.

'The sooner you disassociate yourself from that man, Bill, the better. He is a fool and should be making enough money from his factory alone at the moment, never mind the retail side.'

When I asked him to elaborate, he continued . . .' He has a government contract making raincoats for the navy. These are normally worth a lot of money.'

It transpired that when Jack was demobilised from the Australian army, he rejoined his father's business as a coat-cutter. They had quoted to make many thousands of greatcoats for the Army.

A government official visited the Rothmere factory one day informing them, that their cloth price was acceptable, but they were quoting for far too much material for greatcoats. Jack then outlined how he had dealt with the query by first pretending to throw a temper tantrum. 'You, a master cutter?'

'You tell me, how much material needed for a coat?'

Picking up a nearby roll of cloth, he flung it dramatically across a cutting table. Then picking up various patterns, an extra sleeve pattern for good measure, he threw them on top of the cloth. He stood back, and with much hidden amusement, watched as the government man unsuccessfully shuffled the patterns around. Rothmere, he alleged, obtained this contract and the extra three-quarters of a yard of material for garments was an added bonus.

Shortly after this amusing but enlightening conversation, Arthur Brooking, wanted me to fly down to the Albany Woollen Mills and inspect some of their new materials. As I had previously made firm appointments with large store buyers that week to show a new range – big business here – I declined. Brooking now showed his real colours. He became angry and abusive, insisting I cancel these appointments. As he persisted in such a rude provocative manner, I informed him that, as from that moment, I wished to give up my association with his company. I had not been reimbursed for various small amounts of money I had outlayed and could see trouble ahead.

How clairvoyant can one be? I must have inherited my mother's soothsaying skills.

Both Arthur and Mrs Brooking had spoken to Pat, asked us out to lunch and attempted to mollify the situation.

I refused to have anymore to do with the National Tailoring Company. I had wasted enough time, thought and energy.

Shortly afterwards, the two salesmen left the company, alleging non-payment of salary as the reason. However, Simba Agencies was firing well and the Legassic shop was showing healthy returns. We were moving a lot of stock from King Street to Subiaco.

43. Fremantle Gaol

Things had been too good to be true. Suddenly threatening clouds appeared on the horizon. I received a summons to appear in the local court, in the matter of some $2,000, owing on a recently laid carpet in the East Perth showroom of the National Tailoring Company. Taking my signed agreement with me, I visited the court, produced my documentary evidence, and, as expected, heard the magistrates decision.

'There is no way Mr Northcott can be held responsible for this debt.'

Exit one very relieved agent.

Alfred Sleep had kept reiterating that Perth was controlled by some six or seven families, which he referred to as the Inner Circle. I now realise just what he meant.

A further court action was brought against me for the same carpet. It appeared that I first had to pay the amount owing, and later take a further civil action against Brooking for the recovery of my money. No way. I refused. No more court appearances were thought necessary. A warrant of execution was issued, and I had my first taste of Fremantle, and a debtor's prison.

The Habeus Corpus Act states that Every person who is detained has the right to go to court to determine the legality of that detention. The average law abiding citizen would have no idea of the humiliation suffered in a place like Fremantle Gaol. The admission procedure alone was archaic. The condemned miscreants, 'framed' or otherwise, were obliged to stand, stark naked, in a line for twenty minutes.

The reception area appeared to be a main thoroughfare for all and sundry, with prison officers, trustees and others, wandering apparently aimlessly around. Having been in the services, and with my African experiences, the naked body does not disturb me. But the sordid surroundings and circumstances most certainly did. For some of the younger newcomers it was quite obviously an unpleasant and traumatic experience, something I will certainly never forgive Australia for. When the admission preliminaries and the free nude show was over, our civilian clothes listed and withdrawn, we were obliged to shower and were then issued with disgusting second-hand clothing and very run-down footwear. We were then ushered into an exercise yard.

I was fortunate here. I was recognised by one of my 'Private eye' clients, gaoled for non-payment of maintenance. He quickly filled me in with particulars of the prison routine. He described the yard bosses, the Homosexuals, easily identified by their crisp new uniforms, and most important, he told me whom to keep away from.

To a keen student of human nature with much time to observe and listen to the inmates, prison can be a storehouse of information and learning. I attempted to profit from the experience. I really had no alternative. Sharing a cell with a human wreck, I nostalgically thought of the clean, modern facilities, European prisoners enjoyed, in East African gaols. I fail to remember, how many days I spent in Fremantle on that occasion. It wasn't more than ten days, I believe. Arthur Brooking got his carpet for free. I had just paid for it.

Some of the characters I met at Fremantle were both amusing and interesting, but the habit of mixing young first-offenders or debtors with hardened criminals, murderers and rapists I thought was not in society's best interest. I was obviously receiving special treatment, if only of the wrong kind.

At the central police station on my first arrest I was photographed and not particularly surprised when the police photographer mentioned that I was the first 'debtor' he had ever been asked to photograph.

Someone truly wanted me . . . 'on file.'

A few days after I had been admitted, I was ordered to shave off my beard. Considering this was an infringement of my civil liberty, I objected, but was told that if necessary force would be used.

The backroom boys had definitely been busy.

The WA prison system at that time was obviously founded on the barbaric line of its violent pioneering past. I can reccommend my readers to get hold of a copy of Robert Hughes' book, *The Fatal Shore*.

In it, he dramatically captures the spirit of the Australian penal system. It was almost the same in my time, without the birchings, and will no doubt take a long time to die. Other books which throw light on Australian peculiarities and John Pilgers *A Secret Country* and *Distant Voices*. I have never felt the need, or been able to discuss with my son David – a prison social worker, now superintendent of a woman's prison – as to the changes that must more recently have been made. Anyway, as an ex-community development and rehabilitation officer, for me the whole experience was an eye opener. At last my welcome release came. Pat gave me a warm welcome as she collected me from the prison gate with the old Mercedes Sedan.

Having done my time, I was now a real Aussie. Come off it, Mate. Don't be bloody ridiculous!

Being pretty sensitive, it was not easy picking up the threads of a daily routine again. Perth is a small town, and as I discussed business with buyers my thoughts became tainted – does this person Know? But I am a survivor and it had to be 'business as usual.'

This was not the end of the tailoring affair, though. I never appeared in court again, but was taken off to the debtor's prison on two other occasions. Yes, I know, I had been initially comple-tely cleared in court of this debt, but . . . Habeas Corpus Act again breached, it was easier for Northcott to work the amount off in gaol than for an old established Perth family to honour their debts. Redress through the courts chum . . . It needed money firstly, and anyway, this was in Australia. At least it wasn't for more than three or four days, on subsequent occasions. But how's that for British justice. What a load of cod's wallop!

Rather amusingly, every time I entered Fremantle gaol, something eventful happened. I once saw two escapees go out over the wall. I know it is a dubious privilege and not granted to most law abiding citizens.

On another occasion there was a strike by the whole prison population, who refused to leave their respective exercise yards and return to their cells. These can be dangerous, explosive situations. I have had much more satisfying experiences.

Years later, when for a brief period, I entered the gaol at Chiang Mai as a church visitor, I spontaneously made odious comparisons with Fremantle. I'll take Chiang Mai in preference to Fremantle. The Europeans held here on drug charges are lucky.

I had one final, unpleasant experience with one of these

debts of the NCC. Imagine the scenario: fashion buyers from one of Perth's better class stores, reviewing a range of Exmoor suits at our showroom in King Street. Neville Baker, the managing director of Exmoor was proudly showing his new season's range, with models parading and changing in the office. Enter the bailiff. In a loud voice he said 'Where is Mr Northcott? I've come to list all your possessions.'

'I would be grateful if you would keep your voice down and not go into the main showroom as we're showing a range of suits.'

'I'll say what I want, in the manner I want to and go where I damn well like!'

'How much do you allege I owe you?'

'Sixty-three dollars.'

Into the office where the models were changing . . .

'Jeanette, have you got any money you can lend me?' . . . Ten dollars, Mr Northcott.' 'Margaret?' Five dollars . . .

'Pat?' . . . Twenty dollars. Then into the main showroom. 'Excuse me, Neville, could you lend me twenty-four dollars?'

Back into the stockroom slapping sixty-three dollars on the counter. 'There you are, you bastard. Take your bloody money and get out, before I throw you out!'

'No need for that, sir.'

At this point I unfortunately lost my temper.

'Get out . . . Get out!' I shouted.

Neville said later that the tranquility of the main showroom was suddenly shattered as he heard me shout and saw one very agitated bailiff dart through the passageway from the stockroom, knock over a display stand and hurtle downstairs.

This is not how to run a business; never mind 'face lift' one – and all because of my greed and the 'Inner Circle' system then operating which probably still does. But it was all quite unlawful and so unnecessary. What the devil made me go to Australia in the first place? . . . Listening to a lady again!

FREELANCING
I must mention an unrelated incident that happened whilst Pat and I were running Simba Agencies. A solicitor I knew telephoned the office one day, and requested to see me. It appeared that an Italian client, had unsuccessfully employed several inquiry agents to investigate his wife's activities. He wished to engage my services. No way. I explained that I was

neither licensed to pursue such inquiries, which the solicitor already knew, or was prepared to do so. Could this be another entrapment? On my insistence that I would definitely not give evidence in court, however, on being told, that the Italian was a very wealthy and generous man, I eventually agreed to assist.

Just a few days later, in company with Pat, I followed a certain lady when she rendezvoued with a man in one of Perth's suburbs. They drove in a car towards Central Perth. I recognised the vehicle I was following – a Chrysler Valiant Sedan – as one I had been interested in several years before. My quarry eventually stopped at a small Motel, entering a particular unit. I telephoned from a nearby public telephone box to one of my ex-clients and asked if her husband still owned and drove the Chrysler Valiant, and was she still interested in his activities? He did have the car and she was interested. Good. Could she come immediately to the Terminus Motel and meet me?

On her arrival and after a brief discussion, Pat and my ex-client approached the unit door . . . 'Reception here.' The door was opened and in went one very determined and irate wife.

We visited the Italian gentleman's home and explained that a certain lady's solicitor would have all that he required. He was ecstatic and insisted on a generous donation to the Northcott Widows and Orphans Fund, and upon my suggestion that Pat had actually been instrumental in getting the unit door open, insisted that she accept a cash cheque for the purchase of an expensive dress. He wasn't aware, perhaps, that I had changed my occupation to the more socially acceptable one of a fashion agent.

It was good for one's ego, though, to know that it was still recognised that we could produce results.

Funny things egos. They can cause a lot of trouble!

44. Economics

Occasionally, carrying a selection of mini-skirts over my arm, I would pass, and acknowledge greetings from police detectives. I could well imagine their secret amusement . . .

Despite the fact that we were writing up extremely good business, the commissions were still only paid when merchandise was delivered into store or much later. As we had to meet our routine running expenses; wages, telephone, rent, etc, it was imperative to have some cash reserve.

As some manufacturers defaulted on commission payments, this reserve became critically low. We had our domestic electricity cut off at home on one occasion, for non-payment of the account. Things were getting desperate now, so early one morning I jumped into the Mercedes and drove through an industrial area in Bayswater. Seeing a cement work factory, I parked the car, went inside and applied for a casual job.

'You'll get cement in your beard here, but if you don't mind, you can start work tomorrow at 6.30 am.'

So, to add to my repertoire of jobs, I was now a humble labourer. I shovelled cement for a week until I was able to finalise the electricity account. I would finish at 3 pm, dash back home for a cold shower, into a clean shirt and business suit and rush into town to show my presence around the stores before they closed at 5.30 pm.

Shortly after this physically rewarding period in my life, Pat came into the showroom and said she had got a night job as a nursing aid at the Mount Henry Hospital, starting the next week. I knew she was trying to help, but I felt terrible. The very next day, after a few calls on buyers, I went out and also obtained a night job. Where? The Mount Henry hospital, of course, starting the same day, as a night orderly.

So we augmented our commission, working from 11 pm to 7 am, at the hospital, home for breakfast, a clean-up and into the showroom.

We slept, if possible, from 6 pm until 10 pm. and managed to keep this up for some months, until eventually, we had built the bank up and Simba Agencies was paying its way.

One of my duties was assisting the undertaker to remove deceased persons. A fee of forty cents was paid per corpse. My Kenya training came in handy here. I remember one of the orderlies coming on the day shift, said, 'You found the trolley alright, Bill?'

'What trolley? I just picked the body up, slung it over my shoulder and took it downstairs. I thought the sister looked at me a little askance!'

Once we had finished our hospital stint, completed the next seasons showings, we took, a business-cum-holiday trip. We drove across the Nullabor Plain, in the old Mercedes and visited the Eastern States.

My cousin, Yvonne, Alfred Sleep's daughter, accompanied us on this trip. This was before the road was properly surfaced, and was during the wet season. Some journey! As we drove into Adelaide, the car, with roof rack loaded with water drums and camping equipment, was completely covered, in mud and dirt from the Nullabor Plain. In fact taking one of several detours on the Nullabor I had unfortunately chosen the wrong one and becoming hopelessly bogged suffered the indignity of being towed out by an old Holden sedan.

The service station near Adelaide, at which we stopped for petrol had just had a new car washing service installed, and the owner said he would give the car a free wash, if I would just wait until he could engage the services of a professional photographer.

For something free! But, of course, we didn't object to waiting.

We stripped the luggage off the roofrack and disassembled the racks. Photographs were taken before and after, so that when we finally motored into Adelaide, we looked completely civilised, and where I met Uncle Harold for the second time.

Harold Sleep's European wife, Erna, kept in touch by mail with my mother, until she died. A lovely person, she had first met Harold when he was a cleaner at the Royal Adelaide Hospital. She had been a fantastic wife, which, at that low ebb in his life, was just what he needed.

Desite Harold's very turbulent career in Australia, he was now very much at peace with himself, and had for a long time returned to his early Christian faith. The Sleeps are perhaps a little too sensitive for a pioneering country like Australia. As I was to prove years later.

So with the car nicely cleaned, minus the roof rack, water drums, camping equipment etc, we continued on to Melbourne. This trip gave Pat, her first sight and feel of snow as we drove up the snow-covered road to Falls Creek in Victoria.

It also gave us the opportunity to meet all our manufacturers on their home ground again now with a worthwhile business, unlike our earlier visit as complete rookies to the industry.

We had a few days in Melbourne, then went on to Sydney where we made many new acquaintances, amongst them such nice people as John Beresford, a Sydney agent representing similar manufacturers to ourselves. John had a magnificent showroom at Beresford House in Kent Street and entertained us royally at his home in Hunters Hill. He was also a friend of Neville Baker and represented Exmoor Creations.

Despite the petrol strike in Sydney, we managed to purchase some fuel at Kings Cross, a business centre where I would think it is possible to purchase any other services, legal or illegal – much like Bangkok.

Then we headed home, kindly helped by a petrol tanker driver, 'Captain Midnight', one of the knights of the road fortunately found in most countries of the world. Such characters are legendary.

We stopped at the Parkerville Motel in Melbourne, a nostalgic visit for Pat and I, where our romance had first blossomed. Then back across the Nullabor, sleeping one night in the car which was quite comfortable, it was nice to get a fire going and dine in the open under the stars, away from people and problems.

We had been in the agency business about six years, on paper showing good returns, but the unreliability of commissions influenced us eventually in selling our ranges and calling it a day.

I remember once I met Jack Lew on a Sunday. He arrived in Perth about midnight by plane from Melbourne. We loaded boxes of his samples into the Mercedes, some on the roofrack, which I had installed for the occasion. We drove to the showroom, carrying the coats up the flight of stairs to the premises.

Before unpacking them, I remember I was very tired at the

time, I told Jack to get his chequebook out and pay up his back commission. He somewhat grudgingly did so, but there we were with a full week ahead of solid appointments, during which we would write up many thousands of dollars worth of business, and yet we hadn't received full payment for the last season's showings.

We had tried hard enough again, and for too long. Life isn't meant to be easy, is it? All that maintenance and tax didn't help either!

Neville Baker flew across to Perth when he received our closing notification and attempted to dissuade us. If all our manufacturers had been as honest as Neville, we would probably still be in the business now. We had selected a good agent for him, though we had no intention of letting him down.

The retail business, Legassic, Vera Stock took over eventually as sole proprietor. Exit Northcott from the rag trade. It had been an interesting experience, but the bills unfortunately, have to be paid.

45. The Waterfront

Pat had decided to undergo training as a psychiatric nurse, and commenced her training almost immediately after the business was closed.

My mother had previously sent me $2000 to pay for a trip home to England, but knowing how she had struggled earlier, I decided I would go home, but only when I had sufficient funds to repay her.

I obtained a temporary job as a clerk at the wool dumpers in Fremantle – my first contact with a wool exporting company or experience of a waterfront job. The manager, Reg King, had at one time been an official with a West African railway company. I was to meet his widow some years later in Darwin NT.

After loading dumped wool into containers for some few weeks, I transferred along with two other clerks to a more remunerative position with the firm Seatainer Terminals. One of the other transferees, Russell Robertson, a 'Dinkum Aussie' from Ballarat, has been a friend ever since. He was a real keep-fit fanatic and we used to visit the gym together. He was married to a lovely person called Emily, a Pacific Islander from Nauru. It did at times make me think a little. Here was Emily, a little island lass that Ross had met, when he worked for the British Phosphate Commission at Nauru. She was a wonderful wife, mother and housekeeper, with a basic island education, and yet was so much happier, and efficient in the house than so many more advantaged and privileged western women I had met.

Emily has often told me of unpleasant racial bigotry she has experienced in Australia – rude notes in the letter box and such remarks whilst shopping with her children, 'Don't talk to that coloured boy. Keep away from him!'

She will end her days on Nauru. Of that I am certain, but at present they have a well kept home at Ardross, one of Perth's better suburbs.

The new job was really an eye-opener – over-paid, over-staffed, always people on strike over one fancied grievance or another. There was no discipline whatsoever and eventually, of course it went bankrupt as it had to.

I fell foul of the shop steward very early in the piece. The Clerical Workers Union steward, a pompous little 'Pommie', I am ashamed to say, told me on one occasion that the storemen refused to work with me. Despite the over-staffed situation, off-duty policemen used to perform contract work as storemen. I had two such men on my team one day. Or were they there just to assess my attitude? So many enigmas . . . or am I really still paranoiac?

Fancy, though, men earning in excess of three hundred dollars per week. In those days it was good money standing around continuously, talking about penalty rates etc, actually earning only a portion of their wages, and looking anything but cheerful. Yet I remember the happy African unloading the Dhow 'Aspro' floating forty-four gallon drums of petrol ashore, working in the mud of the mangrove swamp, singing away in unison. pay was just five cents a day, plus food and shelter.

So the week passed and when I had saved enough money, I quit the job, sold the Mercedes and bought Pat a second-hand Austin Freeway sedan.

It had been fifteen years, since I was last in the United Kingdom.

46. England (After 15 years absence)

As I saw my brother's round, smiling, Devonshire face and my parents waiting to greet me at Heathrow airport, I realised how much I loved my family and England. I had arrived on a late evening flight. My parents had slept the afternoon away in a London Hotel, so we drove through the darkness to Plymouth in my brother's comfortable Daimler. The journey passed quickly as I recounted my omnifarious experiences in Australia and the charade of events that had befallen me. We had some good laughs. It all seemed so unreal and far away – now just a hilarious nightmare.

My mother said she knew I had been in gaol, and my father, who had spent a commission in Australia, never liked the country, but even he had some difficulty in comprehending parts of my story.

When we stopped off the motorway for breakfast in one of the rest centres, I realised how much the country had changed.

I had never really wanted to leave England, when I first went to Africa, but at that time it presented a solution to an almost insurmountable problem. Now look at my position. Forty-nine years of age and still far from settled.

Fate or fault? I seem to have tried hard enough! I knew then that England would always be my spiritual home, no matter, wher I lived. As an added bonus on this trip, I met Peter, the youngest son by my first marriage. He was now married himself with two children.

I drove down to Helston in Cornwall to stay with him. He was serving at the RN base at Culdrose, with the Fleet Air Arm. The first evening in Helston we walked from the base into town to collect some English fish and chips, just as I remembered them, and to enjoy a pint of Scrumpie Devonshire Cider. As we were about to enter a pub, Peter said, 'Bill, you're just what I always wanted my father to be!'

Bill, William and Peter

'Why did you say, as a child, that you were going out to Africa to shoot me then?'

'When you didn't send mum her money?'

The maintenance payments, I explained, were sent each month from the Crown Agents of the Colonies. His mother would have received them regularly. I struck up a good relationship with Peter, which fortunately I still enjoy.

Regretfully, I have just been told he has separated from his wife Pauline. More years of heartache ahead for him. I wonder if he had the same reasons as I had when I left Barbara.

My first meeting with my only daughter Anne after an absence of fifteen years was marred for me by the inefficiency of the Australian banking system. I had arranged to take her and husband out to lunch in Plymouth, and first visited a bank to cash some travellers cheques. Anne and her husband, Terry, whom I had just met, waited outside the bank.

The bank teller who was attending to me returned after a short interval away from the counter saying, 'unfortunately sir, we cannot accept the cheques' He then pointed out a microscopic line at the bottom of each cheque which I could hardly read. 'These cheques are not cashable outside the states of Australia,' or words to that effect.

I had explained to my bank manager at the Commercial Bank on Canning Highway in Perth that I was visiting the United Kingdom.

It was a small branch, and he had served me personally as I went through the long process of signing individual cheques, and discussed my forthcoming holiday. I now had the humiliation of borrowing money from Anne to pay for the lunch.

'Dad' was home from Australia! A con man from Down Under.

My brother's bank manager eventually changed all of my travellers cheques, but as he told me on a subsequent visit, it took him some four months to recover the money from Australia. My first, but by no means, the last conflict with Australian finance houses.

The visit home once such incidents were overcome, was terrific. Everything seemed as solid and dependable as I remembered. My brother's business was flourishing, both the petrol and liquid gas division. He seemed to have made much more financial progress than I had ever achieved in Australia.

Great, that is, until dear sister Betty appeared on the scene. The winner, years ago, of a 'typical British girl' photographic competition, she had been first married to a medical practitioner.

My dear, socially conscious Mother had placed her on a pedestal from which she dominated the family with her imperious, disdainful manner. Passing some innocuous remarks as we were returning from a hotel one day, she said,

'You are as bad as that common brother of yours!'

'I have been out of England for fifteen years, dear. That's our loving brother you are talking about.'

She stormed ahead of me and would not speak to me again. When, a few days later her two sons came down to Plymouth, staying at Tor Cottage, my parents home at Hartly, a terrible family row occurred. Unfortunately, too, it was on the evening before I was scheduled to leave Plymouth on my return to Australia.

Betty, 'Rootie' or Bettina as she has variously called herself, has always, for some inexcusable reason, looked down on her

Devonshire family. In fact, would invariably introduce Jack to her social friends in London, as,

'My brother from the country'.

'Aye' Jack would say, 'I be from Devon, that I do.'

This family row did in fact break up our family. Things were said under the influence of the demon drink that should never have been said. In all fairness, though, it was most certainly caused, only by Betty's uncompromising attitude towards her family.

The class system is slowly dying in England, but it still has a long way to go. Breeding purely means privilege, which has been used for too long to cover a multitude of sins. There are so many facets to life, but part of it can be so terribly sad.

I saw my dear old mother at some eighty-five years of age, sitting in her favourite chair and I knew she was continually evaluating her life's work, and constantly comparing, societies changing values.

'You are giving yourself a hard time darling, aren't you?'

'Yes, Bill!' She knew exactly what I meant, and I felt she wished she had behaved less imperiously in the past. It is unwise to be too judgemental, but most of us are guilty of this fault at some stage in our lives. I know I have been. We too can so easily become products of our individual environments and circumstances. Plymouth, like most service towns, has always been social and rank-conscious, with clearly defined perimeters of behaviour.

My mother finally died at eighty-nine years of age. She had been a terrific person, a wonderful wife and mother, and deserved and had earned a much happier end. As I mentioned before, during the war, in the heavy blitz that destroyed so much of the City, Mum had been magnificent. Talking to David, years later, he recounted similar experience to Jack when visiting Betty's home on leave as a corporal from the REME.

'In the army, Dave, I hear, Captain?'

'No, corporal.' End of conversation. Most of Betty's friends didn't associate with non-coms.

So, again, leaving England with heavy heart, I embarked at Heathrow for a flight back to Perth.

Meeting an ex-Malaya police lieutenant on the plane, a kindred spirit, we decided to stop over at Kuala Lumpur, where a friendly 'Mamma Sana' known to my new acquaintance, organised two lovely, elegant and tender, young *demimon daines.* We spent a relaxing four days, during which I blotted my family, and my problems completely from my mind.

But I finally arrived in Perth in a composed and tranquil frame of mind. I realised, though, the family in England would never be the same again. We were all growing older, in a hard, ruthless world and during a time of much social change and soul searching.

47. David and the Family

I was now forty-nine years of age, and with Pat enjoying her psychiatric nursing course, it was now necessary for me to establish a regular cash flow. I still had my day to day living expenses, together with my never-ending maintenance payments, to think about.

We moved into a rented property at Mount Pleasant with, of course, Pat's two children, Debbie and Tony. They were getting older now and had adjusted, and the family began to pull together.

It was at this time that David, my eldest son, applied for his discharge from the British Army, and finally obtaining it, migrated to Australia. He joined us at the house in Mount Pleasant, where I had converted an outside building into a comfortable, self-contained sleeping unit.

David, remember, had been an NCO in the REME (Royal Electrical and Mechanical Engineers) and obtained a temporary job, as a mechanic with a local automobile company. He talked of starting some form of tertiary training, but explained that the only formal education certificate he possessed was a military one. Pat mentioned that a psychiatric nursing qualification would be sufficient to gain entry to a university. So, in his pursuit of an academic training David had his army educational certificate evaluated, and shortly afterwards commenced his three-year stint as a mental health nursing student. His first step up the Australian ladder – fortunately unencumbered by a family or crippling maintenance payments.

Sound Jealous? I was!

As I had previously mentioned, on David's first arrival in Australia, his political views were diametrically opposed to mine, and it wasn't long before we had a serious disagreement. It doesn't need much imagination to realise that his opinions were coloured no doubt by his childhood memories of my first divorce and subsequent move to Kenya. He had, after all, been his mother's principal confidant. From our first meeting as adults I had noticed a veiled hostility. This love-hate relationship has now developed into a somewhat mystifying truce. I know we still love each other. Even the closest of relations can be very unkind and hurtful.

When I was going through my early domestic problems with Barbara, shortly after my demobilisation from the service, the only person I really confided in was my brother Jack.

He, above all people, knew just what I was facing and had offered numerous suggestions in an effort to assist me, most of which I had already undertaken, or carefully considered. Imagine my feelings, years later when under the influence of alcohol and no doubt, a touch of smug self-esteem, my dear brother made a remark, ' when you deserted your kids, Bill, and went to Africa.'

If he had turned around and struck me it would have been kinder. He knew, I had done all I could for twelve agonising years to keep the family intact. From a hopeless start, I had wasted all those years. I think I may have already mentioned a quote I read recently, 'A forced conjugal bond would be a festering sore of hypocrisy.' It certainly had been for me. Yes, it is too easy sometimes, to point the finger.

I wonder if Jack, though, in his declining years, feels as much at peace with himself as I do. Somehow I doubt it. We are all too aware of the mistakes we have made.

48. Engineering

I then applied for a sales manager's job with a firm called Technican Consultants, and was favoured with an interview.

The manager, a Dr Paul Howarth proved to have also been a wartime engineering commander in the RNVR (Royal Navy Volunteer Reserve) He had also been in Ethiopia during the same period as my Kenya friend, BA Allen. They had been together at the Emperors Court and we had an interesting discussion for at least two hours. The specific vacancy advertised, was not what I was looking for, but Paul thought he could help me elsewhere.

A week later, I called at the Technican office, and on this occasion met Doug Oddy, the managing director from Sydney. Four days passed when I received a telegram from Paul requesting a further interview. On my arrival at the office, Paul questioned me closely on my past education, experience and expectations. Eventually he astounded me by saying that the job he was offering me was his own. He wished to return to Sydney and take up his old engineering position on Cockatoo Island.

I knew by this time that Paul, had a doctorate in physics, had lectured at Baliol College, Oxford, and at the University in Johannesburg, South Africa and was a pretty academic sort of a person. Further discussion, however, revealed that Technican Consultants was actually a placement agency for engineering personnel. I realised that my business and administration experience was quite sufficient to manage such an operation. So, I accepted the position, as an assistant manager to Paul until he could arrange the necessary transfer back to Sydney.

During the very first week in the business, I recognised that not only was it unprofitable, it had been mismanaged for months, and actually only had two engineering draughtsmen earning money.

Fortunately, Paul and I hit it off from the start and he endeavoured to give me some insight into the various disciplines, categories and qualifications, that make up the engineering field.

I felt a sense of relief, though, when some three or four weeks later, Paul left Perth, to return to the Eastern States.

One soon learned the basic language of the engineering business and how to confidently discuss air-flow calculations, fan sizeing, piping flexibility, soil compaction, materials handling equipment, structures and pre-stressed and re-inforced concrete.

Being reasonably intelligent, and a good listener helped me of course.

I could now get down to work.

The business was insolvent; the immediate future looked black, but I could sense the opportunities on the horizon. First, the business had to be streamlined down to the bare basics, until it was able to run on a shoestring. It had been practice for managerial staff to book up petrol, as Paul and I already had been doing, on the company account. An inspection of the accounts ledger showed that no petrol accounts had been submitted or paid for many months . . . Why?

I asked the BP station manager to give me an account of what was owing. I asked him not once but on several occasions. Continuing to get fuel for several more weeks, I eventually wrote a letter, saying that unless an account was submitted within seven days, I would have to discontinue doing business with them. The manager informed me on one of my future visits that they were having some difficulty, as a previous Technican manager, A Mr Jackson, owed them several hundred dollars for a vehicle repair account. This, I advised, was a personal matter. I was only interested in fuel accounts. We eventualy ceased doing business with this large service station, and never ever received or paid an account for petrol, which had been provided free for many months.

Quite amazing – inexplicable – this type of occurrence in Australia and as always worried me. There must have been some reason, and the account must have been 'written off' somewhere.

So, I had joined Technican in September, with just two men working in the engineering field. At Christmas, their contracts were terminated and there were just the two internal staff: Sharon, the secretary, who had been keeping the business alive and myself. This was at a time in 1971 when projects were running down or being terminated, and many engineering personnel were thrown out of work. Ever since I have been in Australia the economic climate has always blown hot or cold.

Probably this is similar in many other Western countries, but more noticeable in a sparsely populated, geographically vast country like Australia. In the engineering field too, there is an over supply, or insufficiency of skilled men. Fortunately, being a newcomer to the business, I did not accept the fact that the large projects were the only real source of business.

As I revised the whole office system and updated and simplified the filing proceedure, I started making contact with many smaller firms who did have a need for short-term contract men. As other competitive agencies ran down, Technican started advertising and stepping up activity.

I left the office as much as possible and made personal contact with any engineering company with the potential to employ staff. Men seeking work in any field, like to think they at least have a chance. Slowly, they recognised that I was making genuine efforts on their behalf. I commenced building a rapport with selected men from various disciplines. I listened carefully to their comments and criticisms, and gradually began to feel the pulse. I also formed a close relationship with a few key men. One Bruce Dixon, an electrical engineer has became a life-long friend. Bruce is back in England now, but we correspond frequently, and as a keen yachtsman and navigator, he sends me cards occasionally from various ports to which he has ferried some luxury yacht out from the United Kingdom.

We were members of the same pistol club, and Bruce, also a skilled pilot, took me aerobatic flying on several occasions. We also played squash together at least once a week.

As a grandfather, I first learned to water ski and also did my first loops and barrel rolls in a light aircraft.

The President of Technican from Canada, then visited Perth. I explained to him that he only had a shell of a business. I had previously made the necessary appointments, and together we visited various government industrial development offices and the executive managers of several international engineering companies then listed in WA.

It was Bill Peart, the chairman of Vickers, Hoskin, who advised that it was definitely worthwhile keeping a holding office in Perth as inevitably, the position would improve thanks to the Japanese interest in the iron ore potential of WA. So, after every angle had been explored, it was decided to keep the Perth office open. The president gave me a firm hand to run the business in my own way.

'I like you, Bill. You can do it!'

'It's your money, Ron, not mine.

As soon as I had six or seven men in regular work, I instigated a Friday evening session in the office with a few beers, as the men brought in their time sheets.

This gave me the opportunity to talk to them individually, learn much about their problems, the personalities of the people they were working with and more importantly, details of forthcoming or proposed projects.

We also ceased paying insurance premiums on a building Technican had, a year or two before, used as an engineering model-making shop. Just wasted finance. I was able successfully to chase up some long outstanding debts that had been accepted as 'written off'. Gradually, the business started breaking even, and then very slowly started making a profit. But I was impatient.

A direct by mail system servicing the larger engineering companies immediately paid off. As the offices which we then used were too large, expensive, poorly sited and lacked a certain professionalism, I decided to move.

Selecting two small rooms in Colin Street, West Perth in a large modern building, 'Col-ord House' then, mainly occupied by members of the medical profession and one other engineering consultant.

I considered a new secretary, uncontaminated by a series of inept managers, was also called for.

So I somewhat reluctantly parted company with Sharon and engaged the services of a professional-looking, efficient secretary, Dene Selby. From then on, we really started firing. A replacement managing director from Sydney, Jerry Raynor, visited the new office for the first time.

'Bill, Technican an international company, has never had such a small office.'

'Jerry, we can't really afford a caravan, but just give me time. We'll soon be making a real profit.' . . . And . . . we did.

In that type of business, it is generally accepted that one consultant can only handle about forty engineering personnel personally. Dene, the secretary and I had just over a hundred men working and being administered from that small office.

This is when I began to really enjoy the business, working best under pressure. I found the work challenging and socially stimulating. Dene and I were on the same wavelength and it wasn't too long before the Technican team was recognised and respected on the Perth industrial scene.

As so often in Australia and elsewhere in times of depression, skilled men leave a country to work overseas, and suddenly as the horizon clears there is an acute shortage of competent staff.

It was at one of these low periods that I met again several hungry Australians. One such a well qualified structural draughtsman whom I wished to attend an interview, borrowed some money from me for his bus fare. He alleged he had not eaten for several days and was worried about his hungry children left unattended at home. Realising that he was genuine, I telephoned the social security people who asked to see him. They gave him thirty dollars to tide him over until his first pay cheque.

Luc worked for me after this for several years, but at that time in 1971 I clearly remember I was somewhat shocked by his predicament.

So we weathered the quiet period, but still showed a profit. When the pace began to quicken, the shortage of men soon became apparent and it was necessary to organise my first recruiting trip overseas.

49. Recruiting

After various liaison meetings with the department of immigration, I arranged for a relief from Melbourne.

Accompanied by Pat, I left by air for the United Kingdom.

I first interviewed men at the WA Immigration office, at the Strand in London. The department was very helpful and cheerfully arranged for me to interview men at their offices in Bristol, Masnchester and Birmingham. We had previously run advertisements in the Daily Telegraph, and arranged firm appointments before I left Australia.

Soon securing the services of all the men we needed: engineers, site men and both design and detail draughtsmen, mainly in the mechanical structural and electrical disciplines and having completed the work assignment, we paid a quick visit to my parents in Plymouth. I was naturally somewhat apprehensive after my last traumatic visit. But all was well. My parents seemed genuinely glad to see me, and were soon quite taken with Pat. It was Pat's first visit to England and I knew she was enjoying every minute.

Rather amusingly, when we were recruiting in Birmingham, I returned one day to the hotel for lunch and I found Pat sitting in the lounge reading a book. In her typically Australian way, she said, 'Bill, some of your countrymen are proper prize pricks. Listen to those two at the bar.'

There sat a pair of typical upper-crust lounge lizards, and as I listened to their loud, banal platitudes, delivered in the accent that gets right under an Australian's skin, I had to laugh.

There are cultural differences in countries. I do appreciate that, but plain old-fashioned bigotry I cannot stand. On another occasion, we were in a Cornish pub one Sunday morning at Saltash, just across the river opposite Plymouth. I was talking to a civil engineer. The pub was crowded. Someone passed a remark to Pat, and sudenly I heard her distinctive Australian voice quite loudly 'What a load of crap!'

Complete silence fell, as the patrons stopped talking and turned to look at this tall, strikingly beautiful Australian girl, dressed in a smartly tailored English suit. After a few moments of hushed silence, my brother, with a laugh, said, 'I like that, Pat!' Whereupon there were many laughs and comments. No doubt, though, some were critical. But it was certainly not a 'normal' comment from a young lady in a crowded English pub on a Sunday morning.

Incidentally, Pat only drank pints of draught beer. Whilst most Australians speak disparagingly of our national beverage, Pat acquired quite a taste for it. I must say, she drank as much free beer as we paid for. Male customers were quite impressed with the way she imbibed. Or was it the way she looked?

So the good years passed. Heavy social engagements, engineering 'get togethers', or mental health functions, Christmas parties, entertaining clients and men.

I can remember my brother, years before when he was a circuit manager with Esso, saying how he was physically worn out with entertaining men at business functions. I knew now how he felt. One needed the constitution of an ox to keep up with it all, and, unfortunately, my home became like a social club, instead of the peaceful retreat I needed. On returning from the office in the evening, I invariably found a crowd of psyche nurses - men and women - at the kitchen table, which was just loaded with empty beer bottles.

Pat, successfully finished her three-year course of training and became a fully qualified mental health nurse. She appeared to enjoy the work, but slowly and in many ways, regretfully, we started drifting apart. Most of her close friends were heavy drinkers. I had quite enough of this in the business field. I would have been happy to keep the home a reasonably dry area.

I will always be grateful to Pat, though. She taught me a lot about loving and living, and certainly an appreciation of good music, which had been so sadly missing in our early childhood. My mother had done her best. She had bought, a piano at great sacrifice on which Betty and I were made to practise. But we were never given the opportunity to listen and understand good music. Excuses, old son. Music, like food and drink, should be something that comes naturally. I do believe, though, that the average child of my generation brought up in a narrow, class-conscious family in England, was definitely disadvantaged, compared to its Australian counterparts, and would on reflection not be as well balanced overall. But we are what we are and have to learn to live with it. Having lived so long in Australia, though, I am still proud to be an Englishman.

Integrity, honesty and truth, are still worth something to me. Luxuries, so many people will say, one cannot afford in this day and age.

Back to Technican. Every few months we would hold a managers' meeting in one of the state capitals. These events were both rewarding and relaxing, as we discussed in depth, in comfortable surroundings, our respective business problems and experiences.

A year or so after moving into the Colin Street office, I received a letter, dated 25 May 1973. from the Canadian president, appointing me a Director of the Australian company. Things were coming together for me at last.

50. Trudy

I had continued visiting my two youngest sons, William and Christopher, as often as possible. We had some happy times together at the beaches or away in the country with my caravan. I did waste an awful lot of precious time and petrol, though, seeing the boys at the weekend. The only free time I could see them. Whilst I had repeatedly asked Trudy to leave a note saying at which beach the boys would be, I can never remember such an advice being left. It was a matter of checking the various beaches that were most popular with the boys until I eventually found them. A tiresome business.

On one of these visits to the boys, I discussed with Trudy the desirability of her buying a car. Shopping for a family without a vehicle in one of the most isolated cities in the world can be both time-consuming and exhausting. As she was working as a kindergarten teacher again, I proposed that I pay a deposit on a suitable vehicle and she look after the repayments. Trudy eventually agreed to purchase a vehicle on these conditions.

Contacting various car dealers, I arranged for them to show her a selection of reliable cars. After much long and painful deliberation, she settled on a Morris 1100 Sedan, a clean little car, for which I paid the initial deposit. The car was naturally registered in Trudy's name.

Some few months later, I proposed that the two boys accompany me on a fishing trip to Denmark, a scenic spot down south. We would take the caravan and my small eight-foot fibre glass boat. Trudy said she would like to come down later herself in her own car for a few days if possible and stay at the local motel this was no problem.

We drove down to Denmark, settled into a very nice caravan park and were having a great time.

Young Christopher, had landed a four-foot gummy shark all by himself and was shaking with excitement and elation. I assured him he was the very first male Northcott that I was aware of who had caught a shark on a hand line. Then Eddie Annear, an ex-Kenya mate, and frequent squash partner, suddenly appeared on the scene. His marriage had recently broken up and he was travelling east in his car, which was heavily laden with books, TV set, guns and what have you! Thinking of his children I attempted to dissuade him from leaving WA, suggesting he spend a few days with us to reconsider his decision. He did so, and whilst the four of us were out one day fishing, the dinghy low in the water, a passing power boat hailed us and said I was wanted urgently back at the office. We returned ashore, and on reporting to the office, I was informed that Mrs Northcott had been involved in a serious automobile accident and was in Bunbury hospital with a fractured skull. Pat . . . or Trudy?

Panic stations. As we pulled the boat ashore and loaded it on to the roof of the car we packed up the caravan as quickly as possible and hitched up, heading off as fast as possible to Bunbury. Eddie followed us back towards Perth in his loaded car. It had commenced raining heavily at the time. The road was dangerously wet, and I was wondering what I might shortly have to say to the two boys. This truly was a terrible journey.

Arriving at Bunbury, we booked into a nearby park, unhitched the caravan, and drove immediately to the hospital.

It was Trudy, but she appeared both conscious and rational, as she explained how she had fallen asleep at the wheel, ran off the road, hit a marker post and rolled the car into a ditch. The car, she said, was a complete 'write off'. But the main thing, thank God, was that she was going to be OK.

We spent the night in Bunbury, revisited the hospital in the morning, and learning that Trudy was out of danger headed back towards Perth and home. It wasn't until years later that Eddie, having by then established a good relationship with his sons in Perth told me the real reason he did not proceed east as intended. He had realised his car was overloaded and was worried about hitting bottom, on the rough road across the Nullabor Plain. So much for my rehabilitation technique. I was losing my touch.

51. The Imprest Account

We had been experiencing bad problems some few months later with poor mail deliveries and mens' pays, which were processed in Sydney had not been arriving on time. The Perth office was being held responsible. It mainly affected men working on site in the north of WA.

At the next directors' meeting I requested that the payroll for WA be handled direct from Perth, but this was rejected out of hand by the president. I informed the meeting that we could start losing men if this problem was not rectified – possibly up to twenty men working on outlying stations up north. The session continued until the president said, 'How many men, Bill?'

I could see he was doing a quick mental profitability check, and a few minutes later this was confirmed when he turned to the head bookeeper . . . 'open an imprest account for the Perth Office. Only you can sign the cheques, Bill, even if you are in hospital!' This seemed quite prophetic.

52. Australia's Rough Justice

I had, in fact, signed only one batch of cheques when one day the bailiff appeared in the office.

'I have a judgement summons here in respect of money owing on your wife's car.'

As I had not even received a normal summons or been given the opportunity to appear in court, I told him, in polite, but in no uncertain terms, where to go.

I had been told it had been the practice in WA years before, to issue migrants from Eastern Europe with a 'Warrant of Execution' as a first means, to recover a bad debt. But I wasn't a migrant from behind the Iron Curtain. Or was I? A few days later, the same man reappeared, armed this time with an officially stamped 'Warrant of Execution'. Habeas Corpus Act – once again breached.

Remember please, I had never been given the opportunity to appear in court; had been legally separated from Trudy for many years, and was now a company director. But what difference did that make? And, of course, they now knew I had the money.

I asked Dene to notify Pat immediately; I closed my office and accompanied the bailiff out to his car. 'There is no need for this, Mr Northcott!' 'I have come to the end of my tether with you people let's go.' We drove down to the central police station where my personal possessions were listed. As I moved back from the counter, having signed the pages listing my possessions, the admitting sergeant said 'your watch'. I took it off, but as no effort was made to include it on the list, I insisted.

'Feet apart, against the wall. Don't come that bullshit in here!' I was then roughly searched and physically pushed to one side.

Oh well, I only paid ten pounds to get here, I thought.

I was then placed under lock and key in a holding cell. After walking up and down in the cell for some twenty or thirty minutes, the door was opened and a uniformed policeman placed a meal on the floor.

I kicked it across the cell.

'You aren't hungry, Mr Northcott?'

'Of course, I'm not bloody hungry, just angry!'

All I could think of was getting out in time to sign the next pay roll cheques.

Suddenly there was a loud cry. 'Northcott!'

Ah, release. But no. Once again I was soon on my way in a prison bus to Fremantle Gaol.

Unreal. I could hardly believe how rapidly my status in life was changing. One minute, a respected company director. What was happening to me? No matter how hard I tried in WA, there must have been some dark forces working somewhere against me.

Once again I stood naked in public, as the humiliating admission procedure took place. I had long ago realised the futility of attempting to appeal for any legal redress. Ken Gouldham's expensive experience was too fresh in my mind. He had a worrying eight years to clear his name. No appeal from me could ever get to first base in WA.

However, as soon as I had been showered, kitted out, lost my company director's image, and the usual archaic formalities were completed with the maximum humiliation.

I was accomodated in a second-storey cell, to continue my unhappy meditation. What could I do about the cheques? Professional engineers and others were relying on me. I had completely lost control.

'Northcott!'

Again that welcome shout. This time – exultation. I was to be released. Someone had blundered and over reached themselves.

But for any law-abiding citizen, unlawful imprisonment for any reason is both unjust and immoral. Alright, I have made mistakes – who hasn't – but I am not a criminal, although I now realise I was living in a criminal society.

Most Australians have a sneaking, if not open admiration for their criminal forbears, but those in the administration of justice must surely know right from wrong. Or am I really just being naive. By this time, like the professional models we had previously employed, I was becoming adept at a quick change of garments and role.

I remember on the only night I spent in custody at the central police station, when I was in bed the cell door was unlocked and a group of plain-clothes detectives stood looking in. I pretended to be asleep, but could well imagine their feelings of satisfaction.

53. Success

Back at Technican men were receiving their cheques on time, unaware of the narrow escape they had had, and our reputation was still growing. Dene, I must add, was magnificent. She had visited me at the central police station to see if I needed anything and never made any future comment on the incident. I valued her discretion. Pat was now working with the Drug Rehabilitation centre in Ord Street, within walking distance of our office, together with my recently qualified son David, and another psyche nurse named Sandy Bennett.

The two little offices in Col-Ord house had long proved inadequate. I also badly needed an assistant. Who knows, I might once again get dragged off at Her Majesty's pleasure.

We were lucky. An engineering company, vacated premises in the same building on the second floor of Col-Ord-House. So we selected enough floor space for three interviewing rooms, a large reception area and adequate room for an entertaining section, photocopying machine, filing cabinets and space for the drawing boards. I marked this out, and, purchasing some office wall-dividers, set about assembling our new work place.

I then engaged a technical man as an assistant. This man I understand, is now one of the senior mechanical engineers with Hammersley Iron.

There had been increasing friction and problems, between the nursing staff and doctor in charge, and one day most of the senior staff walked off the job. To ease their situation, I gave Pat and Sandy employment in the business, the latter on the main reception desk. Sandy soon drew my attention to the fact that some of our engineering personnel were regular drug users. I hadn't had a clue.

In this type of business it is helpful if the internal staff are acceptable to the majority of the contract men represented. Unfortunately, whilst my new recruit was sufficiently qualified, he had an abrasive manner which upset several of the key men and he was only with us for a short while.

His replacement proved more successful and together with the new premises, the running of the business became less stressful.

In retrospect, though, I felt the earlier years with Technican when Dene and I were struggling to build the business were the most rewarding for me. I had been told by various men much of the overtime work claimed for had never actually been worked. Several of the consultants were quite happy with the practice, which was virtually a licence to print money. With labour costs already high in Australia, this sort of attitude reflects poorly on management and supervising controls.

'But, Bill, the permanent staff and everyone does it!'

'Don't tell me, I don't want to know it. I have to invoice for hours that have not been worked. Doesn't make me feel too good!'

Easy money is the real name of the game 'down under', and I didn't stick my neck out any further to make an issue of it. Morally I should have done. But, morals in Australia are a different kettle of fish.

So the business continued to profit, blowing hot and cold like the economic climate, but always now at a profit.

Eventually, the three directors in Australia, Mike Purton in Sydney, Graham Pilley in Melbourne and myself in Perth, were given the opportunity to purchase the Australian operations from Technican Canada, the parent company.

It took about another three years to pay off the purchase price, during which period many sacrifices were made, and none of us had any spare cash to play with.

I remember once, on a visit to Graham's home at Lilleydale in Victoria, when his wife said, 'I'm fed up with listening to you men talking business with big money, when I'm finding it difficult to even meet the household expenses.'

The struggle was worth it though. Eventualy the sale was finalised, and we then decided to open three separate companies. In the initial stages of our separate companies it was not easy supporting a big wage bill both Mike and Graham borrowed from Canada. I decided to consolidate my financial situation and then slowly build up my cash reserves. I reduced my staff of contract men to an acceptable economic level. I did this without having to pay out heavy interst on loans. It wasn't long before the financial side of my business was on a solid footing. I was able to pay for Trudy and Christopher to travel to

England on holiday, and leased a Jaguar XJ6 sedan for my own use.

It had been a long haul.

Mike taking New South Wales and Queensland, Graham, Victoria and South Australia, and myself, Western Australia and the Northern Territory.

Mike, another Devon man and myself were the only non-technical executive staff, yet our offices showed the greatest profitability. There were minor disadvantages in not having a professional background, like the time Mike was being shown some detailed drawings of what he evaluated as being of a 'high-rise complex'.

'You've allowed for the wind velocity factor?'

'Mike, the building is underground! 'Quick as lightning.

'Sorry, I meant the earthquake loading!'

54. Augusta

At this time I had purchased a piece of bushland, eight and a quarter acres at Augusta overlooking a rain forest and about four kilometres from the township, a beautiful location in the extreme southwest corner of WA.

We would pick the boys up on a Friday and travel down from Perth, to spend the weekend working on the block. Clearing the land, organising the perimeter fencing and planning for a water dam to be established.

It was a real pleasure for me working on the block with my two young sons,and I know they enjoyed it too. I had a large Sunbeam frypan in the garage, and would put in a chicken or small roast, surrounded by peeled potatoes, every half hour or so, returning to the garage, turning over the vegetables, until a satisfying meal was ready. We worked hard, using a big slasher I had bought a Dexion, I think it was called cutting out the ferns,

Augusta 'Paddock'

planting trees and the ground work, so necessary to hew a rural property out of the bush.

I arranged with the local shire council to grade a road through the property, and shortly afterwards erected an aluminium garage. Once this was fitted out with a number of beds, we were able to sleep on site. Equpping the garage with cooking utensils and other necessities.

One weekend Christopher and I picked up some pickets and rolls of ringlock and barbed wire in the trailer and completely fenced quite a sizeable sheep paddock. I considered this a good weekend's work.

I realised then how much I had missed out on with my first family. So little time to really enjoy my children, which should be every father's right. For example, there was taking time off to do a little target practice with my Martin .22 rifle or a quick practice shoot with my .44 Ruger, black powder revolver, I would then go down to Flinders Bay for a refreshing swim before returning to Perth.

On these safaris to Augusta, we would leave the block on a Sunday afternoon about 3 pm and return to Perth. The car would be absolutely filthy, crossing the waterlogged block or with dust from the bush track into the property. Getting back to Perth about 7 pm. I would take the boys home, return to my place, unload the car, clean it and probably finish work about 10 pm. I did this for several months, but it was worthwhile. This gave me time with the boys, and we were at least achieving something. Next morning: clean car, business suit, and it was back to work.

I should mention here the time I had arranged to pick up fifty poplar trees for planting in the driveway. We harnessed the trailer up in Perth and headed south. Calling in at the forestry department near Pinjarra for the poplars, I wondered if we would get them all in the trailer. The forester opened the boot of the car, and to my surprise put in a wooden box containing fifty small saplings. We travelled from Perth to Augusta and back, a distance of some four hundred miles towing an empty trailer.

I remember by then I had sold my caravan in order to buy the garage. Now I could store more in it, and it was much more practical for an all purpose utility building.

Terry and Anne came out to Australia for a holiday with the two boys about this time to see if they would later migrate from England.

As Terry was a draughtsman in the local shire offices at Ipswich in UK, I was secretly hoping that he could assist me, in running Technican. In fact, he did work in the business for a short while when he eventually arrived from England for good, but subsequently joined the Wanneroo shire, where he did a similar job to his former UK position.

He is quite happy in Australia and is still in the same situation. Anne, who was a qualified nurse in England, did not wish to take up that profession in Australia, but took a three-year teacher training course, now she is doing her masters degree in education.

Peter, my youngest son by the first marriage, wanted to come to Australia, but his wife Pauline, from a very close Liverpool family, would not at first agree. He eventually left the navy, and I paid the family's air flight out to Australia. Pauline immediately loved the country where she too took a teacher training course.

I attended Anne's graduation ceremony, with Barbara, who is now settled in Australia. I must say I felt very proud. Anne received a distinction, won the college council prize and also the Menzaros prize. She was the only graduate to go up to receive a diploma and prize three times.

The kids have all done well, much better I am sure, than if they had remained in England. Thank you Australia. In Augusta I had erected the garage on the block with the assistance of Eddie Annear, William, my son, and a machinist designer called George Skringar. George was a Yugoslav by birth, an inventor, volatile, unreliable, a good dancer and entertainer and, most certainly a menace to the fairer sex. Erecting the garage was a highly amusing pantomime, but we got it to 'lock-up stage' within twenty-four hours. Time left for a swim in Flinders Bay and a few beer's before the long two hundred-mile trek back to Perth.

After trying hard to recapture our former closeness, over a period of some weeks Pat and I split up for good. She was a good lady, intelligent, well read and a good companion. We had some happy years together not always under easy circumstances. Somehow, I could never ask her to marry me. I often wonder, Why not? I understand she is now happily married to an old family friend. I will always think kindly of her and pray she is happy. When she finally drifted out of my life I concentrated my free time on the block at Augusta.

55. Georgeous George

I should tell you a little more about Gorgeous George, He was one of life's more vital characters. It is perhaps to mankind's benefit that his breed is so very rare.

He first walked into Technican's office seeking work and was placed on a few weeks contract as a mechanical design draughtsman with Western Titanium in Bunbury. When the contract finished, he requested another assignment. We had received good reports of his work on this first job. Apparently, George had a factory employing some ten men making specialised machinery for the poultry industry. He had run into serious financial problems, and suggested it would benefit him to close the factory, lay off the staff and work full time for Technican. As we had several long-term projects in the pipeline, I agreed. George closed his business down and worked for Technican for some three years. Despite his poor English and volatile temperament, he did quite a reasonable job. The formal qualifications he held were equivalent to a WA diploma in mechanical engineering. Almost inevitably, however, George ran into big trouble. When he finally ceased working with our company, he started his own business developing a jet surf ski or 'Hydro Glisser' as he called it. He took a large factory premises at Osbourne Park with a grand opening ceremony performed by government officials in the true Skringar style.

He had been working on the invention for several years to the best of my knowledge. It never got off the ground.

We lost touch with George for a year or two until William, my son, met him in Perth. 'He looked terrible, Dad. Very thin and gaunt, and he'd just been in hospital for some stomach operation.'

By this time I had built a house on the block at Augusta and had been in residence for several months. A young Queensland civil engineer was managing the business in Perth and I was then semi-retired. Acting mainly as a financial controller and only visiting the office three days a week.

As I had always been amused by George and his antics and appreciated his effervescent personality I asked William to invite him down to Augusta for a couple of weeks break, the next time he saw him. Eventually, George drove down to the small farm. As William had said, he looked terrible. After installing him in the guest cottage, we had an enlightening talk. He told me his marriage had broken up,his house taken by the bank and he owed many people large sums of money. As I listened to his story it seemed to me like a figment of his imagination. He had received a government grant to develop his invention, which he informed me he had taken to a trade exhibition in Paris. Backing up his story with photographs of his stand at the exhibition, which I saw, with some amazement, was located directly opposite an exhibition of Rolls Royce engines. There was also a photograph of George standing with the President of France, Franáois Mitterand. With even more surprise, I noted that George's stand, solely devoted to his invention, was clearly and boldly identified as 'Australian Technology'. Funny things can happen in places like Australia, as I knew to my cost, but this was ridiculous. The gleaming jet water ski, so proudly exhibited in the glossy, professional photograph, had never even performed. I questioned him about his financial state and asked if I could have a look at his balance sheet. George had never received even one balance sheet since he had first opened his business, but alleged he had recently paid his accountant a $4,000 fee.

'What happened to the development grant, George?'

'When I needed money I would ask the accountant and he would give it to me.'

'How much was the grant, George?'

'I don't know Bill, I'm an engineer. My general manager handled that.'

I was walking up by the forest, a few days later, when I saw a police van pull out of my driveway. As it came towards me, I saw that a uniformed police sergeant was driving the vehicle. Flagging him down, I enquired who he was looking for . . . George Skringar, I have a summons here for him.

I explained that George had been staying with me, but was not then at home. He freely supplied the information that the summons was from the Westpac Bank . . . . for the sum of $30,000. George was in trouble, marriage and house gone, and now this.

A week or two later,when I was making a quick trip to Perth, I suggested that George accompany me and endeavour to obtain a balance sheet from his accountant. We drove together to Perth where we visited a large suite of modern offices located in South Perth. After George had unsuccessfully requested the overdue documents he called me into the principals office.

'I am a semi-retired businessman and sympathise with you handling George's accounts, but he tells me that for several years you have never given him one balance or half-yearly balance sheet,yet I understand he has recently paid you $4000.'

'It's all here,' the senior man said, pointing to a large pile of documents,laid on his desk. 'We will have it ready this afternoon.'

After completing my own business, we finally left Perth late in the afternoon – but with a balance sheet. George told me that when he returned the second time, to the accountant's office, one of the men involved with his books said to him, 'Why have you done this, George?'

On arrival in Augusta, we settled down to a meal,and then I inspected the document . . . Completely meaningless. No mention of a government grant or a lucid breakdown of expenses or wages. George had lost his business, his home and family, and whilst I knew he was a most unusual character, his wife had told me on several occasions, that she loved him dearly. I felt, and still do, that he had been set up and used.

Was there a government grant? Presumably so, as George admitted getting some money! But who controlled it? How much was the grant? And where did the bulk of the money go?

George knew that someone in his office had been photocopying his plans, specifications and patents.

At one time he alleged he had followed his general manager down to the industrial development corporation building in St George's Terrace. I know the WA government had a core of specially briefed and trained men, looking at new bussinesses of this nature ostensibly with a view to promoting industry.

George, being George, would have made an ideal sitting target. After all, the money would have been coming into WA from Federal sources.

On a lighter note, George once amusingly told us how he had taken some home cured garlic sausages that he had made himself into the Metropolitan Water Board where he was working. When he cooked them at lunch time the heavy garlic fumes were picked up by the ducted air-conditioning and permeated the director's suite on the top floor. Quite a hullabulloo followed. George also had a big Alsatian dog that accompanied him everywhere. The very last time I saw him he told me that he was flat broke and shared a tin of Pal with his dog for breakfast. Sad that a skilled engineering man should be reduced to such circumstances. So much for George. A real eccentric. Don't we English value these people? I hope he eventually finds a safe and peaceful haven somewhere.

When William left high school, I had taken him into the business. With my book-keeper's help he had become quite useful, and at one time was able to give me on a Monday a full bank reconciliation which he had prepared himself. In time too Christopher followed William into the Technican business. It was a pity they were not just those few years older. Both would have been quite capable of taking the business over.

Amazing really, all the problems I had overcome and with four sons, I now had a worthwhile business, but was too tired to keep it going long enough for my children to benefit. The final year that I was in business, the tax department did a full audit. Why pick on my Company? I had lost $27,000 in the Darwin office enterprise, and another $20,000 in bad debt. I decided to sell out. I was only sixty-two years old, but I had taken a lot of punishment. It was time to call it a day.

Whilst at Augusta, when I was not worried about earning money to just survive or pay maintenance, I met several Australian-born men and women that I felt completely comfortable with and still hold in much regard. The fact that I was retired and not in competition in any way with them might of course have influenced my feelings.

A few I will name. Vic Roberts the 'sherriff', a cattle man from way back. I found him amusing and interesting to talk to. He lived in what he called the Hollow Log a small hut, used previously as accommodation and as a mustering station. Vic had lived in the district for many years; he was an ex-army commando who had fought in New Guinea. He was at the WA university for several years, studying medicine and geology, qualifying in neither, but quite obviously profiting from his academic experiences. I took several local and overseas guests across to his home in the Hollow Log. They always enjoyed the experience and also Vic's company.

John Williams, the local doctor and a real Australian but a

Vics Home – The Hollow Log

gentleman, and one who was easy to talk to and whose opinion I would value.

Ron Abbott the local butcher – a big amusing Australian, with a cheerful, open manner who gave me some good advice in killing, skinning and dressing sheep.

Bill Jones was an old timber man and orchardist. He told many amusing stories about early Australia. At one time he had worked as a gold miner, well digger and axeman. I was quite interested to learn that as a timber cutter turning out railway sleepers for export to the UK, he was earning several times as much as my father when he was an engine room artificer in the Royal Navy. Bill was a true Christian, and gave me some valuable assistance in pruning the fruit trees planted on my small farm.

My neighbours, Kitty and Noel Warren, were also lovely people. He was an English man who had migrated to Australia as a youth, where he had taken up farming. Noel had been a POW with the Australian forces at the notorious Changi Camp in Singapore.

Russ Robertson, old gym mate, I felt quite close to, but like many Australians who had travelled elsewhere in the world, Russ kept a completely open mind about most subjects, and although easily recognised as a true Australian, was not at all bigoted.

Some Australians I spoke to at Augusta had no desire to travel even to Perth. They had their 'footie', fishing and work at Augusta. These men became quite insular in their outlook. I admit I did have some difficulty in even communicating normally with this type of person – perhaps we were too far apart.

I would also like to acknowledge Christopher Sliwowski and his English wife Beryl. They lived for a while in Augusta. Chris was a Polish gentleman who came to England – a country which he really loves at the beginning of the last war with the Polish Air Force. Both Chris and Beryl worked for many years with the BBC. Chris had actually lived longer in the UK than I did.

I enjoyed my fishing excursions with him and the stimulating discussions about life local government – the Australian psyche – and political trends in Europe. Often held by the poolside on my little farm, as we smoked our harvest from the sea and enjoyed a cleansing ale.

I must recount an amusing incident that happened at 'Torr Shamba' once when Vic Roberts visited me. A senior engineer called George Hyde was staying with me for a few days. His wife had recently died of cancer and he wanted to get away from Perth. The three of us started drinking at about 7 pm that evening, first beer and then whiskey. At 3 am George said he was tired and should go to bed. Vic and I remained at my little bar until about 5.30 am. We stood, as I so clearly remember, on my wide verandah as the dawn broke through. As he had previously spent a night or two in my guest chalet, I suggested that as he had been drinking, Vic should turn in and have a few hours sleep. Vic looked at me from under his wide Australian bush hat and with what I amusingly interpreted as an Aussie's contempt for a Pommie drinker. 'Drinking, Bill. I have some cattle to round up, and you can't call that drinking.' I knew he had an hour's driving ahead of him – terrible wet bush track, often completely under water. Definitely a four-wheel drive journey. But I could appreciate that sort of humour from men like Vic Roberts.

So, I eventualy sold out Technican International WA Pty Ltd.

William and Christopher were making their own way in life, but no doubt profiting from their early experiences in business. I am pleased to say that William is now managing a tourist agency business in partnership with a Kenya-born man.

Christopher, obtaining a diploma in photography from one of Perth's technical colleges, is now working with his half-brother, Peter, at a university in Perth. So exercising the right of the individual to contract out of a state which no longer commands his respect. Here I am still in Thailand.

My children visit Chiang Mai frequently and I have much to look forward to. There are naturally minor problems in living in a different culture, but I do not feel threatened here, and the easy-going Thais make me feel completely comfortable.

No land can be owned by a foreigner. All land must be held in a Thai name. Fair enough. Having initially paid for my townhouse, I have had to get a thirty-year lease on it to safeguard my interests.

The tonal language of Thai is difficult for an Anglo Saxon to master. I have taken formal lessons, understand more than I can express, but accept the fact that I will never become a fluent speaker of Thai. The Banks, however, are straightforward and easy to deal with, and I must say, I enjoy living in the reality of a cash society.

Apart from the family, I have had visits from several good friends, among them, an Australian couple ex-Augusta, Norman and Hele Masters, for whom I have the greatest admiration and respect. Then there was one of my early draughts-women, Marlene Beckett-Cooper, who had only one fear in the early days – that she would be sent back from Australia to Germany. A fantastic person, Marlene. She has worked hard; accomplished a lot and built a lovely home at Gooseberry Hill in Perth. We are always glad to see her.

Also, Russell Sweet, an Australian barrister, from Sydney, who has visited us in Chiang Mai on several occasions. I will mention him again in a further book I intend writing.

We have also had a visit from my friendly ex-Burmese landlady in Perth, Margo Marti, who has recently written to me from Nairobi. Another friendship I really value is of course, the irrespressible Vicki Stint, an ex-New Zealand school teacher, who was our very first visitor and stayed with us here in Chiang

Mai for some two months.

I have written somewhat critically but perhaps understandably, of my experiences in Australia, and I still feel angry too, but I also know and respect many individual Australians, mainly country folk, from whom I have learned a lot.

I have just read the Rise and Fall of Alan Bond, a typically Australian story, the taxpayer again being asked to foot the bill. The ex-state Premier Brian Burke I see has also been jailed for two years. No number of Royal Commissions will unearth the real story; the chicanery in that country goes too deep.

I can say at least that I have been true to myself. Most of us have some character deficiences and I make no excuse for mine.

56. My Conclusions (old age)

Do not go gentle into that good night
Old age should burn and rave at close of day
Rage, rage against the dying of the light . . .

DYLAN THOMAS

I am sure, too, that real peace and universal harmony cannot come from power-hungry, dishonest politicians, or from prejudice-prone law makers, but only with the help of God and through the simple human heart. I have found the ordinary man of any colour, race or nationality to have similar aspirations. Their needs and desires are the same - the chance to live in peace, rear a family and provide the necessities of life to ensure reasonable comfort for their loved ones.

The social upheaval most countries are experiencing is the result of an ever growing awareness of the ineptitude of government bureaucracies, and can only grow much worse.

The writer is amazed that so many learned, professional and government officials pay lip service to worldwide environmental problems, but contiue to tolerate and even encourage the **moral** and **spiritual** pollution that is at present foisted om mankind. How can one justify the vast wasted expense, with its known propensity for secret commissions, on armaments, against the money spent on health or education? Or contiue to tolerate political leaders who are incapable of leading; treasurers who are unable to balance a budget; foreign ministers with no global vision; judges who are tainted with dishonesty; lawyers who misuse and circumvent the law and police and prison services that are not answerable to the public. There **is** a growing crime rate and increasing drug trade with high level penetration and protection; civil servants who are anything but civil, with an ever increasing and costly bureaucracy.

All that is needed for the triumph of evil is that good men do nothing.

No doubt, the world is a comedy to those who think . . . and a tragedy to those who feel. I unfortunately do both.

PROVERBS 20:7

The just man walketh in his integrity:
His children are blessed after him.

'Mine have been!'
'Thank You Lord.'